# The Wonder of
# Worship

OTHER BOOKS BY RONALD B. ALLEN

*And I Will Praise Him: A Guide to Worship from the Psalms*

*Worship: Rediscovering the Missing Jewel* (coauthor)

*Rediscovering Prophecy: A New Song for a New Kingdom*

*Lord of Song: The Messiah Revealed in the Psalms*

*The Majesty of Man: The Dignity of Being Human*

*Liberated Traditionalism: Men and Women in Balance* (coauthor)

*A Shelter in the Fury: A Prophet's Stunning View of God*

*The New King James Version* (coeditor)

*The Nelson Study Bible* (coeditor)

*Nelson's New Illustrated Bible Commentary* (coeditor)

SWINDOLL
LEADERSHIP
LIBRARY

# The Wonder of
# Worship

## A New Understanding of the Worship Experience

# RONALD B. ALLEN
## AND
# CRAIG H. ALLEN

CHARLES R. SWINDOLL, *General Editor*
ROY B. ZUCK, *Managing Editor*

THOMAS NELSON PUBLISHERS®
Nashville

THE WONDER OF WORSHIP

Swindoll Leadership Library

Published in association with Dallas Theological Seminary (DTS):

General Editor: Charles R. Swindoll
Managing Editor: Roy B. Zuck

*Library of Congress Cataloging-in-Publication Data*

Allen, Ronald B.
The Wonder of Worship / by Ronald B. Allen and Craig H. Allen
p. cm.—(Swindoll leadership library)
Includes bibliographical references and indexes.

isbn0-8499-1444-2

1. Public Worship    I. Title.    II. Series

BV15.A386 2001                                           00-068546
264–dc21                                                      cip

*Printed in the United States of America*

04  05  06  07  08  —  9  8  7  6  5  4  3  2

# Dedication

With gratitude to our loving Lord

For innumerable mercies,

And in concert with my wife, Beverly,

We dedicate this book to our grandchildren:

Joy

Joshua*

Joel

Jonathan

Nathan

Emily

Ashley

Alyssa

Kyle

And whoever may join their number in the future!

May God in His grace lead each of you

to worship Him wholeheartedly.

---

\* Died a stillborn

# Contents

# Foreword

A RECENT COVER STORY of an evangelical news magazine summarized the church's current state of affairs. The headline blared two words in large block print: WORSHIP WARS! Can you imagine? Those who have embraced the Lord Jesus Christ and attend a worship service each week, where His name is to be lifted up and extolled, are now at war, fighting over how worship should be carried out.

No doubt you've heard the questions: Should we use an organ or an electronic synthesizer? Would the apostle Paul have welcomed drums into one of his services? Should believers kneel or stand, sit or bow? Are Sunday mornings sacred or is a Saturday evening a convenient time for an additional service? If these issues have yet to be addressed in your fellowship, hold on; they're coming soon to a church near you.

Although these squabbles are receiving widespread coverage, I'd like to think most Christians are beyond fighting over these petty preferences. After spending a week in the marketplace, grinding out a living, most of the believers I know are ready for authentic, sincere, heartfelt worship. For me there is nothing more exhilarating than joining in with a body of ready worshipers.

In her penetrating work, *Up with Worship*, Anne Ortlund writes, "Christians can be grouped into two categories—marbles and grapes. Marbles are 'single units that don't affect each other except in collision.'" Grapes, on the other hand, mingle juices: Each one is a part of the fragrance of the church body. The early Christians didn't bounce around like loose marbles, ricocheting in all directions. Picture them as a cluster of ripe grapes, squeezed together by persecution, bleeding and mingling into one another. Fellowship and worship, then, is genuine Christianity freely shared among God's family members. It's sad to think of how many Christians today are missing that kind of closeness. Sermons and songs, while uplifting and necessary, provide only part of a vital church encounter. We need involvement with others too. If we roll in and out of church each week without acquiring a few grape juice stains, we really haven't tasted the sweet wine of fellowship."

Dr. Ron Allen, an esteemed Old Testament scholar, has made the subject of worship his lifetime passion. As you will soon discover, it shows. This book calls us to be grapes, not marbles.

Dr. Allen is not so much interested in the topic of worship wars as he is the subject of true worship, the object of our affections—*God.* Two of the most critical chapters in this work, in my opinion, are 5 and 6, entitled, respectively, "The God We Worship," and "Worship as Response to God." I urge you to pore over them carefully. It's been my observation through the years that some worship settings are not about God at all, but are about the worship leader, the singers, the sound system, or even the volume level of the sound system. Dr. Allen carefully calls us back to the center of our praise, the One whom we are to admire and exalt.

I believe God is searching for authentic worshipers, those who long to worship Him in spirit and in truth (John 4:23–24). Are there differences in styles, forms, and flavors of worship? Of course. However, I ask you to allow this book to guide you beyond the subjects of form and function. Rather than becoming a casualty of the worship wars, I urge you to let this book lead you onward and upward to the heart of God Himself.

You'll be grateful you made the journey.

—CHARLES R. SWINDOLL
*General Editor*

# *Preface*

NOTHING MAKES LIFE SO SWEET as the fear of losing it. In early 1999 my doctor told me his preliminary diagnosis of a serious disease. While I was waiting for either a confirming diagnosis (and treatment plan), or—in God's mercy—the good news of a favorable report, I jotted down this poem on Valentine's Eve, 1999:

> I would not choose a friend in death,
> but death may wish a friend in me.
> Life is friend. To life I cling,
> yet death has a way of pressing its sting.
> What death does not know
> I'll not reveal—save this:
> Dear life will be my friend again
> if death chalks up its little win.

A few weeks later I learned the results of the second test. An infection had skewed the first test results. All was normal; there was no cause for alarm. Yet the experience was vital to me, for it underscored the importance of the theme of this book. Should God in His grace extend my life, my deepest prayer is that my worship of Him will give that gift its best meaning. For nothing we do as believers in this life—or the life to come—transcends the worship of God!

When Dr. Howard Hendricks delivered the 1999 W. H. Griffith Thomas Lectures at Dallas Theological Seminary, he spoke on the subject of aging. He called the series "On the Edge of Eternity." One of the passages he emphasized was Psalm 71, the prayer of an old man whose desire was to worship God with all his remaining strength. The psalmist wrote, "But I will hope continually, and will praise You yet more and more. My mouth shall tell of Your righteousness and Your salvation all the day, for I do not know their limits. I will go in the strength of the Lord GOD; I will make mention of Your righteousness, of Yours only" (Ps. 71:14–16).

None of us, no matter what our age, has a sure knowledge of how much time is left. All of life is in God's hands. And nothing is more significant in our lives than our worship of Him.

My purpose in this book is not just to discuss, inform, and instruct, but to help readers have a sense of wonder about our great theme of worshiping God. I pray that this book may be used by God to stimulate His people to worship Him more meaningfully and more wholeheartedly.

# Acknowledgments

MOST OF CHAPTERS 14–19 and parts of chapters 3 and 20 in this book have been written by my son, Craig H. Allen, while he was pastor of music and worship at Laurelwood Baptist Church, Vancouver, Washington. He has also assisted in some of the other chapters. As of January of this year Craig begins a new ministry as worship pastor of Southern Gables Evangelical Free Church, Littleton, Colorado.

Many people have contributed to my love for the subject of biblical worship. I wish to mention here my indebtedness to Dr. Gordon Borror for many wonderful emphases on the subject of the worship of God. Gordon served for many years as professor of music and worship at Western Seminary in Portland, Oregon. He served as pastor of First Baptist Church, Milwaukie, Oregon, and coauthored with me the book, *Worship: Rediscovering the Missing Jewel.*[1] He has recently become professor of music and worship at Southwestern Baptist Theological Seminary, Fort Worth, Texas. Some ideas in this present book may have actually come originally from Gordon during the course of our many discussions over the years. Gordon was also the mentor of my son Craig (and many others, including his own sons Greg and Kent).

Phillipe Willems did a number of interviews for me in the early stages of writing this book. Mrs. Karen Giesen read some parts of this book and offered helpful suggestions, as did Dr. Kenneth O. Gangel. Dr. Roy B. Zuck, managing editor of the Swindoll Leadership Library series, has given much encouragement in completing this project and thorough attention to many details. I offer deep appreciation to each of these friends.

# Part 1

# Foundational Issues

*One*

༄

# Leading in Worship

THE AUGUST DAY WAS BEAUTIFUL. Breathtakingly so! While the rest of the country had been painted in simmering crimson colors on the *USA Today* weather map in Friday's paper, the climate in our spot in northern California was a delightful 65 degrees. The skies were an unpolluted blue, a gentle breeze refreshed the air, and the hilltop setting of the church building was exquisite. It was Sunday morning, and my wife and I were in church at Cypress Community Church, midway between Monterey and Salinas.

I knew the day would be wonderful. After church we were likely to have dinner with the pastor and his wife and our dear friends the Hoffmans. After dinner I had planned a bicycle ride of twenty miles or so. The day could hardly be improved on. But ahead were the church services where I was to be the guest preacher.

I was ready for my sermon. The only question I had was how the worship would go. My message was designed to draw people to a greater sense of the grace of God in the person and work of our Savior, the Lord Jesus Christ. But my sermon was just a part of a larger whole. That larger whole was the congregational worship of the living God. And there sometimes is the rub.

## ON THE PLATFORM

The pastors and I wore robes that day, something common for them but less so for me. My shoes were shined and my pants were neatly creased. We had arrived early so there was no unnecessary stress. However, following an older fashion of church etiquette, I was positioned on the platform beside the senior pastor. This is not an enviable position. The people on the platform are separated from the congregation. On many occasions I have found myself wishing I could be nearly anywhere else. I recall more than one "platform party" where the men would seem oblivious to the congregational worship. Worship, they seem to think, is for the people but not for them.

Unfortunately some of the following scenes have become all too common.

- A person seated on the platform makes telephone calls from the phone next to his chair on the platform. Once during a hymn I became aware that the pastor was using the phone to make arrangements for a golf game with the guest speaker!
- The platform people slouch listlessly, cross legs carelessly, chew gum noisily, yawn gapingly.[1] I recall the stern instructions given to those of us on the platform party at a Billy Graham Crusade, warning against these very actions.
- The pastor is shuffling through his notes, impatient for the big event—his sermon. One man has told me that he regards the early part of the service as God's gift to him to review his sermon. Often he finds that contact with the people before the service distracts his thoughts. So he uses the singing time, he says, "to get my mind and heart back on my message."
- The pastor shows annoyance at the time being taken by the "preliminaries."[2] I recall one service in which the pastor interrupted the singing and said to the song leader, "I told you not to do so many verses! I am now ready to preach. Finish your song, if you must, after I am done with my message."
- People on the platform are whispering to each other. At times a necessary note must be passed, but I have been on platforms where

4

they were actually telling jokes to each other as the congregation did "whatever they were doing."

- A minister comes to me and asks a Bible question. I whisper that I cannot answer now because we are singing. He shakes his head and moves away, suggesting perhaps that I have not shown sufficient interest in him or in his question. Well, I am trying to show interest in God.
- Someone on the platform is waving and winking at a woman seated near the front. Yes, they have just become engaged, so perhaps this will not be a recurring behavior pattern.

In any event I do not enjoy sitting on the platform even when I am going to be preaching. I much prefer to sit, stand, and kneel *with* the congregation before I preach *to* the congregation. I want to be known as a worshiper of the living God, not as one of "the platform people."

## A WORSHIPER!

On this August Sunday morning, despite my sense of disquiet at being on the platform, things went very well. The pastor, Wayne Adams, was not merely the worship leader; he was the *lead worshiper.*

I sensed his earnestness in his prayers. I observed his rapt demeanor during the special music. I was unable to ignore his participation in congregational singing. This was a pastor who led in worship by his own actions and attitudes.

My longtime friend Chuck Fromm, founder of Maranatha! Music, told me some time ago that we need to think a bit differently than we usually do when we talk about leading in worship. Truly to lead in worship, he insisted, is to be the lead worshiper. Leading others in worshiping the Lord is not just a position one might have in the church. To lead well in worship one must first be a true worshiper.

## THEN . . . AND NOW

Twenty-five years ago very few books had been written on the subject of worship from an evangelical perspective. Peter Gillquist had begun to write on the subject of worship, a part of his pilgrimage from the free-church tradition to that of Eastern Orthodoxy. Among his early titles was *The Spiritual Side of Being Spiritual.*[3] Robert Webber also wrote on worship; his books make a significant argument for liturgy in the evangelical church. One of his early books was *Common Roots.*[4] Perhaps the first title in the evangelical rediscovery of worship that was centered in the free-church movement was *O Come, Let Us Worship,* by Robert Rayburn.[5] Over the years I have had numerous interactions with both Gillquist and Webber; I have not met Rayburn but I felt his book to be more in the "center" of things in our tradition.

Other names in the early stages of the evangelical awakening in worship include Anne Ortlund,[6] A. W. Tozer,[7] Donald Hustad,[8] and Ralph Martin.[9] But in the 1970s and 1980s these were about the only evangelical authors who wrote on worship. It was in this context that Gordon Borror and I wrote our book, *Worship: Rediscovering the Missing Jewel,*[10] building our title from lectures by Tozer.

Today we can hardly list the number of books written by evangelicals on the subject of worship! Some of these are listed in the bibliography of this book; others are noted in the endnotes. In his book *Worship in Spirit and Truth,*[11] John M. Frame observes that books on worship may be grouped in three categories.

- Some books focus on the history of worship, with appeals for churches today to follow the early patterns of Christian tradition.
- Other books present patterns and analyses of one of the classic strands or one of the new movements in Christianity. For example, a book may be a study of Presbyterian worship patterns or of Latin American (Hispanic) charismatics.
- Other books, according to Frame, are more practical, seeking to deepen, strengthen, and enrich one's worship.[12]

This book fits into the third category. Its distinction is that it is addressed principally to pastors and worship leaders to encourage them in their own worship, and then to help them in leading others in worshiping God.

## AND TOMORROW?

The best way to become a better worship leader is to become a better worshiper. When worship leaders worship, the people will follow happily. When congregational worship is at its best and the worship leader is the lead worshiper, it doesn't matter whether the weather is as pleasant as it was that August Sunday at Cypress Community Church. It can be a miserable day outside. When true worship takes place, weather becomes an incidental and the worship of God is the great reality.

# *Two*

## Getting Ready for Worship

THEN HE SHOWED ME JOSHUA the high priest standing before the Angel of the LORD, and Satan standing at his right hand to oppose him. And the LORD said to Satan, "The LORD rebuke you, Satan! The LORD who has chosen Jerusalem rebuke you! Is this not a brand plucked from the fire?" Now Joshua was clothed with filthy garments, and was standing before the Angel. Then He answered and spoke to those who stood before Him, saying, "Take away the filthy garments from him." And to him He said, "See, I have removed your iniquity from you, and I will clothe you with rich robes." And I said, "Let them put a clean turban on his head." So they put a clean turban on his head and they put the clothes on him. And the Angel of the LORD stood by. (Zech. 3:1–5)

### JOSHUA'S VERY BAD DAY

Joshua the priest was neither a nervous individual nor an incompetent one. But today was *the* day. He was a wreck. He had scrubbed his skin until it was nearly raw. His garments, although brand-new, had been washed repeatedly. Everything had been thought through, everything ordered, everything prepared. Nonetheless tension wrinkled his nerves, an inner turmoil wrestled with his spirit.

*Today he was to lead his people in the worship of God!*

The temple was now complete. All was prepared. All was clean. All was beautiful. Singers and players had rehearsed. The courses of priests had followed their regulations, practiced their rites, perfected their rituals.

When the hordes of Nebuchadnezzar's army had destroyed the temple in Jerusalem decades earlier, many survivors thought that all hope was lost, all promises dissipated, the future but a vapor.

But now there was a new temple in Jerusalem. True, it was modest compared with the building it replaced, but it was completed and the worship of the high God of heaven could commence.

Many people would be involved on this grand day, but no one person was more significant than he. For he, Joshua, was the high priest, and he was to lead the people in worshiping the Lord.

Long before the rays of the morning sun broke over the Mount of Olives Joshua was up and alert. He was in prayer and also in deep thought. He dressed with care, his attendants assuring him that all was clean, that his new clothing was spotless.

At the appointed time amid the excitement of the people and among his attendant priests, Joshua made his solemn approach to the new temple. He mounted the stairs, passed through the gates, entered the courts, and suddenly was transformed.

## WHAT PLACE IS THIS?

The scene had changed. Was he asleep or in a trance? This was not the temple in Jerusalem. He had moved through an earthly gate and had entered the courts of heaven's throne! Like Isaiah more than two hundred years earlier, he now found himself unexpectedly facing the Lord, Yahweh of hosts, the King of heaven. And, like Isaiah, he was nearly destroyed.[1]

Joshua gasped, closed his eyes, felt faint. Without even a glance to the throne he fell, face to the ground, hands over his head. He knew where he was, but understood nothing about how it had happened. He was in heaven's city. He was in heaven's courts. He was before heaven's throne—and heaven's God.

At first all he could hear was the sound of his own heart racing in his chest, the gasping of his breath. Then above the din of his own body's inner noises he heard the sound of an unearthly voice.

He was told to stand. Later he tried to think how he ever managed to do that once simple act. Stand? In the presence of the Creator? Somehow, in some manner, he accomplished this action, but he dared not look forward. He kept his eyes closed and his head down. But there he stood.

And as he stood, he became aware of the most awful of things. It was a smell, the odor of human excrement.[2]

If the glory of the throne before him could not allow him to open his eyes fully, the horror of his own odor caused him to peer briefly at his own garments. And the sight caused him nearly to faint again. His beautiful garments were spattered with waste. And there he stood, before the throne of heaven's glory.

How could this be? He had never worn these clothes before this moment. They had been washed repeatedly, even though they were pristine, new, never worn. Now he could no longer help himself. He looked at his sleeves, the skirt of his robe, his sandals. Everywhere he looked it seemed things were worse than where he had just looked.

When he was first aware that he was standing before the throne of God, he was afraid he might die. Now his fear was that death might not come quickly enough.

And then he began to make sense of the words of the loud, sonorous voice. He stole a glance at the one who was speaking. At first he saw only a dazzling, shimmering phantom being. Then he glanced again, then again, and then he held his gaze, riveted at the strange, bizarre sight.

The sight was simply astounding. He saw a person, a heavenly being. For a moment the being seemed to be the most beautiful and radiant creature one could ever imagine. But when he spoke, the face changed into features more hideous than a nightmare might allow. The voice was like an ocean's roar.

Then the priest heard the words, and even more awful than the words, he heard the laughter. Hateful laughter. Hideous laughter. Haunting laughter. Perhaps the laughter was the worst of all. The dazzling, hateful being was mocking him, deriding him.

Gradually Joshua was aware of something even more insidious. The Accuser[3] was laughing.

"You call this your priest?" he mocked. "Look at him! He is covered in filth." The laughter that followed was as powerful and as evil as might be imagined if there were countless cracks of thunder accompanying a most violent storm in hell itself. And the worst of it was that the accusations were correct. In this case the father of lies did not have to use deception.

## ANOTHER VOICE

But then Joshua heard another voice. The new voice was not loud, but it seemed to have the potential to shatter mountains. Better, this was the voice that could call mountains into being. The new voice was authority. Heaven's authority. And when he heard the words, he could hardly believe them.

The words of the second voice were not directed toward him. The second speaker was addressing his tormentor. And the new voice said to the first speaker, "The Lord rebuke you, accusing one."

The priest trembled again. Someone was speaking in his defense. It might cost him his life, but he dared a glance in the direction of the new voice.

And he was dazzled anew! Whereas the first creature was hard to fix, changing between radiant beauty and hideous repugnance, the second person was as glorious as light.

Both figures, he realized, were angels. The one was the epitome of evil; the other was a holy being. The one was the angel of darkness; the other the angel of light. The one had no real place in heaven; the other belonged next to the throne. The second was the Angel of the Lord (Yahweh).[4]

The Angel of the Lord stood there before heaven's throne in a position of quiet dignity. Clearly this was where He belonged! A glance to the first creature confirmed a growing suspicion in the priest's mind; the first creature did not belong here. He had made an appearance, but it seemed that he had come just because the priest was to be there.

Joshua's thoughts were in a whirl. He heard the words of the Angel of the Lord repeating his condemnation of the Accuser, an announcement of eternal damnation. The Angel of the Lord spoke lovingly of Jerusalem and compassionately of Jerusalem's priest—of him! And as the angel spoke, the accuser slunk back, shrunk down, and was gone.

Joshua still dared not glance at heaven's throne. Had he done so (and lived), he might have seen a gentle nod of Majesty.

Suddenly he was aware of myriads of angelic beings surrounding him. They were above, below, and all around him. Until now he had been completely unaware of their presence—a not unusual phenomenon for God's angels!

Again the Angel spoke, giving a gentle command. Holy angels approached the still foul-smelling priest, extended their arms, obeyed the command, and removed his clothing. Then, gentle as dew on the petals of flowers, they cleansed his skin of any remaining sight or smell of the offending garments.

The Angel spoke yet again, his voice like melodious songbirds, the effect of the waves of sound like the drinking of cool water on a blisteringly hot day. And the words were, "Clothe him, dress him with clean garments."

This the angels did. And while dressing the priest so that he would be truly prepared to lead in the worship of heaven's King, another voice was heard.

The last voice was that of the one who dreamed this scene. He was a prophet of God named Zechariah. Now in the midst of his own revelatory dream he shouted out, "Don't forget the clean turban!"

No chance. The priest was now fully prepared to lead his people in worshiping God.

## SPEAKING OF JOSHUA

More than thirty years ago Merrill F. Unger spoke on Zechariah 3 at the Church of the Open Door in Los Angeles, California. This was during the illustrious ministry of J. Vernon McGee at that venerable church and it was in the context of the West Coast Prophetic Conference.

Dr. Unger wonderfully stressed that the stripping off of the excrement-bespattered garments of the high priest is a poignant picture (a type) of the removal of sin when one is forgiven by the loving, sovereign Lord. He also stressed that God in His saving work does not merely strip away one's sin, but then completes His work by "dressing" that person in the righteousness of Christ. This is the imputation of righteousness, the bringing of the righteousness of Another, where it is lacking in oneself.

But I wish here to make a different point, the preparation of God's leader for God's worship. Left to our own devices, with all the industry that we might personally engender, we—the leaders of God's worship—might appear in heaven's light to be as foul as was Joshua in Zechariah's dream.

Leading believers in worship is a sublime task, and it has extensions and connections to the unseen world about us and the glories of the world to come. Angels attend our worship of God. More precisely, our true worship joins our acts and attitudes with the worship of spirit beings around heaven's throne. Nothing in life could be more impressive than this!

But preparation and presentation are insufficient for our holy task, if they are done in our own strength. Preparation and presentation in worship must be done by God's power, in His Spirit, and to His glory. There needs to be a stripping away of self-engendered concerns and a receiving of heaven's mantle. Also attention needs to be given even to what one wears when leading in worship.

## WHAT ARE YOU DRESSED AS?

For more than ten years I have had a passion for bicycle riding. I do not do mountain riding; I feel that I am much too old and brittle to put myself in a position to do face-plants on single tracks on a mountainside. Instead, I put myself in the relative safety (?) of highway traffic and ride long distances on my racing bike. I am not fast, but I am persistent—and I love it!

I had a painful lesson early in my new passion; this was the first day I rode forty miles in one day. I was so sore that I found it uncomfortable for several days to sit in even a soft chair. That was when I decided to do something I thought I would never do—buy a pair of lycra bicycling shorts.

I determined I would never wear these shorts where someone might recognize me. So on the first day I wore them I drove to the opposite side of the city from where we lived, assured that none of my friends would see me.

As I was taking the bike off the rack of my car, another car pulled in next to me, four of my students got out, and one said: "Dr. Allen, what are you doing over here at Washington Square? I thought you lived near Clackamas Town Center."

I responded, "I am over here so that no one I know will see me wearing these new tight bike shorts."

One day recently I was the speaker for a singles' retreat at a conference center in east Texas. On the free Saturday afternoon I did what I do on most such afternoons: I put my bike together, put on my cycling clothes, and set off for a long afternoon ride. I wear cycling shoes over cycling socks, cycling shorts, a brightly colored (that is, "gaudy") cycling jersey, cycling gloves, cycling cap under a cycling helmet. I rode half of my planned distance and then stopped at a little café in the small town of Hawkins, Texas.

When the hostess saw me, she took one long look at me and said, "And who are you dressed up to be, dear?"

Only then did I realize that it was Halloween!

I said, "Ma'am, I'm dressed up as a bicycle rider." I then took a piece of candy from her bowl as I heard her laugh and say something about my "nice costume."

## AND HOW DO WE DRESS FOR WORSHIP?

How should we dress when we come to lead in the worship of God? In some church denominations, robes or vestments are prescribed. In the free church, issues of dress are conditioned by culture and custom.

These things are under change in our volatile age. I remember the instructions that my classmates and I were given years ago in seminary to always wear a full suit when we preached in church. A sport coat and slacks were not considered dressy enough. We were strongly encouraged to have our coats buttoned when walking to the pulpit. "A sure sign of a sloppy preacher is an unbuttoned coat!"

These days the sharpest dressers in seminaries and churches are likely to be African-American students and professors. One day one of my black students told me that for African-American Christians, dressing for Sunday is a very special tradition. It goes back to slavery days when Sunday was the only day the people could wear their better clothes. Now, with slavery days in the past, the wearing of "Sunday best" is a mark of great pride for African-American families. I do not mean this as "pride" in a sinful sense, but in the sense of joy. These are people ready to worship God in style!

But the rest of us may not do so well. Things have really changed. When I speak at Christian camps and conference centers, I may wear a polo shirt and shorts. I have ironed the shirt and shorts, but they are a long way from a suit!

These days things are far more complex.

Some years ago I arrived at a church in southern California dressed in what I called my "Dr. Jerry Falwell three-piece suit." When I got there, I found that I was likely the only man present even wearing a tie. A friend said, "Perhaps you can at least remove your vest."

I hesitate to speak of paradigm shifts—but they are all about us. In an Oregon church where I have ministered, the pastoral staff members actually do clothing changes for each of three successive services on Sunday morning. In one I was told to wear a suit, in the second to come without the jacket, and in the third to change from a dress shirt and tie to an open-necked sport shirt.

I have spoken in churches in Texas where I felt my wingtip shoes were very much out of place amid so many men (and women!) who were wearing their dress boots. It is not unusual at all in many churches in Oregon to find that hardly any man is wearing a suit or any woman a full dress; rather wool shirts and dressy sport shirts are seen on men and pant outfits on women.

Just when I think I have things figured out, I arrive at a church in Minnesota dressed rather casually only to find that all on the platform are in full suits.

Here, however, are some suggestions:

- Neatness still counts.
- Shined shoes really matter.

- Modesty is still necessary.[5]
- Tastes vary, but ugly is still ugly.

After all, even in casual clothes, we are dressed for worship, not for Halloween.

## ARE YOU NERVOUS YET?

One Sunday I was preaching in a large church in northern California, a church that was meeting in the gymnasium of a public high school. There were three services; each was packed. Toward the beginning of the second service I took a seat in a row near the front (thus avoiding the "platform"). Soon the row was filled with people.

At an early part of the service the pastor encouraged people to greet one another. The woman to my right told me her name was Joan. When I told her my name, she gasped, "Are you the visiting speaker?"

When I told her I was, she asked, "Are you nervous yet?"

I said no, but I thought, "Keep it up and I will be."

She began a whispered conversation of some urgency. Even when the congregation began to sing, she wanted to talk about her fear of public speaking. She told me she was in a class of about twenty people in a course on public speaking. She went on and on about how nervous she gets.

I tried to sing, to orient my thoughts to God. But it seemed that at every slight break she said something about her growing terror—for me! Finally the singing was done, and I made my way to the small pulpit. After the service was over and I had finished greeting a number of people, she came up to me, apologized, hugged me, and then said, "But tell me the truth. Weren't you getting nervous? Just a little?"

Why am I *not* more nervous when I get up to preach the Word of God? Is it because I have done it before in many settings over the span of many years? Did I not used to feel nervous when I would go to the pulpit? Was that not a good thing?

My son-in-law, Jay Held, ministers in an inner-city congregation in Portland, Oregon. Jay has several advanced degrees and is more educated than most of the people in his congregation. He is very fit; early training in football and continued regular fitness and exercise give him a formidable presence. But he tells me that every Sunday morning he experiences a very strong sense of nervous tension. He is prepared for his sermon, he knows what he wants to do, he is fit and strong—and yet he experiences nervousness.

A conversation with Jay reminded me of something my professor of New Testament Greek told me years ago. Professor Zane Hodges said that he was relatively calm when teaching seminary classes and even when preaching in the seminary chapel. If he made an error, he felt he would soon learn about it from his students or colleagues. "But," he said, "when I preach in the barrio assembly in a poor section of Dallas, there is not likely someone there who can correct me if I am wrong. So I work harder at being right because more is at stake."

Joan's nervousness for me was a projection of her own fear of speaking before groups of people. She clearly had no such fear in speaking to just one person; she chattered on and on to me. Was my nervousness in the early days like hers? Was it just a fear of speaking before large groups?

So I ask, When one has become comfortable in the pulpit, standing before a large number of people to present the truths of the Word of God, should there not be some residual nervousness that relates to the prospect of what one is about to do?

The minister of the gospel represents God before His people. The preacher handles the truths of the Bible in a public setting. Lives may hang in the balance. Decisions may be made that impact the direction people's lives may take for time and for eternity.

We should pray, "God, grant me a sense of being nervous, not because of the fright of being in front of a group of people, but with a realization of the awesome responsibility and far-reaching significance of the ministry of your Word."

## JOSHUA'S GOOD DAY

The night vision of the prophet Zechariah described at the beginning of this chapter did not delineate actual events. This was a dream. It was a vision that God used in the life of the prophet in which God was teaching Israel (and us) about His righteousness, mercy, and great grace.

Surely the prophet would have told the story to Joshua. Imagine the impact this dream vision would have had on the young priest of God as he prepared in real time for his initial ministry amid the sacred places in the new temple.

I suspect that when Joshua actually did prepare himself for that first morning, he gave inordinate attention to the cleanliness of his garments. The visionary dream of the prophet was a nightmare for the priest. Surely he also gave considerable attention to his heart. The deeper spiritual issues could not have escaped the understanding of this godly young man of God. So I project that the first day of his ministry for the living God in the holy temple was actually a very good day. It was a world away from the dream that Zechariah had received from God. But Joshua was a true worshiper of the living God.

## A VERY GOOD MODEL

Worship is a participative event. As Robert Webber insists, "worship" is an active verb. To lead well in worship, as Chuck Fromm suggests, is really to be a lead worshiper.

Few in my circle of friends and acquaintances fit this model better than the one for whom this series of books is named. Dr. Charles Swindoll's ministry has been characterized over many years not only by outstanding Bible teaching, witty and practical application, compassionate pastoring, and other excellencies. His ministry has been characterized as well by his active participation in worship in his congregation.

Howie Stevenson and his wife, Marilyn, served with Dr. Swindoll for many years at the First Evangelical Free Church of Fullerton, California. Howie tells me that he always had the sense that Chuck had a significant part in leading the worshiping community.

I observe pastors from time to time in worship services. I do not seek to criticize them, but at times I find myself wondering what is going on in their minds. No one knows the heart but God. But an observer is aware that some don't sing with the congregation. Instead, they whisper asides to people on the platform, they seem distracted—even bored—when they are not themselves "on" at the pulpit.

What we need to do is work on our "preliminaries." Instead of thinking of those parts of the service that are "preliminary" to the sermon, let's use that word to describe our own actions that are "preliminary" to the service itself.

For example, we need to check our clothing well ahead of the worship event. I recall a phone call I made to my pastor when I was a college student. It was early Saturday evening. I apologized for bothering him, but I had a question about the next morning. I remember Pastor Martin Stuck saying, "Well, you got me at a good time. I have just finished pressing my suit for tomorrow."

He had it right. Pressed trousers. Shined shoes. Fresh shirt. He was going to stand at the pulpit as a minister of God.

But I suspect Pastor Stuck and Pastor Swindoll and countless other ministers who understand these things take care of more than their clothing in their "preliminaries." They also give attention to their hearts. They focus on God and His mercy.

They may even get a little nervous.

# *Three*

❧

# The Biblical Role of Worship

## DALLAS SEMINARY AND GOD'S GLORY

FOR MORE THAN seventy-five years Dallas Theological Seminary has had a constant, overarching emphasis in its theology on the glory of God. The concept of *doxology* (which means, literally, "the glory of God") is central. As important as we regard God's work in salvation, we reject what might be called "redempto-centrism,"[1] the idea that the most important thing in Scripture is God's work in man's salvation.

God's glorious work in the redemption of fallen humanity is not an end in itself; it is part of the larger picture of God's work in eternity, which centers in the display of His transcendent glory.

This is the point of Paul's remarkable introduction to the Book of Ephesians. God's great work in Christ Jesus in bringing glorious salvation to fallen beings is designed to bring praise to God's great glory. This merits repeating: *Salvation is not an end in itself. The praise of God is the highest good.* God's work in the lives of His people, according to Paul, is centered in the context of the praise of His glory. In other words God's worship is the divine goal of His redemptive work.

Here is a schematic presentation of the apostle's words in Ephesians 1:3–6.

> Blessed be the God and Father of our Lord Jesus Christ,
> who has blessed us with every spiritual blessing
> in the heavenly *places*[2] in Christ,
> just as He chose us in Him before the foundation of the world,
> that we should be holy and without blame before Him in love,
> having predestined us to adoption as sons by Jesus Christ to Himself,
> according to the good pleasure of His will,
> to the praise of the glory of His grace,
> by which He made us accepted in the Beloved.

This passage ripples with wonder.

These verses also present grand issues that some people find troubling. What is meant by "predestined"? How could God have chosen us "before the foundation of the world"? Why did God choose some and not others?

## AND WHERE IS WORSHIP?

But sometimes the discussion leaves out a central issue. The section begins with the words, "Blessed be the God and Father of our Lord Jesus Christ." The term *blessed* is a New Testament word for praise from the Psalms. To bless God (that is, to call Him "blessed") is to praise God.[3] The passage then builds to the phrase "*to the praise* of the glory of His grace."

Do you see the pattern? "*Blessed be* . . . God" (1:3) . . . "*to the praise of the glory of His grace*" (1:6).

The passage begins and ends with words calling for believers to worship God.

The next paragraph in Paul's letter to the Ephesians also leads to the grand goal of worship. Ephesians 1:7–12 contains some of the grandest ideas of God's salvation work to be found in the New Testament. Salvation is *in Christ*. It is *of grace*. It is all *by God*. Amid powerful (and sometimes troubling) ideas, such as "His blood," "the mystery of His will," "the dispensation of the fullness of the times," "all things in Christ," "an inheritance," "being predestined" (again!), and "the counsel of His will," we find the confession that the principal thing is the worship of God.

Look again at the last words of this paragraph: "that we who first trusted in Christ should be *to the praise of His glory*" (1:12).

Our salvation—as glorious as that is—is not God's final purpose. Our salvation is designed to bring more glory to God. This is a worship theme. This is *doxology!*

But the apostle was not finished with this theme, despite the wonderful language of these two paragraphs. He had another point in verses 13–14, in which he emphasized the role of the Holy Spirit in salvation. The Holy Spirit both seals the believer and is the guarantee of the believer's ultimate redemption. And, as with God the Father in verses 3–7 and God the Son in verses 8–12, the work of the Spirit in verses 13–14 is designed to bring worship to God. For again, all is "*to the praise of His glory*" (1:14).

Three times we have the same phrase (Eph. 1:6, 12, 14). Each of the first three paragraphs of Paul's magnificent letter ends with a call to worship God. Our salvation is extremely wonderful, but it is not the end. Our salvation—and our growing sense of how truly wonderful it is—has one goal and one goal only, that we should be to the praise of His glory. Thus worship is the most important issue in Paul's letter to the Ephesians!

Not salvation by grace. Not the mystery of the church. Not the breaking down of the middle wall of petition. Not spiritual gifts. Not submission of wives to their husbands. Not wearing the armor of the Lord. The most important issue is worship!

## HUMILIATION AND EXALTATION

Philippians 2:5–11 describes the incarnation of the blessed Savior—His humiliation, His suffering, and His death, followed by His glorious exaltation. Paul here described the suffering Servant (the theme developed first in Isaiah 52:13–53:12), the One who humbled Himself in obedience to the Father even to "the death of the cross" (Phil. 2:8). But after the humiliation came the exaltation.

This was revealed to Isaiah seven centuries before the Cross. "Behold,

My Servant shall deal prudently; He shall be exalted and extolled and be very high" (Isa. 52:13).

Paul's use of the term "servant" in Philippians 2:7 is best seen as having come from Isaiah's use of "My Servant" in Isaiah. The prophet Isaiah used three terms to describe the future exaltation of the Lord's faithful Servant: "exalted ," "extolled," "be very high." Possibly these terms suggest three stages of exaltation: His resurrection, His ascension, and His glorification. But more likely these three words are joined together in a form of Hebrew poetry, for the purpose of emphasis.[4]

Two words that are joined together to express one idea are called a hendiadys. An example is in the words of Isaiah 53:3, "He is despised and rejected by men." That statement does not present two ideas, as if He was despised and also was rejected. This is one idea: He was totally rejected.

In the words of Isaiah 52:13 we have what we may call a "hendiatris!"[5] His exaltation will be so glorious that not even two synonyms are able to bear the weight of the meaning of His consummate glory. This "triple" is not unlike the threefold repetition of the word "holy" by the seraphim surrounding the heavenly throne in Isaiah's grand inaugural vision (6:3). By saying the Hebrew word qādôš three times in the hearing of Isaiah, the glowing angels[6] raised the notion of God's holiness to the ultimate level—His holiness is beyond the ability of human language to express.[7] Similarly the coming glory of the obedient Servant, Jesus Christ, is beyond our ability to comprehend.

"He shall be exalted and extolled and be very high" (52:13) means that His glory will be indescribable.

Paul asserted this same consummate glory in Philippians 2. Here is a schematic presentation of the words of verses 9–11.

> Therefore God also has highly exalted Him
> And given Him the name which is above every name,
>> that at the name of Jesus every knee should bow,
>>> of those in heaven,
>>> and of those on earth,
>>> and of those under the earth,
>>> and that every tongue should confess that Jesus is Lord,
>>>> to the glory of God the Father.

Again, the goal of all is *the worship of God*. The exaltation of the suffering Servant (who is also the obedient Son) is limitless. Ultimately every human being will acknowledge the exalted Christ with bowed knee and confessing tongue. And all this will be "to the glory of God the Father."

This is what Joachim Neander may have meant in his words, "All that hath life and breath / Come now with praises before Him!"[8]

> Praise to the Lord, the Almighty,
> the king of creation!
> O my soul, praise Him,
> For He is thy health and
> salvation!
> All ye who hear,
> Now to His temple draw near;
> Join me in glad adoration!
>
> —JOACHIM NEANDER

## MAN'S CHIEF END

Do you see it? The work of Savior Jesus in our redemption is not an end in itself but is God's marvelous means of achieving an even greater end, the manifestation of His glory. The glory of God is the overarching theme of all biblical theology.

The words of the Westminster Shorter Catechism have it correctly, and its answer to the question, "What is the chief end of man?" has never been surpassed. "The chief end of man is to glorify God and to enjoy Him forever."

- We have been created for the worship of God.
- We have been redeemed for the worship of God.
- We will live before Him forever for the worship of God.

John Frame puts it this way: "Redemption is the means; worship is the goal. In one sense, worship is the whole point of everything. It is the purpose of history, the goal of the whole Christian story. Worship is not one segment of the Christian life among others. Worship is the entire Christian life, seen as a priestly offering to God. And when we meet together as a church, our time of worship is not merely a preliminary to something else; rather, it is the whole point of our existence as the body of Christ."[9]

My son Craig has put this powerful idea to music in his song titled "To Your Throne."

> To Your throne, O God, is where we've come,
> eager to hear Your words of love, "Well done."
> To Your throne, O God, is where we've come,
> our heart's desire to magnify the Son!
> We do not seek the praise of men,
> nor to escape the pain we're in.
> But to glorify the Lord on high,
> and forever enjoy Him is our chief end![10]

This was also the sentiment of Neander in the hymn already noted. Here are the words of the fourth stanza of "Praise to the Lord, the Almighty."

> Praise to the Lord!
> O let all that is in me adore Him!
> All that hath life and breath,
> come now with praises before Him!
> Let the Amen
> Sound from His people again:
> Gladly for aye we adore Him.

I love the way Neander ties together the words "praise" and "adore." Here is a grand capture of the words of the Westminster Catechism: "The chief end of man is to glorify God and to enjoy Him forever."

## THE JEWEL OF WORSHIP

As I mentioned earlier, when I was teaching at Western Seminary in Portland, Oregon, Gordon Borror and I wrote the book *Worship! Rediscovering the Missing Jewel.* Our title was adapted from the title of a small pamphlet of addresses to Canadian pastors given by A. W. Tozer: *The Missing Jewel of Worship in the Evangelical Church.* Our idea was that the jewel was being discovered, but that there was a long way to go. The cover of the book, designed by Britt Taylor Collins, won a major award for design. It pictured a heart that was deeply encrusted and pitted, but which had some chipping on one lobe, revealing underneath a lustrous, multifaceted jewel. Behind were many stony hearts on which the chipping process had yet to begin.

It may be a bit difficult to believe today, but when our book was released it was considered by some people as something of an oddity, if not a threat, to have a book on the subject of worship published by an evangelical publisher.

Some people even regarded Multnomah Press as "suspect" because of the publication of our book on worship. Some bookstores packed up all titles from that publisher and returned them because of this "liberal" topic! Worship in 1982 was not a "hot" topic; in some areas it was even forbidden! There were very few evangelical titles on this subject at that time. More than one person wrote or spoke to me about the issue of writing on such a "liberal" topic.

Gordon Borror wrote very strongly on what we both regard as the principal biblical concern in the subject of worship: *Worship is more an issue of the heart than a state of art.* "Throughout the history of Christian worship we can observe a constant art-form modification. Early Christian worship began with little form, primarily brought from Jewish worship by early converts. This was followed by refinements and embellishments and ultimately so much form that the original purpose became obscure or missed entirely. In turn, this was followed by purifying reform which tended to start the cycle again. The lesson which seems to require constant rediscovery is the fact that worship is not primarily a state of the art but rather a state of the heart. By state of heart we mean the driving desire behind the worship life of the believer."[11]

## OUR PURPOSE IN WORSHIP

What is the essence of why we gather weekly in "worship services"? Simply stated, it is *to meet with God.* The emphasis on God is crucial. Yet we must also realize that worship is to be pursued as part of the Christian community, rather than merely as individuals. When we come to public worship, we come *as* the people of God, *with* the people of God, to meet *with* our God together.

### Worship Is for God

Worship should not focus on what we "get out of it." That is obviously self-centered. Our worship is not about pleasing or entertaining each other or our guests. Worship is also not really for unbelievers, for they are incapable of worshiping God. Slaves to sin, they worship things of the flesh.

So if worship is not for people, why then do we attend church? We come to meet with *God*. We come for *Him*. We come with a hunger for the person of God. We come to experience His presence among us. Psalm 27:4 models a worshiper's attitude: "One thing I have desired of the LORD, that will I seek: that I may dwell in the house of the LORD all the days of my life, to behold the beauty of the LORD, and to inquire in His temple."

Like David, we come in worship to gaze on God, to get a fresh sense of His presence, to see again His beauty, to seek anew His will for our lives. And we come to *give—to God!* We come to express our love to Him. We come to feast on His Word so that our lives are renewed and our spirits refreshed. We come to be filled again with the things of God, so that we are recharged to live for Him as His ambassadors during the week ahead. We come as a living sacrifice, offering ourselves to Him.

### God Is Our Audience

When we come to a worship service, we should not come as spectators, to watch an event. We should come to take part. Rather than seeing the pastor and musicians as "performers" and considering ourselves as part of the audience, we need to see ourselves as those who are coming as worshipers, with the Lord as the "audience." He is the Receiver—of our love, our praise, our adoration, our tithes, in short, our worship. The people up front are like player-coaches in sports, or like drama directors and prompters in theater. The leaders attempt to inspire and remind the congregation to offer their worship to God in appropriate and meaningful ways. The question we need to ask at the end of every worship service is not, Did I enjoy it? Instead the question should be, Was God honored by my worship? Was God pleased with my heart and my offering? Can you imagine the difference in our services each week if people came with that perspective in mind?

In Psalm 84 an anonymous psalmist revealed an excellent perspective on public worship. "How lovely is Your tabernacle, O LORD of hosts! My soul longs, yes, even faints for the courts of the LORD; my heart and my flesh cry out for the living God. . . . Blessed are those who dwell in Your house; they will still be praising You. . . . For a day in Your courts is better than a thousand [elsewhere]" (Ps. 84:1–2, 4, 10).

However, if worship is chiefly for God, why do we worship with other people? Is it not adequate simply to worship God in private? Why must we worship Him in public?

*Worship Inspires the Community*

Though God is the Object of our worship, every person present can be a recipient of the overflow of the blessing that worship brings. We come as a group to give to God—and also to receive from Him. And in this process we find ourselves also giving to God's people and receiving from them. As a godly pastor preaches to honor God and His Word, people are challenged to grow. As we sing songs of praise, people are reminded of who God is and what He does. As we see lives changed, we remember that God still answers prayer, and through this our faith increases. We give to God in worship, but we cannot outgive God. He always gives back more— sometimes to overflowing.

One reason we worship in public is to "give unto the LORD glory and strength, [to] give unto the LORD the glory due His name" (Ps. 29:1–2). Psalm 34:3 specifically calls us to public worship: "Oh, magnify the LORD *with me*, and let us exalt His name *together*" (italics added). And one of the reasons for worshiping with others is stated in the previous verse: "My soul shall make its boast in the LORD; the humble shall hear of it and be glad" (34:2).

This is the biblical view. When one believer expresses his or her personal boasting in the Lord through public praise, personal testimony, or the radiance of their joyful singing, others who are struggling are lifted up and encouraged. True public worship fuels edification.

## Worship Is Not an Option

The early church believers were completely convinced of the need to gather together to be built up in the Lord. "And they continued steadfastly in the apostles' doctrine and fellowship, in the breaking of bread, and in prayers" (Acts 2:42). Through this intense devotion they were filled with the wonder of God and even witnessed miracles (2:43). They met together daily both in the temple and in their homes, "praising God and having favor with all the people" (2:47). The result of this intense commitment to worship and fellowship was staggering: "The Lord added to the church daily those who were being saved" (2:47). Dedicated public worship fuels evangelism. When God is at work among His people, unbelievers notice. When God's people are honoring their first commitment to love the Lord with all their hearts, they experience the joy of seeing what He is doing in building His church.

These are the biblical values in true worship. May our gracious God raise up people who will worship Him. May He raise up people who will lead others in His holy worship. And may He instill in our seminaries godly instruction, patterns, and models of true worship.

We began this chapter in Ephesians; here is where we also may end. As noted, Paul began his wonderful epistle with a threefold call for the response of God's people to be "to the praise of His glory" (Eph. 1:6, 12, 14). The work of the Father, the Son, and the Spirit in our salvation is not the end; the end is that God be worshiped, that He be glorified.

Then as Paul reflected on God's grace, he proclaimed these words of doxology: "Now to Him who is able to do exceedingly abundantly above all that we ask or think, according to the power that works in us, to Him be glory in the church by Christ Jesus to all generations, forever and ever" (Eph. 3:20–21).

It is not enough for us to affirm God's glory as a biblical idea. We must also give Him glory as we worship Him.

# $\mathcal{F}our$

# Mere Ritual or True Worship?

NOVELISTS ROUTINELY DESCRIBE religious acts as meaning-less ritual. It is sad to observe, but it is true that for many people, including at times even spiritual leaders, religious acts have very little meaning.[1] In one of his mystery novels featuring horse racing, Dick Francis describes Dorothea, a befuddled older woman, who asked a young friend to arrange for the visit of a Roman Catholic priest to give last rites for her dying brother. Neither Dorothea nor her brother was a practicing Roman Catholic, but with the grim reality of impending death, she wanted to "cover her bases."

When the priest arrived, it was evident that he was not taking his task very seriously. "We waited barely half an hour, long enough only for evening to draw in, with Dorothea switching on the lights. Then the real priest, a tubby, slightly grubby-looking middle-aged man hopelessly lacking in charisma parked his car behind my own and walked up the concrete path unenthusiastically."[2]

The priest took some olive oil with which he made the sign of the cross on the old man's forehead, and then began his blessings in English. Dorothea protested. This should be done in Latin, she said. Neither she nor her brother had attended church since they were children. Somehow, however, she felt that for this to "work" it had to be in Latin. The priest looked at her dispassionately, shrugged, got out his book and began doing it in Latin. "*'Dominus noster Jesus Christus te absolvat. . . .'* Our Lord Jesus Christ absolve you. . . . He said the words without passion, a task undertaken for strangers, giving blanket absolution for he knew not what sins. He droned on and on."[3]

As I read these words, I thought how awful this is. First, I do not believe that a priest has the power to absolve anyone's sins. Only Christ can forgive sins. This major truth is seen in the lively interchange between some scribes and Jesus when Jesus forgave the sins of a paralytic man in Capernaum (Mark 2:1–12). Second, I thought, if one did believe that this fictional priest was actually conveying God's forgiveness on a sinner, then would this not be the most exciting thing he could possibly do? How could such a thing be done "without passion"? How could he drone on and on?

And then I think of our rituals. Is it possible that at times we behave with similar nonchalance when we bow to pray before a family meal? Is it possible that harried pastors occasionally rush through the observance of the Lord's Table because the service has gone too long already? Can it be that hymns are sung without meaning? Choruses sung without thought? Sermons preached without passion? Worship services "gotten through" (completed) without the pastor "getting through" (to God)—or perhaps without God "getting through" to the pastor?

Is the account by Dick Francis simply a fictional tale of a harried Roman Catholic priest conjured up to fill a scene in a novel? Or are we guilty of similar apathy in our worship?

> Let the peoples praise You, O God;
> Let all the peoples praise You.
> Oh, let the nations be glad and sing for joy!
> For You shall judge the people righteously,
> And govern the nations on earth.
>
> PSALM 67:3–4

From time to time we read in the Bible of priests of God who failed to take their tasks seriously, who did not take the needs of people importantly, and—preeminently—who did not view God fearfully.

## STRANGE FIRE

Astonishingly Israel's first high priest, Aaron, the brother of Moses and Miriam, once led the people in paganistic worship—right at the foot of God's holy mountain. The account in Exodus 32 is difficult to comprehend. How could it be that the spiritual leader of the redeemed nation could so easily turn from the worship of God to the worship of idols? How could a man who had seen the powerful works of the Lord turn so quickly from reality to a falsehood? How could one who had stood beside Moses have attributed Israel's deliverance to gods made with human hands? But this is precisely what he did.

Gold ornaments were melted to produce the image of a calf deity. In the ancient Near East the bull was a potent symbol of sexual virility. This graven image was both an echo of Egyptian paganism and a foreshadowing of the principal pagan cult in Canaan, the worship of Baal. In the words, "This is your god, O Israel" (32:4), the people and their priest were corrupting what was most sacred, true worship, with symbols of sexual depravity.[4] Paul fully understood the nature of this incident; he said their sins were sexual in nature (1 Cor. 6:6–11). After eating and drinking in pagan rites before their obscene image, they "rose up to play" (Exod. 32:6; see 1 Cor. 6:7), a not-so-innocent expression! Paul rightly explained that this was sexual activity, not a ball game. The play was sexual congress with persons posing as sacred prostitutes, imitative magic to encourage fertility in the nation.

Just two chapters later in Exodus we read again of these gross sins. Engagement in the worship patterns of Canaan is said to be not only idolatry, but also a playing "the harlot with their gods" (Exod. 34:16). This is much more than a figure of speech. Baal and Asherah were the principal gods of Canaan, male and female fertility deities, whose worship was gross, obscene, debased. It is almost impossible to realize how opposite the true worship of the living God is from the filthy ideas associated with the worship of idols in

Canaan. The divine pattern of worshiping God in spirit and in truth (John 4:24) is in contrast to the pagan, licentious ideas of the ancient Near East.

If Aaron could be led into such apostasy, irreligion, and error—what will spare us from similar grievous sin?

## WICKED PRIESTS

The stories of biblical priests going wrong do not end in the sad account of Aaron at the base of Mount Sinai. We also think of his sons Nadab and Abihu, who "offered profane fire before the LORD" (Lev. 10:1; compare Num. 3:4). Here is a case where the sins of a father are magnified by his sons. What precisely is meant by "profane" (or "strange," KJV) fire is not clear, but the result cannot be missed. Fire (likely lightning) came from heaven and destroyed them. Accompanying the fire were the solemn words of the Lord that must have seared the memory of those standing near the smoking bodies: "By those who come near Me I must be regarded as holy; and before all the people I must be glorified" (Lev. 10:3).

Here is one of the strongest declarations of God's demand for pure and holy worship. Two issues here have overriding importance in our worship of God: His holiness and His glory. Sadly even Moses erred in these issues when he struck the rock unbidden. God's charge to Moses and Aaron is powerful: "You [plural in Hebrew] did not believe Me, to hallow Me in the eyes of the children of Israel, therefore you [plural] shall not bring this assembly into the land which I have given them" (Num. 20:12).

We also read of an apostate priest who was "in the pocket" of his mentor, an Ephraimite named Micah (Judg. 17). Later this priest "got a better offer" from the tribe of Dan (18:19). The symbols of true religion were mixed so thoroughly by both Micah and his priest that likely neither realized how far they were from truth.[5] The chapter is one of subtle satire to demonstrate how foolish people may be when they make up things as in their worship.

Late in the period of the judges Eli, a godly man but an ineffective father, allowed his sons to use their holy office to abuse needy people. These men were "corrupt" (literally, "sons of Belial") and they "did not know the LORD" (1 Sam. 2:12). They used their platform of holy ministry for self-aggrandizement, greed, even sexual assault (2:22). Perhaps the worst effect of their profound wickedness was the people's consequent sense of distaste for the worship of God, which had become so abusive (2:17).

## FODDER FOR THE PROPHETS

The Lord's righteous prophets inveighed against wicked leaders, including priests. For example, the prophet Micah gave a most chilling indictment of wicked spiritual leaders. First he affirmed his authority for his ministry: "But truly I am full of power by the Spirit of the LORD, and of justice and might, to declare to Jacob his transgression and to Israel his sin" (Mic. 3:8).

These words present a formidable basis from which he launched his judgment oracle. The prophet was endowed by no less an authority than the Holy Spirit, and he was animated with a sense of powerful justice (as suggested in the hendiadys "justice and might").

God's purpose for Israel's rulers was that they would emulate His character and provide a standard of righteousness in human government that would be the envy of the world. Instead, the leaders of the nation, drunk with greed, used the powers of their offices for wickedness, expressions of injustice, and outrages of iniquity (3:9–10). The full blast of Micah's divinely encouraged judgment comes in these words: "Her heads judge for a bribe, her priests teach for pay, and her prophets divine for money. Yet they lean on the LORD, and say, 'Is not the LORD among us? No harm can come upon us'" (3:11).

We walk a thin line here. We know that those who serve God in an occupational ministry are worthy of payment for their services; indeed, we believe that such payment should be generous, based on the response of grateful people to the ministries they have received through godly leaders (Luke 10:7; 1 Tim. 5:17–18). But no true minister of God may serve for greed, preach simply for reward, and expect to experience the sense of God's smile. The worst offenders are those who hide among God's promises, which they wrongly appropriate for themselves.

The idea of a corrupt politician is a byword for a jaded citizenry. The notion of a judge who can be bribed spells ruin for a public justice system.

But the concept of a crooked preacher is the worst insult to civility, decency, and order. If "the man of God" serves God only for money (Titus 1:7) or "dishonest gain" (1 Pet. 5:2), he profanes not only himself, but also the God whom he "serves" in the public eye.

What could be more important in the leading of worship than that the leader be a true worshiper? In none other is purity of motive, genuineness of heart, and truth in character more important than in those who lead others in divine worship.

In the days of Micah the prophet, a contemporary of the great prophet Isaiah, the corruption of Judah's spiritual leaders was one of the reasons God announced the destruction of Zion. "Therefore because of you Zion shall be plowed like a field, Jerusalem shall become heaps of ruins, and the mountain of the temple like the bare hills of the forest" (Mic. 3:12).[6]

The enormity of the sins of Judah's leaders is so clearly evident in this verse. The word "you" refers to the wicked leaders, priests, and prophets who "served God" in self-delusion.

## A REALLY BAD IDEA

The wicked leaders in Micah's day were part of what we call today the "temple cult heresy." This is seen in the last couplet of Micah 3:11: "Is not the LORD among us? No harm can come upon us."

In these words they gave false assurances to one another. They reasoned that since the Lord had invested His presence in the holy temple, He, despite their sins, would not punish them. They believed that His presence in the temple was their guarantee; they thought that surely He would not bring down wrath on His own people.

What they had not realized was that the God who came down to reveal Himself could also leave. Ezekiel the prophet was actually given a vision of the glory of the Lord leaving the temple shortly before the judgment came. "Then the glory of the LORD departed from the threshold of the temple and stood over the cherubim. And the cherubim lifted their wings and mounted up from the earth in my sight. When they went out, the wheels were beside them; and they stood at the door of the east gate of the LORD's house, and the glory of the God of Israel was above them" (Ezek. 10:18–19).

So where does that leave us? The promise of the Savior to be present wherever two or three are gathered in His name (Matt. 18:20) was given, astonishingly, in the context of church discipline. Thus we would be as foolish as the sinful worship leaders in an earlier era if we assume that God's presence in our worship services is assured, regardless of our attitudes or actions.

*Part 2*

# Developmental Issues

*Five*

## The God We Worship

- WHO IS THE GOD WE WORSHIP?
- Who are *we* to think that we might worship the living God?
- Why would God desire our worship?
- What does worship do to us?
- What does worship do to God?
- How do we know when we truly worship?

The first thing to focus on when considering the biblical nature of worship is the person of God Himself. J. Carl Laney has written a fine book on the person and work of God.[1] This book should be considered essential reading in preparation for genuine worship. In this section I wish to focus on three significant realities: God is holy, God is merciful, and God is the *ḥesed* God.

## THE HOLY GOD

"In the year that King Uzziah died, I saw the Lord sitting on a throne, high and lifted up, and the train of His robe filled the temple. Above it stood seraphim; each one had six wings: with two he covered his face, with two he covered his feet, and with two he flew. And one cried to an-

41

other and said: 'Holy, holy, holy is the LORD of hosts; The whole earth is full of His glory!' And the posts of the door were shaken by the voice of him who cried out, and the house was filled with smoke. So I said: 'Woe is me, for I am undone! Because I am a man of unclean lips, and I dwell in the midst of a people of unclean lips; for my eyes have seen the King, the LORD of hosts'" (Isa. 6:1–5).

The significance of this great event cannot be overstated. The retelling of the story takes many forms. These are the salient features:

- Despite the longstanding tradition of reading "temple" in verse 1, it is preferable to understand this vision to have taken place in the palace, more specifically, in the throne room of the king, a throne room now woefully vacant.[2] King Uzziah[3] had been excluded from his own palace for seventeen years because of his presumptive sin (2 Kings 15:1–7; 2 Chron. 26:1–23); the throne room was now vacant. Young Isaiah, a confidant of the king and a member of the royal family, may have gone into this room to grieve the loss of this godly king. Then in his marvelous vision he saw the living King!

- The vision of Isaiah was not something he sought, any more than were the visions of Ezekiel or Zechariah. But there was something wonderfully fitting about being in the throne room of a dead king and then being transfixed to a vision of the heavenly throne room in which the King of glory lives forever!

- Everything about the vision is active, dynamic, powerful. The great poetic crafting of Isaiah in recreating his memory of the scene is superlative in this regard. He had a view of heaven's glory, of heaven's King.

- All is described from Isaiah's perspective. He was looking up to see the grandly uplifted throne. He looked out to see the billowing robes. He was aware of angelic beings crowding the scene all about the throne. He sensed smoke, an ominous symbol of God's impending wrath.[4]

- Angelic creatures are especially fascinating. Angels are spirit beings, of course. But from time to time they take on a body in order to be seen by humans. The name "seraph" means "burning one." Imagine spirit beings appearing as if they were on fire. The extra pairs of wings were not for faster travel (!), but for demonstrations of reverence before the living God. We may picture the two extra pairs of wings as enfolding their bodies in such a way as to make them holy angels, completely subservient before their holy God.

- Then we encounter the word *holy*. The visual image is of the throne of God's glory being encircled by singing seraphs, one chanting to another and another to yet another, the same words coming in such volleys of sound that the reverberations shake the foundations of the very palace. Over and over they sang, again and again they intoned, "Holy."[5]

> Holy, holy, holy!
> Lord God Almighty!
> Early in the morning
> Our song shall rise to Thee.
> Holy, holy, holy!
> Merciful and mighty!
> God in three Persons,
> Blessed Trinity!
> Holy, holy, holy!
> All the saints adore Thee.
> Casting down their golden crowns
> Around the glassy sea.
> Cherubim and seraphim
> Falling down before Thee.
> Which wert and art,
> And evermore shall be.
>
> —REGINALD HEBER

The meaning of the word *holy* is critical to our understanding of biblical worship. Some have argued that the basic meaning is purity. But it seems more likely that the meaning is related to the idea "to be different," "to be other," "to be distant." Of course, God *is* pure! But by His holiness the biblical writers wished to assert that He is unique. There is nothing in the entire universe that may be compared to Him. This is what He said through the same prophet, Isaiah, years later: " 'To whom then will you liken Me, or to whom shall I be equal?' says the Holy One" (Isa. 40:25).

This is also the basic meaning of the creed of Israel, found in the famous "Shema," which may be translated, "Hear, O Israel: the LORD our God, the LORD alone is one!" (Deut. 6:4).[6]

So, to say it again, nothing (and no one) in the universe may be compared to the holy God of Scripture. Nothing. No one. As stated earlier, repeating the term *holy* three times is remarkable. A rare occurrence in Scripture, this brings unusual force to the term.[7]

Because of this sense of the absolute holiness of God, Isaiah spoke words of woe and devastation. "Woe is me," he said. "I am undone." In the midst of a scene filled with the sound of the praise of God, he was unable to join the angels. One thought of his being in the presence of the holy One gave him a sense of doom. Not only was he unprepared for the scene; he also knew that no one else would fare any better. Everyone he might have known was exactly like himself; none could stand before the holy God.

The Hebrew word for "woe" ('ôy) is onomatopoetic (as is the English word); the sound itself gives the meaning of the word. Isaiah said "woe"— and so would each of us if we were in his place.

Eight times I have held in my arms a newborn grandchild of mine. And each time I realized that everything that baby knows is in the context of its mother's arms. Then the father comes into the picture. Then perhaps a grandparent. All learning is in terms of making a wider and wider circle of familiar things.

But God is not "familiar" in that sense. God is not another part of the circle of things. Being holy, He is completely outside of our world, our experience, our understanding. In fact, the holiness of God is beyond imagination!

To worship Him without a sense of His holiness is to be impoverished.

## THE MERCIFUL GOD

The picture of God's holiness in the vision of Isaiah is unforgettable. But so is the image of His mercy, which is seen, appropriately, in the same story. "Then one of the seraphim flew to me, having in his hand a live coal which he had taken with the tongs from the altar. And he touched my mouth with it, and said: 'Behold, this has touched your lips; your iniquity is taken away, and your sin purged'" (Isa. 6:6–7).

We don't know how long young Isaiah was suspended in the interval of verses in the text as we read it. It may have been a mere nanosecond before he felt the sense of horror of the Lord's awesome holiness. But it was an experience he would never forget.

Then with a nod from God a pantomime of grace transpired. Isaiah was aware, perhaps in a dreamlike state, of the rustle of angel wings, of a fiery, searing sensation, and then of words that set his heart free of all fear.

The words came from the angel, but they had the authority of heaven's throne. Isaiah had experienced a personal Yom Kippur, his own "Day of Atonement."[8] He was immediately cleansed of all sin. This was not because he deserved it or had earned it. Nor was it because he asked for it. He was cleansed not because of anything in him or of anything that he might do someday. It was all of grace. God's grace.

And he was free! He was free to worship God. Free to serve God. Free to live for God.

And so are we when we too have experienced the grace of the holy God. In every era, in each dispensation, in every covenant, the God of Scripture is a *merciful* God.

Some worship leaders tend to make God more "user-friendly" to unbelievers. I have spoken at length with some who are strong advocates of the "seeker-service" movement. One thing is certain: They have a love for the lost. They wish to do everything they can to take away barriers from belief. If those barriers are obsolete musical forms, archaic language, formal dress, strange liturgies—these items are replaced by less threatening ideas.

But along the way there appears to be a stress on the mercy of God apart from His holiness. Preaching and teaching on the holiness of God is viewed by many as "offensive" to the people they are trying to reach; but God's mercy in Christ is viewed as winsome.

My observation is that the mercy of God can only be appreciated in a biblical manner when it is seen in the context of God's holiness. We do not "do God a favor" by making Him less holy than He is in order to make Him more approachable by the lost. Indeed, the miracle of the gospel is that it is God Himself who acts on behalf of Himself in rescuing the lost. "But God who is rich in mercy, because of His great love with which He loved us, even when we were dead in trespasses, made us alive together with Christ" (Eph. 2:4–5).

- Only with a strong sense of the enormity of sin can the grace of God in the gospel be appreciated.
- Only with a high view of God's holiness can the extent of His mercy be appreciated.
- Only as we realize that the Creator of the universe, the King of heaven, is holy beyond our ability to comprehend, does His mercy become even more overwhelming.

## THE *HESED* GOD

It is difficult to speak or to write with significance on the terms *holy* and *grace*, although they are so rich in meaning and important for our biblical understanding of God. But it is nearly impossible to write or to speak adequately on the word *hesed*, for the reader or hearer may not even know that the word exists!

In 1983 I was in a large meeting of biblical scholars in Chicago. We were assembled to affirm our belief in the inerrancy of Scripture under the aegis of the International Council of Biblical Inerrancy. A beloved seminary professor from years ago was to make a plenary address, a response to a paper on the attributes of God. My professor, Bruce Waltke, began by reading his prepared notes, stating his agreement with and appreciation of the paper he had reviewed. But then with deep emotion he left his text and said something about what was missing from an otherwise fine presentation. The author of the paper Waltke was reviewing had nowhere focused on God's *hesed* love. And at this I remember seeing Dr. Waltke's tears.

It was he who led my classmates and me to a deep affection for this term in the Hebrew Bible years ago. More than thirty years later I feel as deeply about this term as ever. But, as in the case of my professor, I lament that it is known by so few in the church today. Scholars know this word. Academicians continue to debate the fullness of its meaning. But worshipers need to know this word. It is a favorite in the self-revelation of our holy and gracious Lord.

"Now Yahweh descended in the cloud and stood with him there, and proclaimed the name of Yahweh. And Yahweh passed before him and proclaimed: 'Yahweh Yahweh;[9] God merciful and gracious, longsuffering, and abounding in goodness and truth'" (Exod. 34:5–6, author's translation).

The account of Isaiah's vision of the Lord (Yahweh) is often mentioned when people speak of biblical texts that should inform our worship of God. But these verses in Exodus have not received the attention I believe they should have. Isaiah's vision is monumental in the history of redemption. But so is this one. The figure here is also a prophet. His name is Moses.

## THE PREPARATION FOR THE REVELATION
## OF THE *HESED* GOD

The setting is significant. The Exodus was complete; the Lord had brought the people of Israel from Egypt and had made them His people. He had given them His gracious covenant at Mount Sinai. And then Moses had climbed the mountain to commune with the Almighty.

But at the base of the holy mountain, with the compliance and assistance of Aaron, Moses' brother, the people committed the worst of sins. They worshiped a golden calf (Exod. 32), a potent symbol of sexuality, rather than the Creator God, the Giver of all good and perfect gifts (James 1:17).

Exodus 33 begins with Moses and God in the midst of an amazing interchange. The prophet had pleaded for mercy for his people before God; at the beginning of the chapter there is the anomaly of God's grace apart from His presence. He said that He would make complete the journey of the people to Canaan, but that He would not be among them any longer (33:3). Canaan without God? That would be like heaven without Jesus!

Moses separated his tent from the center of the community and found that God met with him in the miracle of the pillar of cloud (33:7–11). I have argued elsewhere that the pillar of cloud is a remarkable example of an appearance of the preincarnate Savior Jesus Christ. The key words are found in verse 9. There we read that the "Pillar Cloud" (as the words may be translated) descended, stood, and talked with Moses![10]

When the Pillar Cloud spoke with Moses, it was "face to face," just as one might speak to a friend (33:11). This is astonishing! In no other prophet's life had there ever been such a close proximity of the presence of God. In this intimate interchange the Lord graciously consented to continue the journey with His people (33:14). And the two continued to talk "face to face."

Yet Moses wanted more. He wanted to experience God's glory (33:18).

But God responded that if he were to experience the fullness of God's glory he would die (33:20). Moses must have persisted, for God seems to have said to him that Moses would see what He could do, but that Moses wouldn't die.

Moses was hidden in the cleft of the rock atop Mount Sinai and the Lord was going to allow him to see more of His glory than he ever had seen before (33:21–23).

The words describing the descent of God are significant. This is God coming near in a way that is different from the "ordinary" sense of His presence. The language is precious; each term is endearing. The cloud that enveloped the living Lord in 34:5 was distinct from the Pillar Cloud in 33:7–11. This is the cloud that obscures God's glory; it is a part of what Samuel Terrien describes as God's "elusive presence."[11]

The wording "to call on the name of the LORD" can be confusing in the Bible. I suspect that most readers think this means praying to God. Think, for example, of these words in Genesis 12:8 concerning Abram. In connection with his building altars to God in Canaan, it is said that he "called on the name of the LORD." This does not mean that he prayed, although certainly he did. The meaning of this phrase is that he made proclamation; he preached! Here is Abram acting as a preacher for the living God amid the pagan peoples of Canaan.

The same phrase is used here in Exodus 34:5, but now the subject is the Lord Himself. He "descended" and "stood" and "proclaimed the name Yahweh." That is, He was now preaching about Himself. The Hebrew wording is the same as in Genesis 12:8, but the proclaimer was now the Lord!

In Exodus 34:6 we read, "Yahweh passed before him and proclaimed,

'Yahweh Yahweh,'" (author's translation). That is, here God was giving the most impressive presentation of the meaning of His name (and character) that He may give. This is the essence of these two great verses.

And on what did He focus? On His indescribable mercy, on His unbelievable patience, and on His abounding *hesed*. The words "God, merciful and gracious" are truly impressive. Here the Lord emphasized His essential deity in the word "God," and he posited His indescribable mercy in the pairing of "merciful and gracious." These are not two different ideas. The two words form a hendiadys, one concept expressed through two words. His compassion is beyond the capacity of human language to express; thus two words are used to indicate the depths of His mercy.

A second divine attribute God mentioned is His patience. The word "long-suffering" in Exodus 34:6 translates a Hebrew expression that actually means "long of nose." In our idiom we may speak of someone having a "short fuse." Well, God has a very long nose and the capacity to restrain Himself from the outworking of His rage.

The climactic phrase in this verse is the expression "abounding in goodness and truth." The depth of meaning of these words is incalculable. The term translated "goodness" in the New King James Version is the word *hesed*. This is the term that is so rich in its biblical use that translators have difficulty expressing its meaning. It is rendered variously as "loving mercy," "lovingkindness," "merciful goodness," "kindness," "mercy," "goodness," "lasting love," "loyal love," "unfailing love," and others.

Bruce Waltke stressed years ago that the most felicitous rendering is "loyal love." This ties together the element of "love and mercy" and "loyalty and steadfastness."

This word *hesed* reveals the name, nature, and character of God in a most impressive way. He is everlastingly loyal to His covenant, to His people, to His promises. Repeatedly in the Book of Psalms, the term *hesed* is the principal focus in the people's praise of the Lord. Psalm 136, for example, has an antiphonal response at every verse that "His mercy endures forever." "Mercy" here is the term *hesed*.

At the heart of the praise of God in the psalms is His *hesed*. Witness these words in Psalm 106:1: "Hallelujah! Praise Yahweh, for He is good, For His loyal love [*hesed*] is forever!"[12]

49

## AND SO WE LEARN GOD

The words of Exodus 34:5–6 are not solitary ideas, lost in the obscurity of ancient laws and practices. They are rightly regarded by the Old Testament writers as some of the most important of all verses on the person and character of God.

One example may suffice. When the prophet Jonah sat moping on a hill, upset that the people of Nineveh had not been destroyed by God's wrath, he quoted from Exodus 34:5–6 as negative praise to God. In effect, this is what he said: "I knew it. I just knew it. This is why I did not want to come in the first place. You gave me a command to pronounce Your judgment on the most wicked nation on the face of the earth. I thought, 'O great! Now He is going to show mercy to Nineveh.'

"Mercy? Well, yes. All the prophets knew that when the God of Israel makes an announcement of judgment it is to the intent that He may show mercy. If God were going to destroy a population, He simply would do it. But by the very fact that He announces judgment, we know that this is the last thing He wants to do!

"So, I thought, I can bring devastation to Nineveh by simply not bringing God's message of judgment. If they don't hear that they are under God's fist, they may do nothing about it, and they will burn.

"But you brought me here, against my better instinct. I gave the message. There was a response. And there they are, alive and well! I can't stand it.

"But this is the way You are. You are overwhelmingly compassionate. You are unbelievably longsuffering. And You act from an overflowing *ḥesed*."[13]


## AND SO WE LEARN CHRIST

The expression at the conclusion of Exodus 34:6 is overwhelming. God said of Himself that He is "abounding in goodness [*ḥesed*] and truth." Again we have another example of a hendiadys (as with the words "merciful and gracious"). The principal word here is *ḥesed*, "goodness" or "loyal love." When used with the term *ḥesed*, the Hebrew word *'emet* ("truth") adds the sense of "steadfastness," "everlasting," "enduring."

Some fifteen hundred years after God revealed Himself to Moses in these wondrous words, the apostle John sought words that would be appropriate to describe the Savior, the Lord Jesus Christ. He used the same words of Jesus as God had used of Himself!

John may never have written better than when he penned the prologue to his Gospel (John 1:1–18). In verse 14 the apostle lavished praise on the Savior, using key Greek words that translated words from the Hebrew.[14]

Many people have looked for the source of John's language in Greek philosophy. But John never attended school in Alexandria, and he was probably never in Athens. His heart and soul were rooted deeply in the Old Testament. It is wrong to look, as so many have, for the source of the *logos* ("Word") in Greek philosophy.

The most expressive of John's terms for Jesus are the words he used at the end of verse 1:14, "full of grace and truth." His words in Greek are *charitos kai alētheias*. He was using the same phrase we have in Exodus 34:6, "goodness and truth." They are the same. The only difference is that the earlier text was written in Hebrew and the later text was written in Greek.

"Grace and truth." "Goodness and truth." What God revealed about Himself in His grand presentation on the mountain—goodness and truth—John revealed about Jesus in his grand presentation in his Gospel—grace and truth.

The God of Scripture is a holy God. The God of Scripture is a merciful God. The God of Scripture is a *ḥesed* God.

The Christ of the New Testament is holy. The Christ of the New Testament is merciful. The Christ of the New Testament is gracious.

As we learn more about who God is, our worship will be rightly directed to His wonders. The apostle Paul put it this way: "Now to Him who is able to do exceedingly abundantly above all that we ask or think, according to the power that works in us, to Him be glory in the church by Christ Jesus to all generations, forever and ever. Amen" (Eph. 3:20–21).

# Six

# Worship as Response to God

IN HIS BOOK *God,* J. Carl Laney develops a chapter, "Responding to God," along these lines:

- Responding with love
- Responding with fear
- Responding with obedience
- Responding with service.[1]

Laney is correct in affirming that worship is response to God. Proper worship—worship that is done in spirit and in truth—is carried out in love, fear, obedience, and service. This present chapter develops the biblical setting for these ideas.

These concepts are found in the Bible in many places, but none is so memorable as the central declaration of Israel's creed, Deuteronomy 6. It is well known that this chapter is of inestimable importance in biblical theology. In fact, the words of Deuteronomy 6:4 are regarded as the quintessence of biblical faith for Israel, the people of God: "Hear, O Israel: The LORD our God, the LORD is one!"

## ISRAEL'S GREAT CONFESSION

The command "Hear" in Deuteronomy 6:4 is in the singular in Hebrew. Sometimes the nation Israel is addressed as a unit; at other times words are given to Israel in the plural, focusing on the many individuals who were a part of the national family.

The singular verb in this verse suggests that the command was to all the people as a group. The distinctive faith of Israel was a national issue; the people were viewed as a corporate solidarity. But the singular also speaks to each individual in that larger entity. Each woman and man in the community received a personal appeal in this strong command. To "hear" means to be an active participant in the community of faith, to be obedient to the Covenant Maker, to be a worshiper of His majesty. The command also has embedded in it the notion of daily renewal. The command calls for a continuing renewal of an active relationship with the living God.

The verse may be rendered this way: "Hear, O Israel! Yahweh our God! Yahweh alone!"[2]

Modern advertisers know the power of a slogan (especially when it is sung) in the lives of consumers. I do not wish to trivialize things here, but in this verse we have, in a sense, God's slogan. In four words (in the Hebrew) grouped in a pair of phrases we have a capsule of biblical truth. These words simply cannot be improved on: "Yahweh our God! Yahweh alone!"

The double shout affirms the reality of an exclusive bond between God and His people. He has chosen to relate Himself to His people in great love; they in turn are to be exclusively attached to Him in holy worship. There is to be none other; He and He alone is God.

Some people tend to think of Deuteronomy 6:4 in isolation. But the richness of the verse can be more fully appreciated when it is seen in its larger context. First, Deuteronomy 6:4 is preceded by a significant, indispensable introduction in the first three verses of the chapter. Second, the section that follows (6:5–9) applies the words of verse 4 in a powerful way. We will look at these ideas in reverse order: the words of application, and then the words of the setting and introduction.

The words of application contain the familiar words of the first and great commandment, the command to love the Lord with all of one's being. "You shall love the LORD your God with all your heart, with all your soul, and with all your strength. And these words which I command you today shall be in your heart. You shall teach them diligently to your children, and shall talk of them when you sit in your house, when you walk by the way, when you lie down, and when you rise up. You shall bind them as a sign on your hand, and they shall be as frontlets between your eyes. You shall write them on the doorposts of your house and on your gates" (6:5–9).

These words provide an essential part of our understanding of biblical worship: *True biblical worship concerns the whole of one's life; its ultimate meaning is rooted in one's wholehearted love for God.* What we do in corporate worship has its prime significance in the context of our daily living. Participating in community worship apart from a full-hearted sharing in the foundational biblical attitudes and divorced from the anticipated biblical actions is to leave one under the sad judgment of a disappointed God: "This people honors Me with their lips, but their heart is far from Me" (Mark 7:6).[3]

Here are several salient points we should not miss from these applicational verses in Deuteronomy 6.

- Everything in true worship springs from one's love for God.
- The knowledge of the Word of God must become a part of one's inner being.
- The commands of the Word of God must become part of one's everyday life.
- The content of the Word of God must be transmitted faithfully to one's posterity.
- One's household is to be a free zone for compliance to the Word of God.

The reason God may *command* love from His people may be found in the nature of the Hebrew word 'ahăbâ, "love." The word is not simply describing warm feelings or romantic attachments. It speaks of both *emotional* and *volitional* concepts. The translation "love" is correct because the word does center on feelings of affection.[4] But 'ahăbâ also centers on one's volitional actions, one's *choice*. To love God is more than to have a warm feeling about Deity; to love God in the biblical meaning is to make one's *choice* in Him, as in the wonderful words of Joshua as an old man: "Choose for yourselves this day whom you will serve. . . . But as for me and my house, we will serve the LORD" (Josh. 24:15).[5]

In a marriage relationship a couple's love for each other may run solely on romantic feelings. But if the romance grows a bit dull, things may fall apart. One even hears of vows that conclude with the words, "so long as we both shall love." Better marriages have dimensions of love that include choice as well as feeling. A husband and wife not only have the deepest feelings of affection for each other; they also have chosen each other, "forsaking all others."

In Jesus' interchange with the religious leaders of His day, He pointed to the command to love God as the first and great commandment (Matt. 22:36–37). He joined love for God with love for one's neighbor (from Lev. 19:18), and then concluded, "On these two commandments hang all the Law and the Prophets" (Matt. 22:40). By this He meant that these commands are the central issues of the Old Testament. As such, they are also central to the meaning of true worship.

## AND WITH ALL YOUR "VERY"!

The command to love God is expanded by the words, "with all your heart, with all your soul, and with all your strength" (Deut. 6:5). The words "heart" and "soul" speak of the inner person. How sad it is to hear some people say that in the Old Testament the emphasis was on external issues and that only in the New Testament do we find an emphasis on the inner person. How could someone be so wide of the mark? God has never been pleased with external actions that are not driven by pure motives, or that do not come as the actions of the human heart. We should not think in later, Western theological categories of "bipartite" or "tripartite" aspects of the human person. The Hebrew concept of the human person is unified, singular. By the terms "heart" and "soul" the command means that one's love for God should fill his or her innermost being.

The Hebrew construction that leads to the words, "and with all your strength," is somewhat amusing; literally it could read, "and with all your very." As Ralph Alexander puts it, these words mean, in essence, "And give it all you've got!"

The true worshiper of the living God begins and ends his or her worship with these great issues in the forefront of his or her thinking. This is why I love the words of Laurie Klein's lovely praise song, "I Love You, Lord." The simplicity of the lyric and the sweetness of the melody are wonderful. The capture of deep theology in these simple words is a marvel.

> I Love You, Lord,
> and I lift my voice,
> To worship You,
> O my soul, rejoice!
> Take joy, my King,
> in what You hear:
> May it be a sweet, sweet sound
> in Your ear.
>
> —LAURIE KLEIN

## THE REST OF THE STORY

Other aspects in the words of application (Deut. 6:6–8) are also wonderful to contemplate. First, the words of God's truth are to be *internalized* by the believing person ("in your heart," 6:6). To repeat, God is *never* satisfied with the external compliance of His people! He *always* seeks the true worship of sincere believers whose hearts are pure before Him.

Second, the idea of teaching these words to one's children (6:7) demonstrates that each generation is responsible before God. The faith of the parents works only for the parents. It is only when that faith is transmitted deeply into the lives of their children that the godly parents may feel that their job is accomplished. Not all children of faithful parents will themselves become people of faith, of course. God makes no such guarantees. Nevertheless godly parents seek to do all they can under the power of God's Spirit to lead their children to experience a "first-generation" relationship with their God.

A third element in these words concerns everyday living (6:7). The most natural thing for people of faith to do is to integrate their precious faith into the context of the things of daily life. Whether sitting or rising, walking or working—all of life is to be integrated into one's knowledge of God. Much of the rest of the Pentateuch is concerned with showing how this may be done. It is remarkable here, however, that the integration is seen first in the context of teaching one's children. This suggests that when a child sees the faith of the parent fully integrated in ordinary aspects of daily living, that child will more likely be deeply impressed with that same faith.

Fourth, one's home is to be a "free zone" for living out one's faith in God (6:8–9). The binding of these verses on one's body and the marking of one's doors and gates with the same is a wonderful physical way of demonstrating that love. The wearing of phylacteries[6] and the nailing of *mezûzôt*[7] on one's doors are strong physical symbols of inward realities. By wearing phylacteries the faithful believer was demonstrating that all of life—thoughts, words, deeds—is to be governed by the Lord. Similarly, his home was a place where he lived for God, whatever may be done in the "outside" world.

All this is part of what the Bible means when it tells us to worship God "in spirit and truth" (John 4:24). God's commands were *in* the believer's heart, love for the Lord sprang from *within* his or her inner being, and outward spiritual symbols expressed those inner spiritual realities.

Of course, a Hebrew person in Old Testament times might have said the right things and have worn the right symbols and still not have had his heart right with God. But it is also true that today Madonna wears a necklace with a cross. Just because these symbols may be abused does not mean that these symbols cannot have been used rightly by people of true faith. After all, the command to wear the symbols came from God!

## INTRODUCTION—SETTING THE STAGE

The introduction to Deuteronomy 6:4 is given in equally powerful words. "Now this is the commandment, and these are the statutes and judgments which the LORD your God has commanded to teach you, that you may observe them in the land which you are crossing over to possess, that you may fear the LORD your God, to keep all His statutes and His commandments which I command you, you and your son and your grandson, all the days of your life, and that your days may be prolonged. Therefore hear, O Israel, and be careful to observe it, that it may be well with you, and that you may multiply greatly as the LORD God of your fathers has promised you—'a land flowing with milk and honey'" (6:1–3).

Several factors present themselves in these great verses.
- Believers are to obey everything God has commanded.
- Obedience is linked with fearing the Lord.
- The Lord's plan in all this was for the good of His people.
- These ideas were to be communicated from one generation to another.

## COMMANDMENTS, STATUTES, JUDGMENTS

It is not unusual to hear people speak of God's Law in the Old Testament as comprised of civil, ceremonial, and moral aspects. They assert that the civil laws relate to government and society in ancient Israel, the ceremonial regulations describe means and methods of worship, and the moral aspects relate abiding principles of God's Law through the ages. While many people find this approach helpful, there is little in this approach that can be sustained from a reading of the Old Testament. We never read that some of God's commands are related to civil or ceremonial issues and that others are formed from basic moral principles.

The Mosaic Law, as in Deuteronomy 6:1, uses the three words *commandment, statutes,* and *judgments.* These words do not themselves describe different categories of the Law; they are used interchangeably. What they do describe are two realities: These laws are from God, and they are to be obeyed.
- The word for *commandment* (*miṣwâ*) is related to a powerful verb meaning "to command." With God as its subject, readers are to understand that His commands are not optional suggestions. The sovereign Lord of creation speaks in the authority of His glory. His commands are simply to be obeyed. A German proverb has it this way, *Gesagt, getan!* ("Said, done!"). So should be the responses of the people of God.

59

- The word for *statutes* (*ḥŭqqîm*) presents the idea of God establishing limits or drawing a line. He has placed limits for the oceans (Job 38:8–11; Prov. 8:27–29); so also He draws lines that place limits on the actions of His people.
- The word for *judgments* (*mišpāṭîm*) has the idea of God making the calls, rendering decisions. Like a baseball umpire behind the plate, He gives the decisions; but unlike some umpires, He never misses the call![8]

When some people see these words *commandment, statutes,* and *judgments,* they may think of them in a negative way. However, since these laws are from God, who is always gracious, His purpose in giving them is not to bring misery and trouble to people's lives. Precisely the opposite is intended. God's commandments are for our good. One of the loveliest psalms on the marvelous acts of God is found in Nehemiah 9:5–38, a psalm that has been called "The Levites' Psalm."[9]

In the marvelous portrayal of God's kind and gracious acts for His people, we read these words about God's Law: "You came down also on Mount Sinai, and spoke with them from heaven, and gave them just ordinances and true laws, good statutes and commandments. You made known to them Your holy Sabbath, and commanded them precepts, statutes, and laws, by the hand of Moses Your servant" (9:13–14).

Amazing, is it not? Readers who are used to thinking of the Law of God as heavy, burdensome, and binding need to come to terms with these sentiments.

## LAW VERSUS GRACE

Many evangelicals believe that a great divide exists between the Old Testament Law and New Testament grace. One of the verses used to support this common view is John 1:17: "For the law was given through Moses, but grace and truth came through Jesus Christ."

Again, we need to make several observations.

- The expression "the law of Moses" is a common shorthand expression, but it is not fully accurate. The law came *through* Moses but did not *originate* with him. The source of the Law was God Himself.

- Therefore the Law is in conformity with God's character. As noted in chapter 5, He is merciful and loving in nature.
- The common contrast between Law and grace is shown to be wrong when one simply looks closely at John 1:17. The term *grace* does not stand alone; the phrase is "grace and truth." The issue is clear: If the contrast is between Law and grace, it must also be between Law and truth. So is there no contrast at all? No. That would also be an error. The word "but" is in italics in the New King James Version of this verse because it is added for clarity, to point to a contrast.
- The key to the contrast is found in the final phrase of John 1:16, "grace for grace [*charin anti charitos*]."

Here then is the marvelous truth: In what we call the dispensation of the Law, God was acting in great grace to His people Israel. The very fact that He spoke to them, entered into covenant with them, made His name known by them, gave His Law to them—these and many other actions demonstrate His love, mercy, holiness, and *hesed*-nature to His people.

God acted in grace. But now in Christ there is more grace than ever!

We err greatly, in my judgment, when we speak of the contrast between Law and grace,[10] because God demonstrated great grace in the Old Testament. The correct contrast is better stated this way: In the Old Testament God's grace and truth were seen clearly, deeply, and wondrously, and in Christ, God's grace and truth are seen even more clearly, even more deeply, even more wondrously.

God abounds in grace and truth (Exod. 34:6), and Jesus is full of grace and truth (John 1:14). It is simply that in Jesus' incarnation we have a grander demonstration of the wonder of God's nature than ever before.

## OTHER CONNECTIONS

Deuteronomy 6 begins with a number of terms concerning the commands of God, terms that take one back to chapter 5 where the Ten Commandments (or as Jewish readers prefer, the Ten Words) were presented for the second time. The Ten Commandments recorded in Exodus 20 were given to the people of the first generation of Israelites who were delivered from

Egypt. Now their sons and daughters received the Ten Words again in Deuteronomy 5. ("Deuteronomy" means the "second" law.)

The Ten Words were never given as a means of salvation. Even though this is a commonly held view, it must be resisted in the strongest terms. Salvation in every age is a gift of God by grace through faith, plus nothing. It was no more possible for people in Old Testament times to earn salvation from God than it is possible for people to do so in our era. The words of Paul in Ephesians 2:8–9 have always been true: "For by grace you have been saved through faith, and that not of yourselves; it is the gift of God, not of works, lest anyone should boast."

God's gracious Law was never a means of salvation. It was given to guide His people in their life of faith.

## THE FAITH OF FATHER ABRAHAM

Genesis 15:6 describes Abraham's faith in God, a faith that God reckoned to him as righteousness. "And he believed in the LORD, and He accounted it to him for righteousness."[11]

The living God looked down on Abram and saw in him faith in God that is the same as what we call in New Testament terms "saving faith." Indeed, the apostle Paul argued this very thing in Romans 4. He called Abraham "our father" (4:1) in a double sense. Abraham is not only "our father" in the sense of being the principal patriarch of the Hebrew people; he is also "our father" (and so is Sarah "our mother"; see 1 Pet. 3:6) in demonstrating saving faith in the living God. Moreover, Paul argued that the record of Abraham (and Sarah) was not written for him (them) alone. For the same imputation of righteousness is made to us as it was to Abraham—and on the same basis, "saving faith." "Now it was not written for his sake alone that it was imputed to him, but also for us. It shall be imputed to us who believe in Him who raised up Jesus our Lord from the dead, who was delivered up because of our offenses, and was raised because of our justification." (Rom. 4:23–25)

These ideas become even more impressive when we examine the language of Genesis 15:6 more closely. We observe first that the verb translated "he believed" means "to cast oneself entirely on." This is the wonderful

Old Testament equivalent of the New Testament Greek word *pisteuō* ("to believe"). Second, the verb is followed by a preposition that means "in," which is attached to the divine name, Yahweh. The idea of Abram's faith, then, is a complete surrender "into" Yahweh. This is saving faith. The same idea is used in the Gospel of John, where the verb "to believe" is often followed by the preposition "into" and the name of Jesus.

God rewards such faith by crediting righteousness to the believer. Abram did not earn, merit, or deserve the righteousness of God; in response to his faith God accounted him righteous. This is why we speak of saving faith as something God graciously does, not something a person achieves. Salvation in every era is by grace through faith. Again, many people know this was true of Abraham, but few know that it was also true of the nation Israel at the end of the events of the Exodus.

## ISRAEL'S SAVING FAITH

While all orthodox interpreters know and champion the significance of the words describing saving faith in the life of Abraham, some seem to struggle to come up with a passage that might be used to demonstrate the saving faith of Israel, the people of God. But Exodus 14:30–31 presents this truth.

After reading how God brought His people through the waters of the Red Sea, we read these very significant words: "So the LORD saved Israel that day out of the hand of the Egyptians, and Israel saw the Egyptians dead on the seashore. Thus Israel saw the great work which the LORD had done in Egypt; so the people feared the LORD, and believed the LORD and His servant Moses."

Each line of this great text calls out for comment.

- Israel was delivered from the Egyptians purely by God's power. This was not something they themselves accomplished.
- The Israelites saw their dead enemies on the shore. This was not something they merely imagined.
- The phrase "the great work" is literally "the great hand." This is just another way in which emphasis is placed on God as the One who brought their deliverance.

- The words "the people feared the LORD" do not mean fright or terror. When the Old Testament speaks of "the fear of the LORD" in a positive sense, as here, the idea is one of reverence, adoration, readiness to worship, and determination to serve Him.
- The words "and believed the LORD" should be translated "and believed *in* the LORD." This is precisely the same language used of Abram in Genesis 15:6. To the people of that first generation their faith, like that of Abram so long before, was reckoned to them as righteousness.

> Marvelous, infinite, matchless grace,
> Freely bestowed on all who believe!
> You that are longing to see His face,
> Will you this moment His grace receive?
> Grace, grace, God's grace,
> Grace that will pardon and cleanse within!
> Grace, grace, God's grace,
> Grace that is greater than all our sin!
>
> —JULIA H. JOHNSTON

The people of Israel *believed in* Yahweh, and so, as with Abraham (and Sarah) before them, they were redeemed. They were delivered not only from Egypt, not only from slavery, but also from eternal judgment. They were now the people of God. Since Moses was the representative of God, his name is also significant in this verse. But Moses was not their Savior; God was.

And so they were redeemed.[12]

As the redeemed, what did they do? They *worshiped* their saving God, as recorded in the first of the psalms of praise in the Bible. Exodus 15 records the lyrics. The words were by Moses, and Miriam led the singing. (More will be written on this in chapter 7.)

## THE CHRISTIAN GOSPEL

We celebrate the death and resurrection of Christ as the central issues of our faith. In ancient Israel true believers looked back to the deliverance of

Israel from Egypt with the same sort of appreciation we have for the gospel. The gospel has two great points. This is the clear, powerful teaching of Paul in 1 Corinthians 15:1–8.

> Moreover, brethren, I declare to you the gospel which I preached to you, which also you received and in which you stand, by which also you are saved, if you hold fast that word which I preached to you—unless you believed in vain.
>
> For I delivered to you first of all that which I also received: that Christ died for our sins according to the Scriptures, and that He was buried, and that He rose again the third day according to the Scriptures, and that He was seen by Cephas, then by the twelve. After that He was seen by over five hundred brethren at once, of whom the greater part remain to the present, but some have fallen sleep. After that He was seen by James, then by all the apostles. Then last of all He was seen by me also, as by one born out of due time.

Many people suggest that the gospel consists of three points: Christ died, He was buried, and He rose again. But actually there are two points to the gospel: Christ died for our sins, and He rose again on the third day.

Two lines of evidence—biblical prophecy and historical experience—buttress each of these two great statements. Thus the fact that Jesus died for our sins is attested by the words "according to the Scriptures" (15:3) and by the historical fact that He was buried (15:4). Similarly the fact that He rose from the dead is attested by the words "according to the Scriptures" (15:5) and by the historical fact that "he was seen" (15:5–8).

A graphic layout of the passage would look like this:

- Christ died for our sins.
    According to the Scriptures.
    He was buried.
- He rose again the third day.
    According to the Scriptures.
    He was seen [by many].

People today come to peace with God not by their works, not by their heritage, and certainly not by their gifts or possessions. The only way to have peace with God is on His terms—saving faith. The same was true in Old Testament times.[13]

## THE "HEBREW GOSPEL"

The question naturally arises, What was the content of saving faith in the times of the people who lived before the Cross? Many respond by saying that these people had to believe in Jesus, who had not yet come. But there are problems with this point of view. It is difficult to assert that only those who knew about the future death of the Messiah could be saved.

The issue becomes more pronounced when we realize that even the disciples of Jesus did not understand the nature of His first advent. In fact, whenever Jesus brought up the subject of His impending death, His followers attempted to dissuade Him. Peter, who rightly announced that the Lord Jesus is "the Christ, the Son of the living God" (Matt. 16:16), moments later attempted to tell Jesus that His impending death and resurrection could be avoided! (16:22). Jesus said Peter's first evaluation came from God Himself (16:17), but that the second came from Satan (16:23). If even the disciples closest to Him did not understand His death and resurrection, how might a farmer and his wife have had this level of understanding, as they lived in Israel in, say, the eighth century B.C.?

So what was the content of the saving faith of people in Old Testament times? It was in believing two things: God delivered His people from Egypt, and this deliverance was for "us" as well as for them.

This is the point of the Passover. When Jewish people celebrate the deliverance of their ancestors from Egypt, they affirm in the words of the ancients, "This was not for them only, but for us as well." That is, Old Testament people were to look back to the first Passover and to believe that this deliverance was done for them as well as for their ancestors.

Here is the analogy. We as Christians look back to the death and resurrection of Jesus, and we affirm biblically that these events transpired not only for the benefit of those who were alive at the time. We participate in these grand events with the same level of benefit as those women who wept beneath the cross and those men who touched His glorified body.

Moses wrote the Book of Deuteronomy for the sons and daughters of the people who were delivered from Egypt. They were not the ones who had been present; for the most part it was their parents, and their parents had since died. But the people of the second generation were told to inform *their* children (people of the third generation) that these events happened "to us." All the events and all the words were to be taught to their children, in each generation. "Only take heed to yourself, and diligently keep yourself, lest you forget the things your eyes have seen, and lest they depart from your heart all the days of your life. And teach them to your children and your grandchildren, especially concerning the day you stood before the LORD your God in Horeb, when the LORD said to me, 'Gather the people to Me, and I will let them hear My words, that they may learn to fear Me all the days they live on the earth, and that they may teach their children'" (Deut. 4:9–10).

Most significant are God's words through Moses in Deuteronomy 5, in introducing the Ten Words. Again, we assert that the Ten Words were given to their parents, as described in Exodus 20. But the words of Deuteronomy 5:2–3 seem to contradict that simple fact. "The LORD our God made a covenant with us in Horeb. The LORD did not make this covenant with our fathers, but with us, those who are here today, all of us who are alive."

So what can this mean? The covenant was made with their parents. Here is where we discover the essential meaning of Deuteronomy—the faith of Israel is *a living faith*, not simply a cultural heritage. We observe with profound sorrow that many contemporary Jewish people think only in terms of cultural heritage. But in the Bible, each individual was to have a "first-generation" relationship of faith with the living God. To be redeemed, every individual must have a personal relationship with God. No one can count on the faith of his or her ancestors. The "faith of our fathers" (and mothers) must become *our* faith.

The same thing was true in Israel. People would look back to the Exodus, to the saving works of God, and by believing in God in the same manner as Abram did, they would be redeemed.

When they looked back in faith, believing, they *had* to respond to God in worship. Their response would be, as Laney posits, fourfold: with love, fear, obedience, and service.[14]

# Seven

The Beauty of Praise

THE MEANING OF "TO GILD THE LILY" is self-evident: Some things are so exquisite in their natural state that anything done to "improve" them may diminish their genuine beauty. The keenest smith who attempts to cover the petals of a lovely flower with a golden sheath will not improve its delicately powerful beauty.

Is this not what Jesus meant when He gestured to wildflowers on the hillsides of the Galilee? The unadorned beauty of these flowers, He asserted, surpassed the ability of Solomon with all his wealth to achieve perfection in his array of garments (Matt. 6:28–30).

Some beautiful things are simply to be enjoyed; they cannot be improved on.

How can we color more fully a dazzling sunset? How could a person adorn more grandly a Beethoven symphony? How could we arc more gracefully the splendor of the rainbow? How could one enhance a statue by Michelangelo?

Some of the works of God and of people cannot be improved on. We may not recolor a sunset, nor may we improve a grand symphony; we are incapable of enhancing either rainbow or statue. If these are truly things of beauty, they are to be appreciated without any effort to "enrich" them.

My wife, Beverly, and I have four grown children and eight grandchildren. When I held each of my children for the first time, I was struck by the wonder of the beauty of that little person! Now as a grandfather I have the same feeling, but perhaps I experience it even more intensely.

The beauty of a baby does not need enhancing. Oh, one may smooth out the hair of a little boy, or fasten a bow on the head of a little girl. But no one puts makeup on a baby!

## THE COMPLEXITY OF BEAUTY

The notion of beauty is exceedingly complex. Who knows how much of the idea of beauty is inherent in an object or a person, and how much is invested by the beholder's eye?

Cultural aspects in notions of physical beauty are especially potent. Physical features prized among one people group may be considered ugly in another. As a Caucasian male of British and German descent, I discovered when first visiting Asian countries that my nose is considered long and my eyes round. Before that sojourn I had never given much thought to the shape of these features.

The beauty of persons is a complex issue, but many believe that the physical beauty of a person may be improved.

## FEMININE BEAUTY

When we think of the word *beauty*, I suspect many in our culture think first of a female model, of the features of a lovely young woman. However, beautiful people, we are told, are often uneasy about their beauty. One supermodel was asked in a television interview if she can ever just "be herself." "Or," the questioner asked, "must you always be the persona of the beautiful model?"

Her response was marked by sadness. "People," she sighed, "have an expectation of me that becomes something of a burden. I can never even slip into a store for a carton of milk without being very concerned about my appearance, my makeup, hair, and clothing."

"Well, poor darling," some must think—figuring they would happily bear some of that "burden" if given the opportunity! Perhaps the most surprising of compliments might be, "She looks pretty even without her makeup." But this is a risk even some models dare not attempt to test.

Her beauty's face—the sum effects of bones and skin, features and animation, tissue and texture—is enhanced by potions and lotions that are all complex and mysterious to the male observer. I once asked one of our then teen-age daughters how a girl learns to put on makeup.

Rachel explained, "It's just what girls do, Dad! You couldn't possibly understand!"

Perhaps only a few men understand such things; the American male is "cosmetically challenged."

It seems to be a given that the lily of feminine beauty may be gilded. Eyes are lined, moisturizers are applied, color is added—all designed to result in a more "natural effect." Don't misunderstand. I am not suggesting that the use of cosmetics is wrong. I simply observe that in our culture it is fully accepted that the use of adorning materials may enhance the natural beauty of a woman's face.

## BUT IT FADES!

A certain sadness, however, is inevitable. There is a deceptive quality about physical beauty; it fades. Thus in the exquisite acrostic in Proverbs 31:10–31 on the worthy woman the writer observed, "Charm is deceptive and beauty is fleeting" (31:30, NIV). The great prophet Isaiah wrote of beauty as "a fading flower" (Isa. 28:4; see also 40:6–7). Unlike beautiful *character* qualities, *physical* beauty is like an open cola container—the fizz dissipates and the taste goes flat.

Thus the most beautiful person plays out what is finally a losing game. Lotions and potions, nips and tucks only delay the inevitable. Flowers fade, and so does physical beauty.

## THE BEAUTY OF OUR GOD

So what shall we say about the beauty of God? If there is anything—or any*one*—in the entire universe whose beauty is absolute, of a certainty it is He, the living God of Scripture—the Father, Son, and Spirit—blessed forever! We may say with utter confidence, *our God is beautiful!*

In His beauty, as in all things, God's holiness comes into play. All comparisons one might make between things we know and understand ultimately fail when we apply them to Him. Here on earth beauty is a comparative notion, but beauty in God is on the plane of the incomparable.

> Beautiful Savior!
> Lord of the nations!
> Son of God and Son of man!
> Glory and honor,
> Praise, adoration,
> Now and forevermore be Thine!
>
> —A CRUSADER'S HYMN

Like the flower, His is a beauty that may not be improved on. But unlike the flower, His beauty is absolute and eternal. If we think of varieties of beauty or degrees of loveliness, God is the summation of beauty and its absolute perfection.

Unlike the beauty of a flower or a lovely woman, His is a beauty that cannot diminish. Since God is perfect in His being, and since beauty is intrinsic to His person, His beauty is eternal. Beauty and God are inextricably bound.[1]

## AND OUR PRAISE IS HIS BEAUTY

Here, then, is the mystery. The biblical notion of praise is one of the most stunning of theological ideas. God, who forever is perfect in His sublime person, actively seeks true worshipers. This is what Jesus said in His unusual seminar-for-one on the subject of biblical worship. To the most unlikely of persons, the woman of Samaria, Jesus said that the Father is seeking true worshipers to worship Him (John 4:23–24).[2]

Here Jesus was bringing to completion the process that began in the first worship scene in the Bible, the authentic worship of Abel as contrasted with the unacceptable worship of Cain, described in Genesis 4. It is fascinating to note that the verb rendered "respected" to describe God's response to Abel and his sacrifice means "to look with favor on" (4:4 NIV). The Lord was seeking true worshipers in the first family; He seeks them still.

And when we worship Him rightly, we do something that is amazing: *In praise we bring new beauty to Him who is altogether beautiful!*

## THE BIBLE'S FIRST PSALM OF PRAISE

The first psalm of praise in the Bible is in Exodus 15.[3] Fittingly, this psalm was in response to the most significant event in Israel's history, God's work in delivering the Israelites from Egypt. The climactic act in God's expressions of kindness (*ḥesed*) for Israel was the crossing of the Red Sea (Exod. 14). When the people of Israel were safely on the far side of the water barrier, and their enemies had been drowned in its resurgent waters, the natural response of the saved and believing community (14:31) was expressed in a great song of praise. The psalm is a poem by Moses (15:1);[4] the singing, playing, and dancing in the presentation of the music was led by his sister, Miriam (15:20).

The worship event commemorated by this psalm may not have been planned in the sense that it was anticipated, and it was not an annual festival in Israel's religious year. There were no precedents; all was new. The event of Israel's deliverance from Egypt could not have been known ahead of time. The event itself is the most significant act of God's deliverance in the whole history of the Hebrew people up to the incarnation of their Messiah. Once the event had transpired, however, we may be assured that the music was both planned and rehearsed and the power of the music was all the more effective because of the enormity of the occasion. I assert that the music was both planned and rehearsed for these reasons:

- The poem is exquisite and highly artistic in its composition; its verbal subtleties rule out the notion of spontaneous composition.[5]
- This is the first act of corporate worship of the people of Israel; it was their national debut in their worship of God. The Passover in Egypt was a family-centered event; this was a corporate worship event that involved the entire nation together.

- We should no more assume that the playing and dancing for this great event were spontaneous than that the writing of the psalm "just happened."
- The fact that an entire chapter in the Book of Exodus is given to the poem, in addition to chapter 14, which is devoted to the prose account, shows that the event here celebrated was of momentous importance.

Any conclusion respecting women and worship leadership must take this account seriously.[6]

Walter J. Kaiser Jr., points out that the poem in Exodus 15 has three main sections, each with a memorable simile of "sinking," with reference to the fate of the enemies of Israel who drowned in the Red Sea.[7] The first section ends in the words, "They sank to the bottom like a stone" (15:5); the second section ends in the words, "They sank like lead in the mighty waters" (15:10); the third section has the words, "They will be as still as a stone" (15:16).

This excellent psalm of praise is a mother lode of theological issues; how sad it is to observe that so many of God's people today are seemingly unaware of its riches. Here is the very first psalm of praise in the Bible. It should be celebrated as such!

## MY STRONG SONG

The key verse in Exodus 15 is verse two. Indeed the opening couplet of this verse becomes the hymnic slogan of God's salvation work in all ages: "The LORD is my strength and song, and He has become my salvation."

The association of words in the first line is arresting. When we see pairings of words in the poetry of the Bible we expect them to be natural synonyms. Thus the word *strength* would more expectedly be linked with a word such as *power*, and the word *song* would more naturally be tied to a term such as *melody*.[8] Here we possibly have another hendiadys.[9] In my view this rare grouping of the words *strength* and *song* is of great importance for our understanding of the use of music in biblical worship. The idea these words yield in combination is something such as "my strong song." Based on this understanding, the verse's first line may read, "The LORD is my strong song."

The idea of God as "my strong song" may mean *He is my reason for singing*. Salvation from the Lord leads to music by His people. When we realize the glory of being saved, delivered, cleansed, purified, justified—we want to sing, shout, clap, and even weep.[10]

## AND THE SONG GOES ON

In June 1997 I had the privilege of meeting with a small group of biblical scholars for a week at Ramat Rachel in Jerusalem to work on a book commemorating the approaching fiftieth anniversary of the founding of the State of Israel.[11] We had been assembled under the leadership of Tuvya Zaretski, a missionary-scholar with the Jews for Jesus ministry. We had each written our essay ahead of the meeting; now we had a week to interact with each other's writings before the book was published. During the course of our wonderful, animated interactions, I directed attention to Exodus 15:2. I pointed out that the words in this verse are quoted in two other great passages of poetry, one that prophetically celebrates the work of the Savior on the cross (Ps. 118:14), and the other that speaks of the coming King in His kingdom (Isa. 12:2).

Psalm 118 is the Passover psalm. When Jews today celebrate Passover, this psalm is the climax of the evening. It is replete with the significance of the impending death and resurrection of Jesus Christ.[12] In the midst of this psalm the words of Exodus 15:2 are quoted by the singer.[13] The connection is simply grand. Psalm 118 is the libretto for Jesus to sing in the context of His passion. He was given the lines of Exodus 15:2 in Psalm 118:14 to encourage Him in the strongest possible manner. The God who delivered the nation of Israel when He divided the waters of the Red Sea was now prepared to deliver the Singer (the Lord Jesus) in His very great hour of need: "The LORD is my strong song; and He has become my salvation."

The words of Exodus 15:2 come once again in the most stunning of contexts, the singing of the redeemed in the millennial kingdom. This song is recorded in Isaiah 12. Isaiah 1–11 alternates between passages of the gravest judgment awaiting Judah and words of exquisite loveliness in anticipation of God's future kingdom on earth. Chapter 11 is one of the most graphic prophetic portrayals of that coming kingdom found in the prophets. This chapter speaks of the beautiful Branch (Isa. 11:1; see also 4:2; 6:13) from the stem of Jesse, of the fullness of the Spirit resting on the messianic King (11:2), of His superb rule in equity and mercy (11:3–5), of former carnivores becoming herbivores and once venomous snakes becoming the friendly playthings of little children (11:6–9). This is also a grand prophetic chapter describing both the conversion of the nations (11:10) and the regathering of Israel in the language of a second Exodus (11:11–16). Isaiah 11 is a great prophetic chapter on Israel's future glory.

The future blessings in the millennial kingdom described in Isaiah 11 are followed immediately by a psalm of the kingdom (Isa. 12).[14] Isaiah 12 is in two stanzas (12:1–3 and 12:4–6), each introduced in the same manner, "And in that day you will say."[15]

In the first movement of this millennial psalm we read for the third time the words we first discovered in Exodus 15:2. Here they are in Isaiah: "For Yah-Yahweh is my strong song; He also has become my salvation" (Isa. 12:2, author's translation).

The one difference in Isaiah 12:2 as against both Psalm 118:14 and Exodus 12:2 is that the divine name Yahweh (conventionally rendered LORD in English versions) is here joined with the short form of the same name, Yah (the same element we find in the Book of Psalms in the word "Hallelu-Yah"). This doubling of the divine name is similar to the use of "Yahweh Yahweh" in Exodus 34:6, discussed in chapter 5. This rare emphasis makes Isaiah 12:2 even more potent: Our reason for singing is found within our relationship to Yah-Yahweh, our Savior God! This could hardly have been stated more strongly than it is here in Isaiah 12:2.

The Exodus, the Cross, the Millennium—each of these monumental works of God is celebrated by the same lyric in the hymnody of Israel.

## AND SO WE SING

The second couplet of Exodus 15:2 ties together the ideas of praise and beauty. "He is my God, and I will praise Him; my father's God, and I will exalt Him."

Biblical Hebrew has more than a score of words to convey the idea of praise.[16] This verse uses two of them, one in common use and one that is remarkably fresh. The verb "exalt" means "to hold high, to uplift."

Here is true mystery: God, whose majesty is infinite, is "lifted up" by the praises of His people (see also Ps. 22:3).[17] When we sing praise to Him, following the pattern established so long ago in the redeemed Exodus community, there is a sense in which we "lift up" the exalted Lord. Do we actually *do* something to God when we sing? Logic and theology would say no. He who is infinite cannot be expanded; He whose glory is beyond measurement cannot have more glory added. How, then, can finite, frail people bring more glory to the Creator God, the triune Deity of eternity?

In one sense, however, the praises of God's people, given in spirit and truth, do bring new glory to our awesome God. When we sing of His awesome wonder, we affirm the truth of His wonder and we also add wonder to wonder. These praise words in the Bible are designed both for the worshiper as he or she responds *to God,* and for God as He responds *to their praise.*

I suspect that when we are in heaven, we will be simply astounded as we learn dynamics of worship, at which Scripture only hints.

> For Thou, O Lord, art high above all the earth;
> Thou art exalted far above all gods.
> For Thou, O Lord, art high above all the earth;
> Thou art exalted far above all gods.
> I exalt Thee, I exalt Thee, I exalt Thee, O Lord.
> I exalt Thee, I exalt Thee, I exalt Thee, O Lord.
>
> —PETE SANCHEZ JR.

God, who is absolute in glory and infinite in wonder, stands in need of nothing in the universe—least of all, from fallen, frail, feeble human-kind! And yet when we sing praises to the One who is exalted, in some sense His dynamic exaltation is made even more grand.

When we sing with Moses and Miriam, "I will exalt Him" (Exod. 15:2), we are both acknowledging His exaltation and, in one sense, adding to it. Psalm 97:9 affirms that God is high above all He has made, and certainly

He is high above "all gods": "Surely You, Yahweh, are Most High[18] over all the earth; You are exceedingly exalted above all gods" (author's translation).

So in the words of hymn writer Pete Sanchez Jr., we first acknowledge that God *is* exalted. He is the Most High, the Sovereign of the universe, resplendent in intrinsic glory, resident in magnificent station above all He has made. And then we sing, "I exalt You."[19] In doing this we join believers in the millions through time. In doing this we join the chorus of ancient Israel at the time of Moses and Miriam. In doing this we link hands with believers on all continents, from all kinds of cultures, ethnicities, and languages. In doing this we join innumerable choirs of angels. In doing this we bring new exaltation to the exalted One!

In this context we find the biblical significance of all other ministries. We don't learn Scripture just to know more about God's revelation. We don't involve ourselves in evangelism just to lead more people to salvation. We don't promote world missions just to reach the lost. These ministries and many others have wonderful meaning in their own terms; but all of them, when done in the power of God's Spirit and to God's glory, have one end—the worship of God.

## AND *NEW* BEAUTY

There is even more mystery in the Hebrew verb rendered "praise" in Exodus 15:2. The verb *nāwâ* means "to beautify, to make beautiful."

When we praise the Lord in spirit and in truth, something happens that we could never have anticipated. In our praise we bring more beauty to Him. The last two lines of Exodus 15:2 could be translated, "This is my God and I beautify Him; God of my fathers and I exalt Him!"

In our corporate worship of the great God of Scripture, we, the believing Christian community, join with the redeemed of the Exodus in bringing new beauty to our beautiful God.

Praise *does* something—to the individual, to the community, and to God. Another psalmist wrote, "Hallelu-Yah! Surely it is good to sing praises to our God; for it is pleasant; praise is beautiful!" (Ps. 147:1, author's translation).

After the opening Hallelu-Yah (see also the closing Hallelu-Yah in verse 20), this psalm of the returning exiles[20] speaks in verse 1 of praise as good, pleasant, and beautiful. These wonderful words can describe things on three levels. First, praising God is good, pleasant, and beautiful to the individual worshiper. When one first comes to a worship service, there may still be much of the cares of the world hanging on one's shoulders, sagging at the back. Yet in an almost magical way—better, by way of a miracle—the singing of God's praises with other believers draws one away from personal cares.

Second, praise is good in the community. One person's voice joins another; voices join instruments. The congregation sings, and angels join. And in heaven—who knows, but perhaps the Savior sings as well! And we are not alone. Diverse people with contrasting lives and backgrounds join together in the most important thing people can do together—worship God. This is good, pleasant, and beautiful.

Third, praise is good for God. As He hears these voices, when His people come in spirit and truth, He smiles on them and calls the praise good, pleasant, and beautiful. The term rendered "beautiful" in Psalm 147:1 is related to the verb "to beautify" in Exodus 15:2. God looks down, as it were, on the people who worship His beauty, and He receives their actions as new beauty for His Person.

The lily may not be gilded; its beauty would be reduced if it were sheathed in a delicate filigree of gold. A lovely woman may be adorned; cosmetics and jewelry may enhance her natural loveliness. The beauty of both lily and lady is destined to fade, but God is altogether beautiful, and His beauty never fades.

However, we do enhance the lily of His beauty when we worship Him in biblical praise. He accepts our praise as new beauty added to His infinite, intrinsic beauty. And by definition, His beauty lasts forever. This is wonder indeed. Imagine beautifying the beautiful One as we praise Him!

# Eight

## Worship in Spirit and Truth

WITHOUT DOUBT the words of the Lord Jesus in John 4:24 on the subject of worship form the most impressive capsule on this topic in the Scriptures. In fact Jesus' words to the Samaritan woman provide what I call "the full bloom" stage of the "opening of the rose of Scripture" on this topic. That is, this great passage serves to demonstrate the usefulness of an analogy of Scripture that I have been using in my teaching for many years. I call this is "the analogy of the rose,"[1] in which I suggest that Jesus' teachings on moral and ethical issues were not new, novel, or unexpected. Rather, in His teaching He demonstrated that He is the Teacher of Righteousness (Joel 2:23)[2] as well as the Prophet greater than Moses (see Deut. 18:15), principally because He taught the heart of the Law with unparalleled power and unqualified insight. Not only did He fulfill the Law; He also explained most fully what God's intentions were in the Law.

The principal way we see that Jesus is a Prophet greater than Moses is in the way He spoke, not just in the content He gave. That is, He could not contradict Moses and be truly the Messiah. Were Jesus to contradict Moses, He would be speaking against God. The Messiah could not contradict the Law, for the Lord, not Moses, gave the Law.[3]

What then is the significant difference between Moses and Jesus in their teaching ministries? When Moses spoke, he attributed his utterances to God. The most common phrasing in the Law is found in the many ways in which Moses said He spoke for the Lord.[4] But when Jesus spoke in an authoritative manner, He did not say, "The word of the Lord came to me, saying" or "Thus says the Lord." When Jesus spoke, He said, "Most assuredly, I say to you" (for example, John 3:3).[5] In His conversation with the woman at the well, Jesus used a variation of this formal introduction in the words, "Woman, believe Me" (4:21). No mere prophet would call such attention to himself as the authority figure; only the Messiah could speak with such personal assurance. The woman who listened with great interest came to recognize this great truth (4:25–42).

## THE TRUTH OF WORSHIP IN THE FULL-BUD STAGE

In the analogy of the rose I posit the idea that the books of Moses display the major ideas that Scripture develops later. Not all details are present, of course; but these five books present the basic issues. They are there in the sense that the fullness of the flower is present in the full bud. But the full beauty of the flower is only partially understood when it is in the bud stage.

The story of Cain and Abel in Genesis 4 gives us the first lesson in the Bible on the true worship of God. However, many Christians assume that God did not accept Cain's offering because he had not brought a blood sacrifice. Pointing to the produce offered by Cain, they quote the words, "and without shedding of blood there is no remission" (Heb. 9:22).

Here is the standard syllogism:

Premise one:     Only blood sacrifices can atone for sin.
Premise two:     Cain did not bring a blood sacrifice for his sin.
Conclusion:      There is no remission for Cain's sin.

It is strange, however, not to hear someone then add that it is not just the "shedding of blood" that avails for sin. The same writer of Hebrews wrote not only that the shedding of blood is necessary, but he also wrote that it can't be just any blood: "For it is not possible that the blood of bulls and goats could take away sins" (10:4). Thus if Cain were in trouble because he brought only grain and not a blood sacrifice, how did Abel get "off the hook" when all he brought was the sacrifices of animals? The one verse cannot be used against the one brother without the other verse coming into play with the second brother. I believe something else is at work in Genesis 4.

## WHO BROUGHT UP "SIN"?

Genesis 4:3–5 says nothing about remorse for sin as the motivation of the two sons' worship. True, much of the instruction the Lord later gave through Moses about sacrifice does concern sin and atonement. In fact, I suspect that when Christians think of the idea of sacrifice in the Old Testament, the image that usually comes to mind is that of the burnt offering (see Lev. 1:1–17), an offering specifically concerned with the issues of atonement (1:4).

The second chapter of Leviticus, however, discusses grain and firstfruits offerings, with no mention of blood or atonement. Not all sacrifices commanded by God in the Mosaic Law pertained to animals, blood, and death. Some sacrifices were to be made of plant produce. Some sacrifices were simply celebrations of God's blessings in one's life, markers that He and He alone is the Source of all such blessing.

## BRINGING ONE'S VERY BEST

A close reading of Genesis 4:1–5 brings out some remarkable contrasts between the actions of Abel and those of Cain.[6]

Several observations may be noted about these two sons.[7]

- The occupations of the two sons (farmer and herdsman, 4:2) do not suggest moral issues; like siblings in many families, they simply had different interests.
- The phrase "in the process of time" (4:3) suggests that they had now reached sufficient maturity to bring sacrifices to the Lord on their own.
- No mention is made of the origin of the notion of sacrifice in their lives; presumably God Himself had instructed the family about worship. Perhaps the Lord had given instructions to Adam and Eve before they left Eden.[8]

- If the report of Cain's offering had been given alone, we might have had great difficulty in assessing the issue. However, as noted already, God did not judge him because he had not brought an animal sacrifice. He was a farmer; and farmers are to acknowledge that their crops are a gift from God.

- It is only in the relatively lavish praise of Abel's sacrifice that we see deficiencies in Cain's sacrifice. The Hebrew contrasts Abel with Cain by using unusual word order, adding the words "even he," and—most importantly—giving the qualifying words, "the firstborn" and "of their fat."[9]

- Thus Abel brought of the very best, whereas Cain brought "just stuff."[10]

When the Lord later regulated offerings for Israel, He gave specific instructions about the grain offerings His people were to give Him (Lev. 2). The wording there speaks of "fine flour," "firstfruits," and "full heads" (2:1, 14); in addition, we read of the use of oil and frankincense along with the grain (2:1, 15). These details suggest that only the very best could be used in grain offerings, as in all of God's holy worship. "This *grain offering* was prepared and presented at the altar in the same way as those already described [in Lev. 2]. As they had to be prepared from fine flour, so this one had to be prepared from the first of the year's grain harvest. The principle was reaffirmed: Only the best of a person's resources is good enough to offer to God."[11]

So the contrast between the offerings of Cain and Abel is this: The issue lay in the *quality* of the respective offerings, not in the presence or absence of blood in them.[12]

## AND THE HEART

There is another significant contrast for us to discover in a close reading of Genesis 4. The issue was not just between what the two sons brought to the Lord; there was also a significant difference in their hearts. "And the LORD respected Abel and his offering, but He did not respect Cain and his offering" (4:4–5).

In each case God considered *first the person* and *then the offering*. In looking at the person He was looking at his heart.

In all eras true acts of worship include both who a person *is* and what he or she *does*. For one's worship to be acceptable, both need to be in accord with God's truth. Thus we may think of a grid something like the following.

| Heart right | *Heart wrong* |
|---|---|
| Offering right | Offering right |
| Heart right | Heart wrong |
| *Offering wrong* | Offering wrong |

True worship happens only when both heart and action are right before God. To have a heart for God but to do the wrong thing, or to bring the right offering with the wrong heart (in the italicized words in the box)—both lead to disappointment. As for Cain, it seems things were even worse: he was wrong in both his heart and his actions.[13] Abel, on the other hand, had both heart and actions that were pleasurable to God.

In Genesis 4:4 the verb translated "respected" in the New King James Version means "to look with favor on." I believe that when Jesus spoke to the woman at the well, He may have had this verse in mind as He spoke of the Father *seeking* true worshipers, those who worship Him "in spirit and truth" (John 4:23–24).

## THE OPENING OF THE FLOWER

As the rose of Scripture opens in the prophetic books and the Writings, we find various themes touched on that were first mentioned in the books of Moses. One of these passages on true worship is Isaiah 1:10–15. These verses present the strongest possible condemnation of the worship of the people of Judah, as it was being practiced in Isaiah's day (after 740 B.C.). Isaiah did not condemn idolatry, paganizing practices, or waywardness. (This is entirely different from the diatribes of Jeremiah, who spoke against the pagan practices of the people of Judah in his day, some of which were practiced within the very precincts of the holy temple.)[14]

The sins of Judah that Isaiah addressed did not consist of the actions they were doing, for they appeared to be doing all the right things. But they were doing them for all the wrong reasons. They were bringing whole burnt offerings, burning incense, attending sacred assemblies, keeping New Moon festivals (Isa. 1:12–15)—these were all practices God Himself had commanded in the Mosaic Law. But God rejected it all. He said, in effect, "Who needs this?" Even when He looked at their hands lifted up in prayer, He saw on them the bloodstains of daily atrocities against others (1:15). All this was a polluting of His presence, a trashing of His courts. None was accepted by Him as true worship.

In rejecting the worship of His people God said, "I do not delight in the blood of bulls, or of lambs or goats" (1:11). This verse is quite arresting! The word translated "delight" (ḥāpēṣ) has the idea of "taking enjoyment in, smiling about something, receiving joy from something." The Creator of the universe is not some heavenly sadist who finds perverse pleasure in the bleating of sheep and then in the bleeding of helpless animals, with blood everywhere, entrails bespattering His priests, flies all abuzz under Judean sun.

Of course, God had demanded sacrifices from His people, and among them were those that called for the slaughter of animals—whole burnt offerings (Lev. 1), sin offerings (Lev. 4), and trespass offerings (Lev. 5). Each of these involved "blood and gore" aplenty. But God does not find joy in dead animals or smeared blood. If God is to take pleasure (ḥāpēṣ) in the sacrifices that He has commanded, it will be because both the sacrifice and the one bringing it are right before Him. Worship that is acceptable to God cannot be simply a "going through the motions," not even when the motions are the very ones He has commanded.

*God always looks at the heart of His worshipers.*

## SAUL'S SAD SAGA

The prophet Samuel spoke very strongly to King Saul about these very issues. At one point in his sorry career as Israel's first king, Saul became impatient at Samuel's failure to arrive in what he believed was a reasonable period of time. Meanwhile Saul was aware that his troops were beginning to sneak away from the camp; he was in danger of losing his army before the battle against the Philistines had even begun.

So, somewhat understandably, Saul took things into his own hands and offered the requisite sacrifice to the Lord so that the battle with his enemies might ensue. I suspect that Saul offered the sacrifices with scrupulous care; he probably did everything correctly. Yet he was not the one permitted to do these acts; his clear instructions had been to wait for Samuel's arrival (1 Sam. 10:8). We note with sadness that there were more enemies in Saul's life than the Philistines and the Amalekites; among his enemies were his own rash behavior and impatience.

Just as Saul finished his sacrifice, Samuel arrived. The prophet took in the scene and then asked the chilling question, "What have you done?" (13:11). Saul gave his rationale in words that have a certain reasonableness to them. But Samuel's evaluation was stern: "You have done foolishly" (13:13).[15] Samuel had given Saul a specific command, but Saul had disobeyed the prophet—and God. Saul's actions were in the context of worship, but in the process he had not brought pleasure to the Lord.

King Saul's misadventures with true worship did not end in this story. In yet another battle, this time with the Amalekites, the king of Israel spared both his royal counterpart from the army he defeated, as well as the choicest of animals. These actions were in clear disobedience to God's command through His prophet Samuel. The Amalekites were under the ban (*herem*) of the Lord; no breathing thing was to escape destruction (15:1–3).

For reasons not clearly stated, Saul spared both Agag, the Amalekite king, and the very best of the animals of the defeated peoples. Perhaps Saul spared the animals for his own use, but why did he spare Agag? In any event, when confronted by God's prophet, Saul boasted of his achievement and lied about the rest. Finally the prophet Samuel could take it no longer and told him to "Be quiet!" (15:16).[16] Saul, in folly, did not obey this simple command, but, when pressed, he continued to excuse his behavior. His most tragic words were uttered when he blamed the people for sparing the best of the animals, but then suggested that he could use them to worship God in sacrifice (15:21).

The words of God's prophet to the disobedient king are unforgettable. These words should be known by all who lead in worship. "Has the LORD as great delight in burnt offerings and sacrifices, as in obeying the voice of the LORD? Behold, to obey is better than sacrifice, and to heed than the fat of rams. For rebellion is as the sin of witchcraft, and stubbornness is as iniquity and idolatry. Because you have rejected the word of the LORD, He has also rejected you from being king" (15:22–23).

Just as with Cain, so here too God looks on the heart of the worshiper as well as on what the worshiper might bring before Him. Even if one brings the very best offerings to the Lord, the more important issue is heart motivation. Saul was unable to cover his sin of disobedience by suggesting a lavish act of sacrifice to God. The story of Saul makes me think of a latter-day Mafia don giving a magnificent cash gift to his parish priest to beautify a church building. The gift might buy a wonderful window, purchase an organ, or repair the roof. But the gangster may not pay off God as a way of escaping the consequences of his personal sin.

Saul was somewhat quick in his thinking, but not quick enough for Samuel—and certainly not quick enough for God! *Worship of God that does not proceed from obedience to Him is not worship at all.*

So again we confront the notion of worship and the *delight* of the LORD. First Samuel 15:22 begins with the words, "Has the LORD as great delight in burnt offerings and sacrifices, as in obeying the voice of the LORD?" The noun "delight" (*ḥāpēṣ*) is related to the verb *ḥāpēṣ*, which we saw in Isaiah 1:11. As in Isaiah, so here God does not take pleasure in, smile over, or enjoy the sacrifices of a person who does not bring them for the right reasons, even if the sacrifices are otherwise acceptable. As we saw with Cain, so we see with Saul: *what* one brings and the *heart* with which one brings it are both significant to God. Saul's acts of disobedience ruled out God's acceptance of his sacrifice. To make this even more clear, Samuel's poetic indictment states that Saul might as well have practiced pagan rites of idolatry and witchcraft (1 Sam. 15:23), for his rebellious actions were as detestable to God as those awful acts would have been.[17]

We need to remember the grid: Only when right action is coupled with a right heart may one then sense God's pleasure. Anything less is not biblical worship. I love the way Sondra Corbett captures these ideas when she speaks of worship as "what I want to do."

> I worship You, Almighty God;
> There is none like You.
> I worship You, O Prince of Peace;
> That is what I want to do.
> I give you praise for You are my righteousness.
> I worship You, Almighty God;
> There is none like You.
>
> —SONDRA CORBETT[18]

## DAVID'S HEART

David has left us so many psalms that we may feel we know him as a dear friend.[19] No psalm of David deals with the subject of worship and one's heart more powerfully than Psalm 40, particularly verses 6–8: "Sacrifice and offering You did not desire; my ears You have opened. Burnt offering and sin offering You did not require. Then I said, 'Behold, I come; in the scroll of the book it is written of me. I delight to do Your will, O my God, And Your law is within my heart.'"

When I first read these words, they seemed to be almost unbelievable. How could David have spoken of the sacrificial system the Lord had established as something that He did not "require"? This seemed astonishing. If God did not "require" sacrifices, who did?

Some critical scholars have seized on verses such as these to assert that there was an antisacrificial party in Israel that opposed the prosacrifice party. These liberal scholars assert that the prosacrifice party won the battle but did not sufficiently cleanse the Bible of the words of their opponents. They say Psalm 40:6 is an example of such an unexpurgated verse!

Yet, we must ask, how could David speak of God-ordained sacrifices as neither desired nor required by God? The key is to be found in the verb translated "desire" (ḥāpēṣ) in verse 6. The point here is the same as in Isaiah 1:11 and in 1 Samuel 16:22.

God does not take pleasure in the blood of animals. Instead He is pleased with the believer who comes to Him in worship with a glad heart, a broken heart, a true heart. His people pleasure Him. True, they must bring the sacrifices—but they bring them gladly. God looks first at the people and then at what they bring. And then He smiles![20]

Many writers suggest that the clause "my ears You have opened" (Ps. 40:6) relates to a verse in Exodus 21 regarding a freed slave who wished to remain in slavery for family reasons.[21] However, David spoke of God opening (boring through) each of his ears, not just piercing the lobe of one ear, as in the case of a slave. He meant by this that he was a responsible worshiper. The Lord has given us ears to hear; when He speaks, His people respond. David knew the errors of his predecessor. Saul thought he might "fix" disobedience by a lavish act of worship, but David knew that obedience is a part of true worship.

For this reason David said exultingly, "I come!" (Ps. 40:7). He knew that what he did in worship was written in the scroll, that is, in the Books of Moses (namely, Gen. 4). This was deep within his heart (Ps. 40:8). True, he brought a sacrifice. But he also brought himself. This verse is wonderfully anticipative of Paul's familiar words in Romans 12:1: "I beseech you therefore, brethren, by the mercies of God, that you present your bodies a living sacrifice, holy, acceptable to God, which is your reasonable service."

David was not simply bringing animals to offer to the Lord. He was bringing himself as well. Like Abel so long before, David knew about the true worship of the holy, merciful, loving God. And so he worshiped Him.

Now here is an astounding thing. Psalm 40:6–8 includes a pairing of words, an *inclusio*,[22] that ties the passage tightly together. In verse 6 we read, "Sacrifice and offering You did not *desire*," and in verse 8 we read, "I *delight* to do Your will, O my God" (italics added).

The word translated "desire" is the same Hebrew verb translated "delight." They both mean "to find pleasure in" (*ḥāpēṣ*). I find this to be simply wonderful. If we put both verbs in the positive force we discover the wonder of biblical worship; when worship brings pleasure to the Lord, it also brings pleasure to the worshiper! In true worship *we bring pleasure to God, and that brings us the greatest pleasure of all!*[23]

## THE FULL BLOOM

The idea of the analogy of the rose is that the grand truths of Scripture are seen first in the "full bud" of the Books of Moses, then in greater clarity in the "opening phases" of the prophetic books and the Writings, and then are seen at their very best in the "full bloom" of Jesus' teachings in the Gospels. Thus Jesus' words to the woman at the well of Sychar form the grandest text in Scripture on the basic meaning of the true worship of the living God; but these words are also the culmination of the flow of Scripture beginning in Genesis 4. In Genesis 4 we saw the truth in the *full bud* form; in 1 Samuel 15, Isaiah 1, and Psalm 40 we saw the truth in the *opening of the rose* form. Now in the words of Jesus we see it in the *full bloom* form.

Here are some major ideas from Jesus' words to the woman in John 4:21–24.

- As already noted, Jesus was speaking with great authority. In His words "believe Me" (4:21), He was asserting divine authority. He spoke as the greater Prophet, as the Coming One, as God.
- Jesus could not have chosen a less likely setting or audience for this magnificent statement. One might have thought He would give His description of true worship to priests in Jerusalem, not to a despised woman of Samaria. But He who knows what is in a person (2:25) knew that in this desperate woman there was one who would not only believe Him, but who would even evangelize her entire town!
- Jesus marked out the errors of the Samaritan system, simply and firmly. The Samaritans worshiped the Father at the wrong place (Mount Gerizim); only Jerusalem was the site for worship during the temple period. Thus, even if one in Samaria had a right heart, that person was at the wrong place. A right heart with a wrong action does not equal true worship.
- Jesus affirmed the correctness of both the place of Jerusalem and the people of Israel as the centers of true worship and God's salvation. Truth is never to be compromised in worship. Jesus did not seek to salve her feelings; these were deeply emotional issues, but He told the truth in love.
- Jesus also affirmed that a time is coming (and was upon them) when the place of worship would no longer be the important issue that it had been for a thousand years. This looked forward, of course, to the New Testament era when one may worship God with the people of God in any location in which they gather for worship.

- The most important issues in Jesus' remarks take us far beyond the argument about the place of worship and deeply within the heart of the worshiper.

## THE TRUE WORSHIPER

Jesus' words about the coming of a new era ("the hour is coming," John 4:23) take us back to His same words in verse 21, "the hour is coming." In both cases Jesus was emphasizing the change of eras from the period of expectation to that of realization. The new era had begun. The Lord Himself was speaking!

Jesus also had a strong focus on the Father as the Object of worship. While it is true that each person of the Trinity is to be worshiped, it is also true that the more usual wording of Scripture is that we worship the Father through the mercy of the Lord Jesus and in the power of the Holy Spirit.

Jesus emphasized as well that "God is Spirit" (4:24). These words must have a distinctive importance in this context; otherwise why would Jesus say such a "simple thing?" The importance of the phrase may lie in our need to remember that in worshiping God we should have a sense of His presence in our midst. God may not be seen in the way an idol might be visible in a pagan temple. God is Spirit. His presence will not be tasted, touched, heard, seen, or smelled. But as we worship Him in spirit and truth, there He is!

Wherever we are, if we are truly involved in the corporate worship of God, we are on holy ground. When Moses stood before the burning bush at the base of Mount Sinai, God told him to remove his sandals (Exod. 3:5). In Eastern custom one removes sandals when in a person's home. The proximity of the bush had become the dwelling place of God. Moses later memorialized this great fact in these words of blessing: "And the favor of Him who dwelt in the bush" (Deut. 33:16). Now if Moses was on holy ground before the burning bush, so are we when we come to worship the same God whom Moses adored.

> This is holy ground,
> We're standing on holy ground;
> For the Lord is here
> And where He is is holy.
>
> —CHRISTOPHER BEATTY

## IN SPIRIT AND TRUTH

We come now to the phrase "in spirit and truth" (John 4:24).

- On one level the words "in spirit and truth" are another hendiadys that speaks of the internal genuineness of the worshiping person. These words point to the heart, to the inner man. We are to worship from the heart (in spirit) and with sincerity (in truth). The heart of the believer is of first importance to the God we worship.
- The word "spirit" may be thought of as though spelled with a capital letter: "in Spirit and truth." That is, it is not enough to be sincere, because one may be sincerely wrong. Our worship must be empowered by God's Spirit and in accord with His truth.[24]
- The words "in spirit and truth" relate both to the inner person and to the outward acts. These must occur together, and when they do, true worship occurs.
- God the Father actively seeks for such worshipers—worshipers to whom He responds in gracious favor, in full smile, as it were.
- Another observation about Jesus' words to the woman at the well is that He did not merely make a suggestion about true worship. His words are in fact a command. "Those who worship Him *must* worship in spirit and truth" (italics added). True worship, in spirit and truth, is so important to the God of Scripture that anything less is simply inadequate.

*Part 3*

# Implementational Issues

# *Nine*

✦

# Word, Water, and Wine

MANY PEOPLE TODAY think of worship exclusively in terms of music. It is not uncommon to hear people speak of "traditional worship styles" when they think of the use of hymns, and of "contemporary worship styles" when they focus on praise choruses. A review of a number of articles in *Worship Leader* magazine shows writers (including writers of letters to the editor) speaking of "praise and worship" churches. But in all of this the center is on musical style, as though music alone defines the worship of God.

Within our churches we hear similar sentiments. In my travels as an itinerant Bible conference speaker in churches across North America I frequently hear the worship leader say, "And now let's worship," as he picks up his guitar or reaches for the microphone. The surprising thing is that he says this at a point well along in the service.

What were we doing before that moment? And what will we be doing when the singers sit down and the cords go slack on the many microphones? Has the current emphasis on music led people to conclude that worship and music are interchangeable terms? Does not worship occur in other elements of the service?

This chapter focuses on several elements of worship that seem to have been minimized in the current passion to make so much of music. My son Craig describes this as "music-driven" worship. As important as music is in worship, we need to remember that worship is much broader than music. Music may be one of the important elements in worship, but it is only a part of the whole.

Several weekends each year I do bicycling events in towns in Texas as well as in cities across the country. Often the ride is on a Saturday and I preach in a church on the following day. On some occasions I have the "day off" and simply visit a church on Sunday morning. I have been calling this "Discovering Texas—by Bicycle and Bible." One weekend I stayed in a bed and breakfast in a small town in Texas. After my bike ride on Saturday, the woman at the B&B invited me to join her family the next morning in their church—the small Anglican church across the street.

The priest began the service with an announcement. The husband of the organist had died early in the week; the funeral had been on Saturday—as it turned out, during my bike ride! "So," he said, "we will proceed with our service this morning without the organ, and apart from any music." He mentioned that the organist was simply not able to serve that morning.

Music is so much a part of worship that it is hard to imagine worship apart from it. But that morning this is precisely what we did. We engaged in prayer. We heard the reading of the Word. We engaged in the liturgy with lovely responses from the congregation. There was a biblical message. There it was—the people of God, the Word of God, the service of God, the worship of God, but none of the music of God. It worked, but I am glad it was but for a morning.

## THE PLACE OF THE BIBLE IN GOD'S WORSHIP

My parents came to faith in Christ through the ministry of an evangelical Lutheran pastor in southern California. That church, Emmanuel Lutheran Church of North Hollywood, was one of the most innovative churches in the region in the 1950s. Along with many then-new ideas, this was the first church to have an early drive-in service before the regular services. Long before Robert Schuller made a similar innovation in the Crystal Cathedral over in Orange County, our church had services that people attended in their cars. As people drove up to church, they parked their cars in the large playground of the Christian school—and stayed in them during the service.

The pastoral staff and some singers would lead in the service from a raised platform. An outdoor sound system flooded the area with the sounds of the service. People would come dressed for the beach (this was California!), stay in their cars for the service, then motor off for a family outing. These services were particularly pleasing to my father. Since an automobile accident had left him paralyzed from just below his neck, he found the drive-in services to be a convenient option to getting into his wheelchair for Sunday mornings.

Our pastors were deeply spiritual men. Norman Hammer was exceptionally creative (the drive-in was during his ministry), and his successor, Erling Wold, was a wonderful orator with a keen intellect. They both gave deeply impacting biblical messages. But neither of them was an expositor. As Lutherans, they would follow the Bible passages for the Sunday of the church year and would form their messages from the passages selected.[1] I owe these men much in my early spiritual formation.

After I was married and in college, my wife, Beverly, and I began to attend a Bible church, the Arcadia (Calif.) Union Church. Under the ministry of Martin Stuck, we discovered the wonder of verse-by-verse, passage-by-passage expository preaching. This book-by-book ministry of the Word was simply marvelous to us. Occasionally we would visit the Church of the Open Door in downtown Los Angeles during the ministry of J. Vernon McGee. I remember vividly the first time we were at a Thursday evening Bible class at that church (known as COD). Dr. McGee announced a passage and there was a new sound to us, one of great loveliness: four thousand people paging through their Bibles to locate the passage for the evening. The rustling of the pages was akin to angels' wings beating through the air.

In the Lutheran church much was made of the reading of the Bible, but in the Bible church much was made of the preaching of the Bible.

The reading of the Bible in the Lutheran church of my youth was a major part of worship. The reading of an Old Testament passage and the reading of a portion from a New Testament epistle were given from the lectern with the congregation remaining seated. Then came the reading from one of the Gospels. The congregation would stand to hear this section as it was read from the pulpit. After each reading there was a brief congregational response in song.

In liturgical churches few people ever bring their Bibles with them; in the Bible churches (and in the Baptist churches we later attended) almost everyone brings his or her Bible to church.

In Bible churches the reading of a Bible passage, if done at all, often serves as the basis for the sermon. In the course of time we found that in a number of churches the Bible reading was rarely given the importance we had sensed in our Lutheran church. Though the passage was read, it was clear that the more important issue was the preaching that was to come. The reading of the Bible was important, but it was not generally seen as an act of worship in itself. In fact, the inane little prayer that often followed the reading of the Bible, "May God add His blessing to the reading of His Word," suggested that the reading was not an important thing in itself. But God does not need to "add His blessing to the reading of His Word." The reading of His Word is *in itself* blessing indeed. And when it is read as an act of worship, it brings blessing to God.

## WHERE IS THE BIBLE IN THE BIBLE CHURCHES?

In several experiences in the last several years where Beverly and I have attended services in varied cities, I have discovered something very disquieting.

The Bible is almost missing from current Bible churches![2]

Perhaps not from yours. But time after time I have noticed that in those churches whose middle name is "Bible" the Bible is seldom used. This is almost unbelievable. In hardly any services that I have simply attended in the last few years (as against those in which I have had a part as the visiting preacher) do I remember much being made of *reading Scripture as an act of worship*. This seems almost to have disappeared.

It is not simply that there is a lack of the three readings (Old Testament, Gospels, and Epistles), as in the experiences of my youth; it is that there is no reading done at all. Today—as I type these words—it is a Sunday afternoon. The morning service is fresh on my mind. The music was wonderful. The prayers were stirring. Worship was planned, and worship occurred. But there was no reading of the Bible whatever, except for a few verses in the sermon. The Bible is no longer being read as an act of worship, not even in churches that claim to be "Bible churches." This is simply astonishing—and disturbing.

I am not alone in this observation. Ron Owens has noted the same phenomenon. "The reading of the Word of God no longer holds a central place in the worship services of many churches in North America. We still say we love God's Word and base our lives on it, but if we gauge our love and commitment by the amount of time we give to reading it when we gather as God's people, there is reason to question our claim. When is the last time you heard an entire chapter read during the gathering? We say there just isn't enough time."[3]

A graduate student from India, Mazie Nakhro, recently completed his doctoral dissertation at Dallas Theological Seminary. He wrote on the topic that the Book of the Revelation is a worship document, designed to be read as a part of worship of the church. Along the way, Nakhro observes the irony of the paucity of Bible reading in contemporary Christian worship among those churches where the Bible is said to be so very highly regarded. He writes, "Unfortunately, many conservative Christians today, who rightly defend the belief of *Solo Scriptura* and accept the Holy Scriptures as the authoritative Word of God, often fail to include Scripture reading as a worship act in their services."[4]

Later in his study he writes the following concerning the Book of Revelation and the worship of God: "The significance of the Book of Revelation for the corporate worship of the church seems evident in view of the fact that the book is addressed to and written for all the churches so they may use it in their corporate worship of God. Furthermore, it is conceivable that the Apocalypse, being the last inspired Scripture, may have been God's last word on Christian worship."[5]

## BIBLES, BIBLES . . . EVERYWHERE!

People need to hear the reading of the Word of God in public worship now more than ever. We live in an era where the Bible is more accessible to more people on the planet than at any time in history. Courageous and highly skilled pioneer missionaries in organizations such as Wycliffe Bible Translators have brought the Scriptures in whole and in part to people groups in some of the most remote places in the world.

We in the industrialized West, particularly in English-speaking countries, have so many varied ways of accessing God's Word that it staggers the mind. We have Bible schools and seminaries, and many of them have numerous extension sites in addition to their main campuses. Churches have Bible classes and study groups. Bible Study Fellowship, an organization I champion, may have more people meeting in organized study groups in one week's time than any other ministry has ever had at one time in the history of our faith. We have tape ministries, video courses, and innumerable resources on the worldwide web.

And think about the Bibles. We have the King James Version and the New King James Version. We have the Revised Standard Version and the New Revised Standard Version. We have the New American Standard Bible and the New American Standard Bible, 1995 revision. We have the New International Version and soon the "New" New International Version. Revisions have revisions! There are the New English Bible, the Jerusalem Bible, the New Living Translation, and the Torah (JPS). We have Phillips's Paraphrase, *The Living Bible*, and Eugene Peterson's paraphrase, *The Message*. We have Bibles with notes. We have Bibles with pictures. We have Bibles with full study materials. On a world scale it is somewhat embarrassing to realize there are so many options in English, particularly when there are still so many people groups in which the Bible has yet to be translated at all (despite the great work of Wycliffe Bible Translators and others, as mentioned above).

Our Bibles are available in leather and in paper. They are hardbound and softbound. They are even in denim! Bibles are still being produced as illuminated manuscripts in very small numbers, but they are also produced electronically. Dallas Seminary professors have produced the NET Bible, designed especially for Internet users. Bibles are available on audiocassette tapes, CD-ROM versions, and in hand-held electronic tools.

So I repeat, at no time in human history have more people on the planet had more ways of accessing the Word of God. And for those people whose language is English, the means of access are exhausting just to list.

Yet there seems to be less general knowledge about the content of the Bible among otherwise informed people than at any time in post-Reformation history. In a recent television quiz show program, this was one of the questions: "Which one of the following individuals led Israel to freedom from Egypt in Bible days?" The four choices for the answer were Moses, David, Joshua, and Spartacus. The response given was correct that time (!), but easily could have been wrong. Many people today have as little knowledge about Moses as they do about Spartacus.

I recall an advanced elective course in English poetry that I enjoyed in my college years. My professor was one of the best, but she had some gaps in her knowledge base. One day in class we read and analyzed a poem titled "Provide, Provide." It described in lovely lyric poetry a very beautiful woman named Abishag. I recall my professor saying that she loved the poem but hated the name. "Why," she asked, "would a poet describe a beautiful woman with that rather ugly-sounding name?" When I told her the source after class, she was considerably embarrassed. But then she said, "But then, no one can be expected to know the Bible in our day as they might have in earlier generations."

Here is my point: We need to have the reading of the Bible and the exposition of the Scriptures as major elements of our worship services more than ever. Never has the reading of the Bible been more critical than in our day. The Bible needs to be read aloud in our services because even people who *have* Bibles tend to be biblically illiterate.

## READ THEM OVER AGAIN TO ME

The reading of Scripture needs to be done well. In fact it should be rehearsed.

Ordinarily the pastor is the one who reads Scripture as an act of worship in the church services.[6] But others too may do so. I love how our pastor in Oregon has readings done by women as well as men, by children as well as adults. Sometimes he has a family come and read a passage, with different members reading different sections. Sometimes he will have a trio of women standing at music stands, not to sing, but to read in creative and powerful ways.

Reg Grant has done memorable Bible readings in seminary chapel services and at other special meetings, as has our colleague John Reed. Both of them emphasize in their seminary classes that the reading of Scripture can have a strong impact on the worship of God's people.

Yet I still chafe at the memory of a church service I attended in which no reading of Scripture was included in the worship service and the Bible wasn't even opened during the sermon. The visiting speaker did quote a verse a couple of times, but he did so out of context—in fact to the opposite effect of the intent of the verse. The scene was nearly comic. He paced back and forth on the platform, waving a Bible that he didn't open even once. Nor would anyone else in the congregation—at least not in this service. And this was in a church with a strong heritage of expository preaching of the Bible.

When the Bible is read, the reader should actually have a Bible before her or him. There is a growing tendency that is troubling to me in this regard. Speakers these days tend to come to the lectern with a manila folder holding their notes, and they come without a Bible. They may have Bible verses written in their notes and they may read them well in the course of their message, but they don't have the visual symbol of a Bible in their hands.[7]

Yet a powerfully symbolic act transpires when one makes a point of opening the Bible to a passage and then reads, not from one's notes, but from the printed Bible. This is a way of elevating the Bible in the eyes of the people as well as in their ears. In my seminary classes, I use my full leather-bound English Bible and my Hebrew or Greek Testament. They are prominent on the podium. I don't read the Bible from a computer screen or from notes in a folder. I read the Bible from the Bible.

God is a God of visual symbols. Think of His use of the elements of natural phenomena, of features of creation. For example, He planned for His people to use two mountains near Shechem for the reading of covenantal cursings and blessings in the land of Israel (see Deut. 11:26–32, especially v. 29). One mountain, Mount Ebal, is rather barren; this was the setting for the reading of the cursings. The other mountain, Mount Gerizim, is regularly green; here the Israelites stood as the blessings were read (Josh. 8:30–35, especially v. 33).

God is the God of visual symbols. He wrote on tablets with His finger. He descended on Mount Sinai with many attendant wonders. God roared from Zion in the preaching of His prophets.

How can we fail to use the grandest symbol of all when we stand up to convey His message? A preacher who rises to preach without having his Bible in his hand is like a violinist arriving at a concert saying he can hum the tune.

At times I preach from passages that I could quote from memory; I don't need to have the Bible opened to preach from these passages. But I take my Bible with me, I open it, I look at the page, and I read from it. Why? Because I want the visual symbol to be clear: This is the Word of God and I honor it by reading from it.

It is a simple ceremony, this opening and reading aloud from the Bible. But it is one of the most significant things we do in worship. Only we who have always had the Bible nearby fail to appreciate the significance of actually holding and reading God's Word.

## THE TREASURE IN OUR HANDS

In December 1991 I taught a course on the Book of Psalms in the Ukraine at Svet Evangelia, near Donetsk. My interpreter told me that the students had no textbooks; my lectures would become their text. Sure enough, I observed that when Demitri Romanov translated my words a sentence at a time, the fifty students each wrote word-for-word dictation in their notebooks. In doing this for their textbooks, they were doing what they had done earlier for Scripture. In the days of Soviet control, one person in their church who had a Bible would read a passage and each member would write down the text word for word. One couple showed me their "Bible." It was a notebook into which they had copied large sections from both Testaments in word-for-word dictation over the years.

One person told me that in those many years of Soviet oppression preachers were forbidden to visit his church in order to transmit materials other than personal letters from friends in other congregations. So a visiting pastor might stand and say in church, "I have a letter from Sister Olga," and he would read the letter. Then he might read another letter from Brother Ivan. Last, with a wink, he might read a letter from Brother Paulus, and the people would write each word as they would add an epistle of Paul into their hand-printed Bibles.

We have the treasure of God's written Word at hand. Let us renew our devotion to God by making more of the public reading of Scripture in our worship.

## CEREMONIES OF OUR FAITH

The simple acts of opening a Bible and reading it well in the congregation are wonderful elements in our worship. Other simple acts are wonderful as well. In some churches they seem to be nearly as much at risk as is the reading of Scripture.

Water baptism is one of the great opportunities for congregational celebration of our holy faith. When a person who has received Christ as his or her Savior is baptized in a public setting, what a wonderful gift the congregation can enjoy with that person. Yet I report with sadness that in many churches in which the message of salvation is preached with power, grace, and wonder, the biblical act of publicly celebrating that faith— water baptism—has also fallen on hard days.

Recently I was told by one pastor that the worship would be curtailed somewhat because they had to have a baptism. He seemed to convey that baptism was a kind of "tack on," and not a genuine part of worship.

The simple, beautiful symbol of a person being immersed in water and then raised from it is exquisite both as a teaching tool and a celebration of grace. This is an act of worship. It is not intrusive. It is not something that takes away from worship. Properly presented, baptism is a wonderful part of our worship of God.

Similar comments may be made about the Lord's Supper. Timothy Ralston argues strongly that historic worship patterns have two foci, the Word and the "Table." Passages in the Book of Acts and notices in the records of the early church suggest that celebrating the death and resurrection of Jesus in the Lord's Supper was a regular feature of worship in the early church. Ralston has a splendid presentation he uses in class to urge the weekly celebration of the Lord's Supper along with the preaching of the Word of God.

My own view is less emphatic on this point. I may be speaking more from my own traditions and experience than from lessons in early church history, but I remain very comfortable with the practice in many churches of celebrating Communion monthly rather than weekly. The issue of frequency, to me, is a choice one may make, rather than a command to be followed.

But I share with Ralston the distress he feels in the tendency toward minimizing the Lord's Supper in believing assemblies. So often this act of worship is tacked on to an already full service. It is not unusual to see people sit down, glance at the bulletin, and then grimace a bit when they realize that "this will be a longer service" because of Communion!

Again I point with joy to the pattern that our church in Oregon has used over the years on Communion Sundays. On these days the entire service is geared toward the celebration of the Lord's Supper. The sermon is briefer; all the music and readings are directed toward an aspect of the Lord's death and its profound significance. Noting is rushed. There is time to pray, to reflect, and to weep. People do not groan when they learn it is Communion Sunday; they know that this will be a service in which the Cross will be central, and in which one of the ever-significant elements of our faith will be celebrated in a most meaningful manner.

Here again, a "music-driven" worship pattern may be wrong-headed, if some Christians conclude that worship is minimized on Communion Sundays. True, the role of music is so important in biblical worship that it is difficult to imagine worship apart from it. Nevertheless worship is more than music, and few acts of worship are more significant that the congregational participation in the Lord's Supper, in which they together remember the Lord's death and anticipate His coming.[8]

## ARE THERE RULES OF WORSHIP?

The Bible, I believe, gives considerable latitude for the worship patterns of the church. God gave an enormous body of material to ancient Israel through His prophet Moses on the manner and meaning of their sacrifices (Lev. 1–7) and in the design for their great worship tent (Exod. 25–31). He spoke with great detail on the qualifications of priests (Lev. 8–10) and on the nature of

Israel's festivals and fasts (Lev. 16, 23). But He seems to have given considerable freedom in the orchestrating of their worship services. We read about major worship services, such as the dedication of the temple in the days of King Solomon (2 Chron. 6–7), but no divine instructions were given on how those services were to be conducted. In the psalms we read of the emotions of God's people in holy worship (see, for example, Ps. 100), but nothing is said about the order of their acts of worship. We read of their music, but we have no scores to reproduce it. We read of their sacrifices, but we know little of what accompanied those acts.

In the New Testament we have even less to go on. Passages such as Acts 2:40–47 are sometimes taken as templates for Christian worship. While informative, these passages should not be thought of as presenting the "rules of worship." The Book of Acts describes the transition from temple worship to the earliest Christian house assemblies. If this passage is used as biblical authority for celebrating the Lord's Supper on each occasion of Christian worship (2:42), does it also demand that Christians today engage in communal living (2:44), as some groups insist? If the passage suggests anything about the regularity of the Lord's Table, it might be thought to be daily (2:46); also every day more people came to Christ for salvation (2:47). And all the while, these new believers in Jesus were continuing to worship God in the temple (2:46).

Paul wrote of doing everything "decently and in order" (1 Cor. 14:40), but he wrote more about the problematic issue of women's head coverings (11:1–11) than he did on how Christian worship services were to be organized, and he said virtually nothing on what the "order of service" might have been. He certainly emphasized the meaning and importance of the Lord's Supper (11:34), but he did not say how this sacred rite might relate to the rest of a "Christian worship service."

We face two issues in the writings of the New Testament that may be disconcerting to some. One is that the Book of Acts is a record of the earliest Christians in transition from Judaism to their distinct new identity; the other is that the Epistles are "occasional letters,"[9] not thorough treatises on Christian doctrine. We believe that these documents of our faith are enormously important; but we also find that in some areas of Christian practice, there are often as many questions as answers.

I suggest a positive approach to this issue. Rather than lamenting the fact that we do not have more direction on our worship services from the pages of the New Testament, let us rejoice that God in His kindness has given us considerable liberty. The church, He knew, would go through numerous permutations in the practice of worship through its rather convoluted history and in its growth in worldwide ethnic diversity. The many varieties of Christian expression, so long as they are deeply rooted in biblical truths that *are* unchangeable, provide divine opportunities for many diverse people and people groups to worship the living God.

## A NEW RITE OF CHRISTIAN WORSHIP

Here is an example of a new rite of Christian worship that is particularly suited to a distinct people group and setting. Beverly and I spent about a month in ministries in Japan in the summer of 1992. I taught concentrated classes in two seminaries and spoke in a number of churches.

Our last day in Japan was a Sunday. The pastor of a church in Tokyo told us that he would get us to the airport in time for our flight, but that the timing would be close. I knew that our flight was not scheduled until late afternoon, so I wondered why he spoke as he had. "Oh," he said. "We have a bit of an adventure planned for you before we go to the airport."

Adventure it was! We joined a caravan of cars filled with church members, winding around a number of roads, until we came to a cemetery. Then the pastor explained that the entire church body was coming to the cemetery for a resurrection service.

In Japan unsaved people supply gifts for their dead relatives and pray for them. When Japanese people come to faith in Christ, one of the charges of their families and friends is that they are deserting their responsibility to the dead, that they are leaving their dead loved ones to some sort of unsupported limbo. Wonderfully creative Christians decided to face this issue by developing a Christian alternative to presenting gifts to the dead and saying prayers for them. They have periodic services at their church cemetery where they affirm their belief in the resurrection, and thus show their ongoing love for those who had died before them.

Because cremation is mandatory in land-poor Japan, and because land for burial is quite expensive, churches have banded together to purchase burial sites. Each congregation has a burial area, where the urns of the ashes of their church members may be kept. Chairs had been set up at the entrance to the mausoleum. The people gathered in solemnity. We prayed and sang, there was a message of hope, and the service ended in joyful anticipation of the physical resurrection of the body at the return of the Lord Jesus Christ.

Here were people in a special situation inventing a new type of Christian worship service. Not only did it lead to renewed personal hope in the resurrection, but it also served as a witness to their unsaved relatives and friends that in becoming Christians they were not deserting their loved ones.[10]

Similar things happen when ministries are developed in our own country for special groups of people. We all know about ministries designed for team members in professional sports; there are also ministries developed to reach motorcycle club riders, cowboy rodeo wranglers, and racecar drivers.

Worship is multifarious; the true worship of God concerns many issues and can be realized in a wide variety of ways. In many churches today worship is music-driven; but worshiping God is far more complex than the type of songs one may sing or the styles in which they may be performed.

# Ten

## Worship as One's Manner of Life

"WORSHIP IS MORE THAN SINGING SONGS to God on Sunday morning!" These words are true, but I was a bit surprised when I heard them expressed very strongly not long ago. Unexpectedly they came from a minister of music, Ron Man, who for many years was minister of music and worship at the First Evangelical Church Memphis, Tennessee.

The setting for these words was also somewhat unexpected. Ron Man and I were presenting alternating lectures in a conference on worship at the Biblical Theological Seminary in Wroclaw, Poland. We spoke through several interpreters over the course of our lectures.

### MORE THAN SONGS

When Ron began one of his lectures with the words, "Worship is more than singing songs to God on Sunday morning," he was right!

And in fact the singing of songs to God on Sunday morning may not in itself even be true worship. Many people who may engage in the songs have not engaged with God. We hear more and more about the shallowness of people's response to God in contemporary North American life. Our most illustrious American pollster has released a new study of religious affection. George Gallup, Jr., suggests that "God is important but not primary in people's lives."[1] Although there has been a significant growth in church attendance, it seems that far too many people have added a layer of religion to their lives rather than being radically transformed by a vital relationship with the Lord Jesus Christ.[2]

Think about what happens each Christmas season in the public arena. No wonder Jewish people become offended. *Everyone* sings Christmas carols! Sinners join saints in these songs. Secularists sing along with the spiritual. Drunks sing them in bars. Soap opera characters sing them. Situation comedy programs have their "Christmas episodes," with Christmas carols along the way. Hollywood entertainment types, Nashville singers, Seattle rock stars, and Broadway dancers join each other in one Christmas special after another. Opera singers are featured with a full orchestra, singing a great carol on a program such as *Saturday Night Live.* Puppets sing. Animated creatures sing. In malls, elevators, restaurants—carols are inescapable. Everybody sings! They sing holy words of a holy night and a holy Child—but these are sung seemingly apart from holy intentions.

Of course, not all these songs are songs of Christ. We are assaulted by muddled messages of nostril-enhanced reindeer, good-hearted snowmen, chubby gift-givers, singing chipmunks, roasting chestnuts, and dreams of snow on Christmas. But amid the fluff and foolishness, we also hear the carols of the newborn Christ, old and new, that mark out Christmas as a time of nearly overwhelming song. Songs are such a part of Christmas that it is scarcely impossible to imagine a celebration of it apart from music.

Today's climate is one of openness toward everyone.[3] In the winter holiday season of 1999 there was an unusual convergence of Christmas, Hanukkah, and Ramadan, not to mention the neo-rite of Kwanzaa.[4] In a newspaper article Christine Wicker wrote of schools that are attempting to incorporate some participation of Ramadan, the Muslim month of fasting during daylight hours. She reported that one local educator said, "We'd be happy to include Ramadan songs in our holiday choral program, if there are any."[5] When we think of Islam, we don't immediately associate music with it. But when we think of Christianity, things are different.

Worship is more than singing on Sunday morning. But lots of the singing of great worship music may not be true worship.

## WORSHIP AND LIFE

Worship, biblical worship, is more than music. It is more than actions or routine procedures. Worship, true worship, is something that animates all of life. The fact of worship being a part of one's entire life is taught in a variety of ways throughout the Bible, and especially in Deuteronomy.

As I mentioned in chapter 6, worship is to permeate every aspect of a believer's life; it is not just an occasional attendance in a worship service.

The words of Deuteronomy 6 provide an essential part of our understanding of biblical worship: *True biblical worship concerns the whole of one's life; its ultimate meaning is rooted in one's wholehearted love for God.* What we do in corporate worship has its prime significance in the context of our daily living. Merely to participate in the sacred rites of community worship, apart from a full-hearted sharing in the foundational biblical attitudes, and divorced from the anticipated biblical actions, is to leave one under the sad judgment of a disappointed God: "These people . . . honor Me with their lips, but their hearts are far from Me" (Isa. 29:13).

The *focus* of worship in the Old Testament is on the acts and attitudes of the community of believers gathered together for corporate responses to God. But the Bible never conveys the notion that mere acts of worship could make up for a life that is not lived as a "living sacrifice." Those who join with others in worshiping God do so as people whose lives are marked by attitudes and actions of true worshipers.

## WORSHIP AS LIVING SACRIFICE

Sometimes we hear that the New Testament makes greater demands of worship than did the Old; that in the Old Testament there was only concern for worship acts as such, but that in the New Testament the idea of worship was expanded to the whole of one's life. Romans 12:1–2 is often quoted to this effect. If one thinks that the only issues in Old Testament times were rites, rituals, and regulations of an external nature, then words in Romans 12 might seem to stand in strong contrast to the Old Testament.

But if one has drunk deeply at the well of biblical spirituality as presented in the Old Testament, then we can look to these wonderful words in Romans 12 with a sense of deep appreciation of the continuity of biblical teaching on worship in spirit and in truth.

After all, think again of the story of Saul. If God were merely concerned about animal sacrifices, why was Saul blamed for rushing the task? The story of Saul is one of the clearest Old Testament passages to make the very point Paul later made in Romans 12. As I wrote in chapter 8, Samuel made known to Saul a basic biblical reality: *Obedience to God is more important than worship of God.* To put it in another way, worship of God that does not proceed from a life of obedience to God is really not genuine worship at all.

Samuel asked the king, "Has the LORD as great delight in burnt offerings and sacrifices, as in obeying the voice of the LORD?" (1 Sam. 15:22).

Again, the term *delight* is key here. The Lord does not take pleasure in, smile over, or enjoy the sacrifices of a person who does not bring them for the right reasons, even if the sacrifices are otherwise acceptable. As with Cain, so it was with Saul: What one brings and the heart with which one brings it are both significant to God. Saul's acts of disobedience ruled out God's acceptance of his sacrifice. To make this even clearer, Samuel stated that Saul might as well have practiced pagan rites of idolatry and witchcraft, for his rebellious actions were as detestable to God as those awful acts would have been (15:23).

## WORSHIP AND THE HEART

Regularly we read in the Book of Psalms of wholehearted worship. Here are just a few verses that make the point strongly:

> I will bless the LORD at all times;
> His praise shall continually be in my mouth.
> My soul shall make its boast in the LORD;
> The humble shall hear of it and be glad.

Oh, magnify the LORD with me,
And let us exalt His name together. (Ps. 34:1–3)

Bless the LORD, O my soul;
And all that is within me, bless His holy name!
Bless the LORD, O my soul,
And forget not all His benefits. (103:1–2)

Oh, give thanks to the LORD!
Call upon His name;
Make known His deeds among the peoples!
Sing to Him, sing psalms to Him;
Talk of all His wondrous works.
Glory in His holy name;
Let the hearts of those rejoice who seek the LORD! (105:1–3)

Praise the LORD!
I will praise the LORD with my whole heart,
In the assembly of the upright and in the congregation. (111:1)

I love the LORD, because He has heard
My voice and my supplications.
Because He has inclined His ear to me,
Therefore I will call upon Him as long as I live. (116:1–2)

Search me, O God, and know my heart;
Try me, and know my anxieties;
And see if there is any wicked way in me,
And lead me in the way everlasting .(139:23–24)

These passages speak of one's whole heart, one's entire being, one's full course of life. These verses join the corporate worship of God with outreach in global evangelism for His worship among the nations. These passages speak with joy and depth of feeling because they come from forgiven sinners and from people who have experienced deliverance by

God's hand. True worship, biblical worship, worship in spirit and truth, *always* join corporate actions with private piety, the outward act with the inner heart. Bringing an animal was never an acceptable act in itself. Believers who lived in the period of animal sacrifice also presented themselves as living sacrifices to their living God. Paul's words in Romans 12:1–2 are not revolutionary. They are not new. They are simply a powerful expression of what God has always expected from His worshipers.

These same ideas are found in other biblical books. Surprising as it might be for many Christians who have not lingered in some of the riches of the Old Testament, such ideas are found in 1 and 2 Chronicles as well.

Chronicles emphasizes worship. Worship is not presented as something one does casually or apart from daily living. One commentator put it in this way: "In Chronicles it is not sufficient that Israel observe the letter of the law, i.e., bringing contributions to the temple and being present for its ceremonies. What is required is obedience with a perfect heart (1 Chron. 28:9; 29:9, 17), contributions willingly given (29:1–9, 14, 17), and participation with joy (29:9, 17, 22)."[6]

## WORSHIP AS AN ACT OF SUBMISSION

Writers on the subject of worship rightly speak of the various words for "worship" that are used in Hebrew, Aramaic, and Greek, the languages of the Bible. If "worship is a verb," as Webber states, then it is time to get the verb right!

Barry Liesch writes this about the principal Hebrew word for worship in Scripture.

Another emphasis can orient us away from the superficial and the cosmetic. It's an area where evangelicals are chronically weak. The symbolism of the body can powerfully point toward authentic worship. In fact, the primary word that defines worship in the Old Testament makes explicit reference to the body.

*Shachad*, translated "worship" in the NASB eighty-one times, means literally to "bow" politely or respectfully, to "prostrate oneself," to "make obeisance," or to "bend low." Worship has a profound physical dimension in Hebrew culture. It "emphasizes the way in which an Israelite fittingly thought of his approach to the holy presence of God. He bows himself down in lowly reverence and prostration." Prostration means to touch one's nose to the "ground" (see Gen. 42:6), a gesture representing *absolute submission*—hardly cosmetic worship! The Old Testament word for *worship* is not primarily propositional; it is visual, gestural, attitudinal, and often involves the relinquishing of rights.[8]

What Liesch says about the importance of this verb is correct, but *the verb he mentions is not correct*. Or to put it more fairly, we now know that this verb has long been misunderstood.

Older reference tools give the verb in question as *šāḥâ*, the verb certainly *intended* by Liesch when he writes *shāchad*.[9] Now, however, we know that the verb in question does not begin with the letter "š" (pronounced "sh") at all. The root for the verb is *ḥāwâ*.[10]

The form in which this verb occurs in Hebrew is unique to this verb. I find it utterly fascinating that this form has the idea of "making oneself do something."[11] The *something* here is significant—it has to do with the physical aspect of one's worship of God. This is one of the verbs describing body actions in God's holy worship. It would seem that in God's providence He allowed this one example of an old verbal form to continue to be used in the writing of His Word so that people would finally discover the nexus between the believer's heart and God's holy worship: True biblical worship does not simply happen. The true worship of God is purposeful, deliberate living. Worship is something we determine to do. When the prompting is by God's Spirit and is in accord with His truth, then worship takes place "in spirit and truth."

One of the great texts in which this verb is used of worship is Psalm 95:6–7. "Oh come, let us worship and bow down; let us kneel before the LORD our Maker. For He is our God, and we are the people of His pasture, and the sheep of His hand."[12]

Verse 6 actually includes three verbs that speak of bowing down to God. The first is the word under discussion (*ḥāwâ*), often translated *worship*. The second and third verbs, "bow down" and "kneel," simply carry on the idea of the first. They all present the same idea, but by using three different verbs the psalmist emphasized his point more forcefully. Although worship proceeds from the heart, it extends to the body.

In worship we are acknowledging the reality of God, the presence of

God, the wonder of God, the care of God, the judgment of God, the mercy of God—in short, we make God count in our lives when we worship Him.

Philip Yancey quotes Eugene Peterson to this effect: "Worship is the strategy by which we interrupt our preoccupation with ourselves and attend to the presence of God."[13]

How better to show this grand "interruption" than by kneeling before His glory? How better to demonstrate our sense of God's presence than to bow before His majesty? And how wonderful that the verb in question is one that means "to cause oneself to bow down" in humble adoration!

## AND WITH THE NATIONS

A second place in which this verb is used wonderfully in the psalms is in Psalm 96:7–9: "Give to the LORD, O families of the peoples, give to the LORD glory and strength. Give to the LORD the glory due His name; bring an offering and come into His courts. Oh, worship the LORD in the beauty of holiness! Tremble before Him, all the earth."

From the beginning God's intention was to bring the message of His grace to the peoples of the earth. Grace and world missions did not begin in the New Testament. Psalm 96 is a natural outflow of the covenant promises God made with Abram (later Abraham) in the beginning (Gen. 12:1–3). The last of the seven elements of God's promise to Abram was that all the families of the earth would be blessed in him (12:3).

When the Israelites were thinking (and singing) rightly, they realized that their own worship of God in the temple was indeed wonderful, but was far too limited. Psalm 96 is intensely global and missionary in nature. The nations needed to know God's glory. The peoples of the earth needed to turn from idols to the living God. Their gods were "nothings,"[14] but God had made the heavens.

Psalm 96 presents the idea of world missions in terms of God's worship. Missions exists because the true worship of God does not! John Piper has come to the same conclusion. He begins his book on world missions in this manner: "Missions is not the ultimate priority of the church. Worship is. Missions exists because worship doesn't. Worship is ultimate, not missions, because God is ultimate, not man. . . . [Missions] is a temporary necessity. But worship abides forever."[15]

One day every knee will bow before the risen Christ, but, sadly, not all will bow in joy. One day every tongue will confess that Jesus is Lord to the glory of the Father, but not all will do so in love. One day people will be made to acknowledge Him, and some will do so in terror.

But we have the opportunity now, in this life, to worship God. We can cause ourselves to bow down in reverent worship. Further, we may be a part of God's program worldwide to extend His worship in spirit and truth to people who do not know Him. For no one in heaven or on earth is worthy of our worship besides our holy God.

> Praise the LORD!
> Praise the LORD, O my soul!
> While I live I will praise the LORD;
> I will sing praises to my God
> While I have my being.
>
> —PSALM 146:1–2

# Eleven

# Are There Stages of Worship?

> Worship the Lord in the
> beauty of holiness!
> Bow down before Him,
> His glory proclaim;
> With gold of obedience
> and incense of lowliness,
> Kneel and adore Him:
> the Lord is His name!
>
> —JOHN S. B. MONSELL AND TOM FETTKE,
> "Adoration" © Lillenas Publishing Co.

I WOULD LIKE TO THINK that there is no one who loves the Book of Psalms more than I do. But at times I hear of ideas drawn from the psalms relating to Christian worship that I find troubling. One of these ideas, my son Craig tells me, is one of the most commonly stressed teachings in popular conferences for worship leaders. In fact, this is now regarded almost as an axiom of contemporary worship. But it is still a misconception. I speak of the notion that there are "stages" or "steps" in the worship of God that are prescribed in the psalms. Many worship leaders today believe that by using these stages one may lead the people from where they are to where we would like them to be.

Judson Cornwall represents this point of view in his book *Let Us Worship*.[1] He uses Psalm 100 for his teaching template, arguing that this psalm presents three or four steps to the worship of God. The words of verse 4 are pivotal for this approach: "Enter into His gates with thanksgiving, and into His courts with praise. Be thankful to Him, and bless His name."

In his presentation Cornwall treats the key worship words of verse 4 as progressive steps in an ever-more intimate experience of worship.

- *Thanksgiving.* This is the stage in which the people may enjoy singing songs of testimony. When they are at this stage, they are in the "priestly encampment," but not yet ready to move close to God.
- *Praise.* Here is where they move from thanking God for past favors to the more important element of praise for His present mercy. Now they are in the larger outer court; it may take a great deal of singing to get them to move further.
- *Be thankful.* Now the people have moved into the Holy Place; they were singing about themselves but now they sing of God inside the Holy Place.
- *Bless His name.* At last, all thought is of God; the people are now in the very presence of God and may savor the sense of His presence.[2]

Several things are troubling about this approach, not the least of which is the presumed pattern of the temple that underlies this teaching. We are not Jewish people living in the Old Testament world. We do not worship God in the temple in Jerusalem. But even if we were ancient Hebrews and worshiped in the temple, the plan of worship that Cornwall and many others describe does not fit the meaning of Psalm 100.

## PROBLEMS WITH THIS VIEW

The problem with this approach is that it is in the mind of the writer, not in the text of Scripture. What we have here is an all-too-familiar pattern of eisegesis (reading into the Bible something that is not there) rather than exegesis (reading out the true meaning of the text). Cornwall has made points with this verse that simply are not in the text.

Psalm 100:4 is a wonderful verse of Hebrew poetry. As in all Hebrew poetry, parallelism is its structural format.[3] Ordinarily one finds two lines of poetry in each verse in the English versions. To the uninitiated the two lines seem somewhat repetitious. But actually the second line enhances, shapes, and reinforces the first line, and this is done in a variety of ways. Some verses, however, like this one, have three lines, and they too reenforce each other.

Cornwall and others see a certain "progress" in this verse. He says the psalmist had in mind the tabernacle, so that the worshiper moved from the *gates*, into the *courts*, and then *into God's presence*.[4] But there are overwhelming problems with taking the view that this verse is the template for contemporary worship leaders to employ. I make much of this point only because it is stressed so strongly and commonly in contemporary worship seminars.

Here are the salient issues:

First, if the idea of this verse is that of the worship leader moving the people from "outside" to "inside" (by which is meant the presence of God), we need to remember that there was only one person who could actually enter the Most Holy Place. This person was the high priest, and even he could make this journey only on the holiest day of the religious year, the Day of Atonement (Lev. 16; 23:26–32; Num. 29:7–11). The priest did not lead anyone into the holiest place; it was a sacred precinct only he could enter. Thus this verse in Psalm 100 cannot refer to leading people by steps into God's presence. Those were steps they could not have made!

Second, a false division is made in this approach between the terms "gates" and "courts." To enter His gates is the same as entering His courts. These are not separate stages; to go through the gates is to come into the courts.[5] There is not one kind of song to sing in the gates and another in the courts. When one has passed through the "gates," he or she is in the "courts."

Third, in Psalm 100:4 the terms "thanksgiving," "praise," "be thankful," and "bless" are all synonyms! It is fallacious to attempt to argue that there is a divinely intended progression in these terms. In fact the first word, "thanksgiving," is the noun form of the verb "be thankful." Each of these terms describes precisely the same thing—the worship of God!

So it is an error (no matter how well intended) to attempt to use this Bible passage as a pattern of steps to follow in singing or in stages of worship.

The Hebrew words for the noun "thanksgiving" and the verb "be thankful" actually do not refer to giving thanks in the way we usually think of it. These translations are concessions to English language and usage. The basic meaning of the Hebrew root *yādâ* is *public acknowledgment*,[6] as Claus Westermann pointed out many years ago.[7]

## IT IS ALL ONE

Each of the three lines in Psalm 100:4 and each of the key terms describe the same thing, not different or progressive stages. "Worship" is not a higher plane than "praise." "Praise" is not a higher stage than "giving thanks." The point of the verse is to say the same idea in several ways—to make the point all the stronger. There is nothing more wonderful than the praise of God. There is nothing higher than public acknowledgment of His works and wonders. There is nothing more sublime than His worship. But these are all the same thing.

This verse is often employed by worship leaders as a script or a recipe for effective progression in musical worship. They assume that the "thanksgiving and praise songs" will be loud and lively, and that progress will then be made to "worship songs" which are slow and reflective. There is no question that moving from one style of songs to another in this manner can be an effective means of using variety in musical style and content in worship. But that idea should not be drawn from this passage.

## WHAT ABOUT BOLDNESS?

Perhaps the two arguments often used to sustain the "stages-of-worship" viewpoint are these: It works, and it fits with the New Testament boldness motif. Our response to the first idea is one of no contest. We may all agree that the skillful crafting of musical ideas and modes can be used powerfully by God's Spirit among His worshiping people. Moving from one style to another is part of skillful planning and can be blessed of God.

Second, we may also agree that there is a new dimension in the worship patterns available in the era of the church that was not enjoyed in the days of temple worship. This has to do with a new sense of boldness, based on the priestly ministry of the crucified, resurrected, and ascended Lord Jesus Christ. This is one of the great teachings of the Book of Hebrews. Jesus is a better Priest than Aaron; His covenant is a better covenant than God gave through Moses, and our access to the living God is more wonderful than ever imagined in Old Testament times. As the writer of Hebrews encouraged us, "Let us therefore come boldly to the throne of grace" (Heb. 4:16).

Frame comments on this major issue in biblical worship: "The great changes from the Old Testament to the New imply that there will be changes in worship. As the new Israel in Christ, the church worships in a way that is parallel to that of the Old Testament, in that every ordinance of the Old Testament is fulfilled in Christ. We too have a covenant, a priesthood, sacrifices, a tabernacle, circumcision, atonement, and feasts. But in our actual practice, there are great differences, for all of these institutions now exist in Christ and in Him alone. And our worship in Christ presupposes the once-for-all accomplishment of the redeemed to which the Old Testament Jews looked forward."[8]

Some things do change. But what does not change is the meaning of the biblical text. Psalm 100 is a spirited call for joyful worship of the living God. In various ways it calls for believers to praise, worship, and acknowledge Him. But this psalm does not present stages of worship. All it says is that the person and work of God call for true worship of His people. Indeed, a careful reading of the psalm shows that not only are God's people to praise Him, but so are the peoples of the earth. Our reason for engaging in evangelism and global missions is so that more and more people will come to know Christ and thus join with God's people in praise and worship.

So let's forget the stages and simply worship Him.

*Twelve*

## Those New Praise Songs

⊕FEW ISSUES HAVE PROVOKED MORE FERMENT in our churches in the last few years than the emergence of the "new choruses." Some churches have seized on the recent changes in musical style, often termed "praise and worship music," and have flourished. Other churches have resisted this trend with equal fervency. Many churches and not a few of their pastors are caught in the middle, often unsure about both biblical and musical issues. I write this chapter with an interest in the development of the praise-song movement; this means that some of the issues I describe here may seem antiquated to some readers. But I believe this broad scope is necessary to help other readers "get up to speed" on the most significant musical shift in recent worship experience—the development and spread of the "new praise songs."

### SEVEN-ELEVEN MUSIC?

Criticisms of the new praise songs are often harsh and judgmental. "Seven-Eleven music."[1] "Cheap sentimentalism." "Fluff." "Charismatic music." "Little ditties." "Boring." "Repetitive." "Worship Lite." "Dumbing down."

Yet while some continue to eschew "those choruses," an astonishing number of churches across the country and in many countries throughout the world have been transformed as they have embraced this new and vital form of music in their worship of God.

In the past few years of my own preaching ministry I have been in churches in virtually every part of America. In church after church the one inescapable reality is that the revolution has happened in church music. Whether I am in a Lutheran Brethren church in Paramus, New Jersey; a Presbyterian church in Salinas, California; a Baptist church in Powell, Wyoming; a Bible church in Florida; or a Mennonite church in Oregon, the story is the same. People everywhere are singing those "new praise songs."

The sweep of the new praise songs has extended across ethnic lines in this country as well. Eddie Lane, an African-American faculty member at Dallas Seminary, pastors Bibleway Bible Church in south Oak Cliff in Dallas. Praise songs now predominate in the worship services of this African-American church as commonly as they do in the mostly Caucasian churches of north Dallas.

Many people champion the use of the older, standard hymns in worship, and do so passionately. They argue that the church is "dumbing down" by using "choruses." Hymns are regarded as pure congregational music, solely suited for the worship of a holy God, and choruses are thought to be cheap, inane, and repetitious. Choruses, it is alleged, cheapen our view of God. They focus on the worshiper, not on the One to be worshiped.

Are these criticisms valid? And how did this musical revolution take place? If some of these criticisms were valid at one time, are they valid today?

## AN OLD BATTLE

Changes in musical style—and the battles that ensue—are not new. Gordon Borror has a presentation on the history of this debate that traces musical styles in the worship of God through church history. Time and again, new musical styles have competed with established, traditional patterns. Hardly any aspect of what today is thought to be traditional patterns in church music came to be regarded as traditional without a battle.

In fact I have a pet theory concerning musical style issues even during the period of the Old Testament. Imagine a young Hebrew mother looking with exasperation at her ten-year-old son, sometime in the eighth century B.C. She says, "I want you to stop singing those Canaanite songs." He replies, "But mother, the Levite youth choir leaders are teaching these songs in the temple!"

While a few choruses have been part of the singing of our churches for a long time, it is only in the last few years that the new praise songs (or "choruses") have become a major part of congregational singing in many churches. Indeed in some churches they are now the *only* part of congregational song. The distinction between hymns and choruses is often drawn far too sharply, and the word "choruses" is not a sufficient term to describe the new music.

While this new musical style began more than thirty years ago, it is only in the past several years that it has spread so broadly as to be regarded as nearly the universal model of contemporary Christian worship music. A recent cover feature in *Christianity Today* is titled, "Triumph of the Praise Songs: How Guitars Beat Out the Organ in the Worship Wars."[2]

## OLDER CHORUSES

For perspective, consider some of the choruses that we older Christians sang in the past. "I'm so happy, and here's the reason why, Jesus took my burdens all away." Here was a simple, cheerful song that celebrates the forgiveness of sins. It was particularly effective, it seems, for children. Another is the song "Do Lord." This happens to be one that I never liked, but I may have been alone in that. This song was sung in my youth countless times. I felt there was something wrong in a song that asked God not to forget me, since so many passages of Scripture assert that God has an active remembrance of those who are His people.

These songs, as I recall, were usually sung in Sunday evening services, youth meetings, or camp settings. I do not recall songs such as these being sung in morning worship services—at least not in the church where we worshiped. Also songs such as these seemed to be used more in children's settings than in adult contexts. "Jesus Loves Me" or "The B-I-B-L-E" might be sung by the whole congregation, but they were normally sung in children's classes.

One song that I found particularly annoying years ago was based on the great Hebrew word of praise "Hallelujah." The words of the chorus were "Hallelu, Hallelu, Hallelu, Hallelujah, Praise ye the Lord." Some song leaders seemed to think it was highly effective to have one section of the congregation stand on the "Hallelus" and the other side stand on the "Praise ye the Lords"—a sort of congregational calisthenics. But I never sensed that this song led to a deep sense of the presence of God, nor of deep desires to worship Him.

Another was "Deep and Wide," all done to hand motions. This was "fun" when I was little, but later on in life I felt it was tiring.

So I have a theory that when some older people think of the new praise songs ("choruses") negatively, they do so in part from memories of the choruses of their early church experience when the songs were childish and the "motions" annoying. Those songs were not really worship songs. Many older Christian adults, including their leaders, have an out-of-date understanding of choruses, and they have rejected the new praise songs without really realizing what has happened in the world of worship music in the last three decades.

## WRITING THE NEW SONG

A second element that leads to a critical spirit concerning the new praise songs concerns notable weaknesses in writing, especially in the early days of this newer musical form.[3] The early "praise-and-worship" movement was not done by design or plan. It seems to have been a more-or-less spontaneous eruption of a new musical style. People did not sit down at conference tables at Christian music publishers' meetings and attempt to mark out a new strategy to sell new songs for the church. This "just happened." But those who are a part of the new music believe there was more to it than that. They believe that this was a work of the Spirit of God in bringing a new dimension of personal and corporate response.

We may think for a bit about the "just-happened" approach. The first writers of the new praise songs were not trained theologians or Bible scholars. They were largely part of the Jesus Movement in the late 1960s and early 1970s, centered in but not limited to the beaches and beach towns of southern California.

The writers of the new music loved music, freedom, and simplicity. They were not part of the then-current establishment; in fact many were antiestablishment to the core. When they came to faith in Jesus, they made commitments that were total, without reserve. It was a wondrous period of time when many men and women turned from the cultural banes of the 1960s—drugs, free sex, and antiwar protest—and embraced the Lord Jesus Christ.

Their earliest songs were simple. They had melodies that are learned easily, lyrics that are simple to remember, and, yes, they were repetitive. But they were also fresh, naive, and alive! The songs may be thought of as love songs to Jesus. And they, and songs like them, have spread throughout the world. In fact one of the most exciting elements of church singing is the development of ethnic or indigenous musical forms among "new" people groups. Byron Spradlin of Artists in Christian Testimony alerted me to this happy movement. He worked for some time as a musical consultant with George Patterson, missionary to Honduras, to help achieve an indigenous worship music there.

## THE INSIDE STORY

Chuck Fromm, one of the founders of Maranatha! Music and its leader for many years, was invited to present a paper on the music he called "New Song" at a research conference held at Oxford University in 1983.[4] Much of Fromm's paper surveys the association of new musical forms and revivalism in the history of the church. He says the beginning of the new praise-song movement, can be pegged to 1968 with the beginnings of the Jesus Movement, more than thirty years ago.

"Calvary Chapel, in Costa Mesa, California, played a particularly important role in the development of New Song during those decades, and continuing even to the present day. Prior to the rising spiritual tide of 1968, the church had a congregation of 150 people, grown from its original flock of thirty when Chuck Smith, an affable, soft-spoken pastor arrived in late 1965. Today, the church numbers well over 20,000 in weekly attendance and has spun off over 250 daughter churches, some with congregations in excess of 5,000."[5]

This is amazing growth by any standard. Chuck Smith is Chuck Fromm's uncle. Pastor Smith encouraged Fromm to take a leadership role with the many new Christians who began coming to Calvary Chapel. A number had instruments and it was thought that they might find a ministry through their music. Thus was born Maranatha! Music; in the beginning it was the music ministry of Calvary Chapel. Fromm writes, "The early years of the Jesus Movement were also marked by the emergence of the modern Christian music group employing conventional pop instrumentation—electric guitars and keyboards, as well as a full array of percussion instruments. The band Love Song is a telling example of such a group. Love Song was initially a secular rock and roll band that earned its living by playing at bars and nightclubs. In the late sixties, group members lived together communally, experimenting with drugs and dabbling in Eastern mysticism."[6]

Tommy Coomes, the leader of Love Song, tells the touching story of his first visit to Calvary Chapel with some of his musician friends. "Towards the end of the service the people began to sing. I found that the worship and the singing were really touching. The melodies were pretty— a little old fashioned but they were very warm and it made me feel good to sing them. It was really quite beautiful. The feeling I got was of elation. My impression was that these people really knew who God was."[7]

Some readers will seize on the term "feeling" in this report and will react negatively. Faith, many insist, is a matter of knowledge, not feeling. Yet is not music primarily the vehicle of emotion? Was it not that the Jesus Movement began with people who felt things deeply and acted on those feelings for ill—or for good? And are not feelings a part of the Christian experience? By emphasizing feelings, Tommy Coomes was certainly not minimizing thought, doctrine, and belief. After all, to come to Christ from the drug culture of the 1960s took a bit more than happy feelings found in a couple of songs.

Coomes and some of his friends became Christians, and they began to write songs about their personal journeys. Fromm reports that "Welcome Back" was one of the first songs of the (now Christian) Love Song group, which Coomes and his friends played for Chuck Smith in the parking lot after a church service. Here are the words:

> Welcome back to the things you once believed in,
> Welcome back to what you knew was right all along;
> I'm so happy now to welcome you back,
> Welcome back to Jesus.[8]

These words present both the strength and weakness of many of the early choruses. The strength is in the genuineness one senses, what Fromm describes as "the intensely personal nature of early Jesus Music."[9] Here is the joy of the new believer, exulting in the sense of having come "home" to Jesus.

The weakness in the words of this song is their lack of specificity (and in unclear pronouns). The song seems only to make sense if it were sung not by Coomes and friends, but by someone in the congregation (the pastor?) welcoming new believers "home" in the church. It is this exasperating junction of wonderful feeling and unclear reference that troubles many people who look closely at the lyrics of some of the early choruses.

But these weaknesses are not found in new praise songs alone. They may also be found in some hymns. Consider the words of James Rowe's hymn, "Love Lifted Me":

> I was sinking deep in sin,
> Far from the peaceful shore,
> Very deeply stained within,
> Sinking to rise no more;
> But the Master of the sea
> Heard my despairing cry,
> From the waters lifted me,
> Now safe am I.[10]

This sort of testimonial hymn also has some limitations of exactitude when sung by a congregation. An old boozer who has come to Christ would sing it best. A young lad who gave his life to Christ at the age of three might be able to sing the chorus with gladness ("Love lifted me! / Love lifted me!"), but he would know little of the "sinking deep in sin" of the verse.

But singers of hymns would respond, "A hymn does not have to display the personal experience of all of its singers to be a fine song for congregational singing. Indeed, hymns help to create a type of story with which many can identify." That is correct. And the same ideas can be said for many of the new praise songs.

## STRENGTHS IN THE NEW PRAISE SONGS

It seems to me that the greatest strength of the early choruses in the New Song movement is in the way they allow people to speak directly to Jesus or to God the Father. Laurie Klein's song, "I Love You, Lord," is a case in point.

> I love You, Lord, and I lift my voice
> To worship You, O my soul rejoice.
> Take joy, my King, in what You hear;
> May it be a sweet, sweet sound in Your ear.[11]

This, to me, is a wonderful example of a good praise song. The melody is quite sweet and fits the text well. The song is easy to learn. Though not written for children, the story has the simplicity of a child's song. Most "choruses" can be learned in the first singing—a part of the genius of this form. The lyric is intensely personal but can be sung well in a congregation by everyone who is a believer. Laurie Klein did not use archaic pronouns ("I love Thee, Lord"). And she has captured a significant feature of biblical theology—that our music is designed to bring joy to the Father.

The story of the writing of this little chorus is as simple as its content. In 1974 Laurie and her student husband were living on four hundred dollars a month in a mobile home in central Oregon. One day at home, when she was feeling sad, she began to sing these words to God. And now this song is sung by fellowships of believers in settings around the world.[12]

## SING THEM OVER (AND OVER)

Well known is the fact that many of the new praise songs have problems. But some people attribute issues to the New Song choruses that are not necessarily a part of the music. When one says that the songs are repetitive, that may be a bit of misdirection. The songs are usually too short to be repetitive. What gives the impression of repetition is not the songs themselves, but the practice that some worship leaders have had (especially early on) of singing them over and over (and over and over!). The repetition is not necessarily in the songs themselves but in the way they have been used.

Repetition in the music of worship cannot be entirely bad, for some hymns also have considerable repetition in them—especially in the chorus section. Look, for example, at the chorus of the W. H. Clark hymn, "Blessed Be the Name."

> Blessed be the name,
> Blessed be the name,
> Blessed be the name of the Lord;
> Blessed be the name,
> Blessed be the name,
> Blessed be the name of the Lord.

The only difference in singing this chorus repeatedly is that the chorus in the hymn is interspersed with the stanzas—and this hymn is from the nineteenth century. The singer of the hymn may not be as aware of singing the same repeated phrases four times because of the intervening stanzas—but the repetition is there nonetheless. To repeat over and over that the name of the Lord should be blessed is a very salutary sentiment; it is essentially biblical. Witness the repetition of the words, "His mercy endures forever" in *every* verse of Psalm 136.

## OLD WINE IN NEW SKINS

One valid and common problem in some of the new praise songs concerns issues of language. Some of the early choruses quoted parts of verses from the King James Version, with its use of "Thee," "Thou," and "Thy." Pastor Chuck Smith was using the King James Version exclusively in the early 1970s when many of these songs were written. This practice provided a natural impetus for these young writers to adapt the same text in their new music. They could quote the King James Version without having to pay royalties for the use of a newer translation, such as was required if they used the New American Standard Bible.[13]

The problem became more complex when the writers added their own words, using "You" for God. This mishmash of archaic language and contemporary usage is a stylistic blunder that is deeply disturbing.

Think, for example, of one chorus that is deeply loved, but which has this anomalous feature:

> As the deer panteth for the water,
> So my soul longeth after Thee.
> You alone are my heart's desire,
> And I long to worship Thee.[14]

The melody is lovely and the sentiment is precious, but moving from "Thee" to "You" to "Thee" is troublesome. However, this can easily be fixed by changing the two occurrences of "Thee" to "You."[15]

The use of the archaic forms of the personal pronouns when referring to Deity is not confined to the writers of choruses. Many hymns do the same thing (and many who love these hymns do the same thing in their prayers). Many dear Christian people still feel that the use of these old forms of the pronoun for God is a way to show more reverence to Him than the use of more ordinary pronouns would. This mistake is not easily corrected. Emotions run deep here.

In 1611, when the King James Bible was translated, the English language was marked by the use of "thee," "thy," and "thou" for singular referents, and "you," "your," and "you" for plural. The languages of the Bible (Hebrew, Aramaic, and Greek) also have singular forms of the pronoun "you" along with plural forms. But never in the Bible is the mere presence of the singular pronoun a mark of respect or reverence to God. It is just the singular! If David were to write a psalm in which he spoke lovingly and adoringly of God, he would use the singular form of the second person pronoun to speak to God. But, if on the same day, he were to give instructions to his general Joab, speak to his son, or commune with one of his wives, he would use the same form of the pronoun. There was no special form of the pronoun to show reverence.

I lectured on the theme of worship in Japan in the summer of 1992 at two seminaries, the Conservative Baptist Theological Seminary of Sendai and the Tokyo Bible Seminary. In both places I was told that the issues are different in Japan. The highly complex language tradition in Japan has different forms of pronouns depending on the relative status of the one addressed. The form of the pronouns used to speak to one's friends would be inappropriate for addressing one's superiors. Special forms are used to address the emperor and thus to address God. All of this takes considerable finesse and experience.

But in English things are simpler. It was appropriate several hundred years ago to use "Thee," "Thou," and "Thy" when addressing God. This is not the language of choice today, for those forms are no longer current. They do not promote reverence so much as a sense of irrelevance. Most importantly, the use of these forms is not based on Scripture. It is merely a convention (largely of older Christians in our day).

Most modern translations have eschewed the use of the antique pronouns. A notable exception is the New American Standard Bible. In this translation, favored by many evangelical preachers, there is a statement in the introduction of the policy to use "you" in all cases, but to retain the old pronouns "Thou," "Thy," and "Thee" for Deity. This approach was finally abandoned in the revised edition of the New American Standard Bible, published in 1995.

For songwriters the issue is particularly hazardous. Many are unable to carry off the use of these old forms for more than a line or two, and they are also ill prepared to use the antique forms of the verbs that these pronouns demand. If one uses "Thou," then he or she may not use the modern form of the verb. Try this: "Have Thou a plan for me?" See what I mean? One would have to write, "Hast Thou a plan for me?" Further, one cannot follow "Hast Thou a plan for me?" with the words "You do because of Your love." There needs to be agreement: "Hast Thou a plan for me? / Thou dost because of Thy love." And it is precisely here where many of the early examples of the new praise songs can be faulted.

The solution is simple. Drop all antique forms. The whole point of the new praise songs is to provide a contemporary expression of love for God. Why ruin the contemporary sound by using language from another era? Why compound the problem by using old forms of language wrongly?

## I FAIN, YOU FAIN, SHE FAINS?

Moishe Rosen, founder of the Jews for Jesus ministry, gave his testimony in a chapel service at Western Seminary several years ago. He included a number of hilarious examples of misunderstanding that he as an adult Jewish man had to overcome on first coming into a traditional Baptist church. One concerned a hymn that the rest of us have loved and have sung for years, perhaps without a thought to its archaic language. He said he stumbled at the words of the hymn "Beneath the Cross of Jesus," with its line, "I fain would take my stand."

"What in the world does 'fain' mean?" he asked the seminary students— and their professors. No one spoke. I suspect most were like myself. We simply have sung this song so many times that we have never stopped to think how strange is that word "fain." No doubt most of us never encounter the word "fain" in our conversations or reading.

So I looked up the word in the dictionary and learned that this is an archaic adverb meaning "gladly." But I had never really seen the strangeness of this expression until it was pointed out to me by someone who came "from outside" and asked the question.

## MORE PESKY PRONOUNS

In some praise songs the lyrics have disagreement in subject and verb, dangling participles, and the like. But as I've suggested, the most noticeable and common errors concern the use of pronouns.

Here is a place where preachers and songwriters share the same malady. None of us would say something like, "God loves I." But some songs have the wording, "God loves you and I." None of us would say, "He called and invited I to lunch." But how often do we hear the hapless preacher say, "He called and invited my wife and I to lunch."

The issue is so simple; it is something that we were taught (or were supposed to have been taught) by third grade! Object pronouns are used as objects; subject pronouns are used as subjects. This is not rocket science, but the misuse of pronouns by careless preachers and songwriters sounds to many in the congregation like fingernails scratching an old blackboard.

True, God is more concerned about the state of one's heart than the state of his or her art. But a desire for a heart for God is not incompatible with an equal desire to do things for God in a manner that is in line with His truth and glory.

Reflect on the details that God gave for the construction of the tabernacle and its furnishings. Or think about the details from heaven concerning the temple. God, not just the devil, is in the details. Further, some of the charges of "dumbing down" would be less stabbing if our writing were "a bit more smart."

The most important thing in the life of a Christian songwriter is his or her commitment to the Lord Jesus, a pure desire to serve Him, and the sense that the song being written will be pleasing to God, even as the gift to write it comes from Him. Still, it is honoring to God to do one's best to use correct English grammar.

At times, of course, grammatical anomalies are purposeful in reflecting the dialect or idioms of a particular group. No one has to call the grammar policeman when a choir sings a traditional (African-American) spiritual or a Stephen Foster song. Folk music has its own charms—and its own rules. But those who preach from today's pulpits and who lead in song from today's platforms should themselves use standard English with pride. It is the King of glory whom we adore. Using standard English in praising Him is a matter of politeness. It is an act of civility. Surely this cannot be too hard to master—these are only pronouns!

## BUT WHAT DOES IT MEAN?

Other problems exist in some of the New Song music. Consider the words of the following song by Andy Park, titled "Holy Love."[16]

Many waters cannot quench Your love,
Rivers cannot overwhelm it.
Oceans of fear cannot conceal Your love for me. (repeat)
Your love for me.

Holy love, flow in me, fill me up like the deepest sea,
Like a crashing wave pouring over me,
Holy love flow in me.

Many sorrows cannot quench Your love,
Darkness cannot overwhelm it.
I will not fear, your love is here to comfort me. (repeat)
You comfort me.

When I find you I find healing,
When I find you I find peace,
And I know that there's no river so wide
No mountain so high,
No ocean so deep that you can't part the sea.

Let me make several observations about this song.

- The song is based in part on Song of Solomon 8:7, which speaks of the passion (fire) of sexual love that cannot be quenched by many waters; but the author of this song is ascribing that love to God, as though that were the meaning of that verse. One might make an application to God's love from this verse, but the Shulamite's words to her beloved have to do with sexual passion (contrasted with the fiery jealousy she spoke of in 8:6).

- The last section of the song makes no sense. One can say that there is no ocean so deep that God cannot part the sea, but what does a mountain so high have to do with His parting the sea?

- Even more pointedly, what is the meaning of "holy love" in the chorus? It would seem that this is a phrase for the Holy Spirit in a charismatic context, but where does it come from in the Song of Solomon?

- One of the problems of some of the contemporary praise songs is this ambiguity. The tender lyrics and intimate music may certainly speak of one's love for God. But at times the lyrics are so vague as to leave one uncertain about who is celebrating whom—or what!

## IS THE NEW MUSIC A "DUMBING DOWN"?

One of the strongest written challenges to the use of the new praise songs in Christian worship has come from Marva Dawn in her book, *Reaching Out without Dumbing Down*.[17] Hers is a stimulating but argumentative presentation that comes down rather hard on the "chorus" movement without achieving either a sense of balance or a historical perspective on changing musical styles in the worship of God. She is a passionate writer who strikes too hard on her theme. She maintains a constant critique of new worship patterns. Here is an example: "If, in their attempts to revitalize worship, churches merely speed it up and lower its substance, then they trivialize both God and the neighbor. They don't respect their neighbors enough to offer them the solid food of God's fullness. Moreover, too small a God leads to too small a concern for the neighbor in both evangelistic care and passion for justice."[18]

The most thorough critique of her book is John Frame's *Contemporary Worship Music: A Biblical Defense*.[19] He argues that Dawn is often petty in her criticisms of the new praise songs, using language that gives many "deprecatory metaphors and epithets" that, if carried far enough, would logically extend to the biblical texts that these songs have set to music! He writes, "But let's get down to specifics, if Dawn will not. What about Michael W. Smith's 'How Majestic Is Your Name?' Is it resigned sentimentality? Spiritual Wonder Bread? Does it lack roots, depth, sustenance? The first part comes literally from Psalm 8:1, and the rest is Psalms language. Do we want to suggest that God's Word is less than adequately deep, that it furnishes inadequate roots? Does this song have an 'easy listening' tune? I think not; in my judgment, the tune has a real bite to it, especially with the accompaniment used on the recorded version."[20]

Despite the problems that may be found in some songs (especially among some of the earlier ones), I believe the new praise-song movement is one of the most powerful, pervasive, and significant musical forces in contemporary church experience.

The new praise-song movement, when used as a part of the full music ministry of the church, brings a remarkable freshness and a level of joy and intimacy that, frankly, for many people, had ceased to be present in the singing of old hymns.[21]

This movement is *not* what it was just a few years ago! "Seven words repeated eleven times" may sound like a cute criticism, but it is neither accurate nor fair. We have come a long way in this movement to continue to speak of repetition.

Nor is it accurate or fair to describe the new praise-song movement as being consumed with the first-person pronoun. The use of "I" and "me" in many of these praise songs is not because the songs are about the singer; it is because they follow the biblical models fully established in the Book of Psalms to be personal in one's response to God.[22]

Some writers of praise songs include Graham Kendrick ("Shine, Jesus, Shine"), Billy Batstone ("Everlasting Father"; "Your Everlasting Love"), Kelly Willard ("Most Holy One"), Michael W. Smith ("Great Is the Lord"), Diane Ball ("In His Time"), Rick Founds ("You Are the One"; "Lord, I Lift Your Name on High"), Twila Paris ("He Is Exalted"; "We Will Glorify"), Martin Nystrom ("Shepherd of My Soul"; "As the Deer"), Rich Mullins ("Awesome God"), Debbie Owens ("Hear My Prayer"), Leonard E. Smith Jr. ("Our God Reigns"), Amy Grant ("Thy Word"), Karen Lafferty ("Seek Ye First"), Tom Coomes ("The Sweetest Name of All"), Buddy Owens ("Face to Face"), Jamie Owens-Collins ("The Battle Belongs to the Lord"), and Marty Goetz ("Oh Lord, Our Lord").

These and many others have enriched the English-singing churches of the world immeasurably. What riches these songs bring into our lives. What joy they give to millions of believers globally. And most significant of all, what glory these songs bring to God when sung in spirit and truth.

These new praise songs are not a dumbing down of worship; they are vehicles for the warming of the heart of the worshiper in bringing glory to God.

## SING TO HIS MAJESTY

The New Song of the contemporary praise-song movement is a powerful phenomenon. First, in summarizing this chapter several things need to be said. I believe that God is pleased with all manner of music that is played and sung to His glory by persons who truly worship Him in spirit and truth. There is no one "correct" musical style for worshiping God.

Second, I need to affirm that my taste in music is not God's taste; His is far broader than mine.

Third, I believe that the writing of these songs may continue to improve; writers may use more care in their use of biblical texts, in simple issues of grammar and in making good sense.

Fourth, as I will argue in the next chapter, the new praise-song movement may actually help "save" the singing of hymns for another generation.

Fifth, as these new praise songs continue to develop, the distinction between them and the idea of the "traditional hymn" may become less and less distinct.

I close this chapter by quoting the words from a new praise song that I thoroughly enjoy—and in doing so, I join a host of believers the world over.

> Majesty, worship His Majesty.
> Unto Jesus be all glory, honor, and praise.
> Majesty, Kingdom authority,
> Flows from His Throne, unto His own,
> His anthem raise.[23]

Jack W. Hayford, composer of this chorus, pastors the Church of the Way, Van Nuys, California. He tells the story of the writing of this song in his book, *Worship His Majesty*.[24] I find it fascinating that he wrote this powerful song after touring Scotland and England with his wife, Anna, viewing both magnificent countryside and then Blenheim Castle, associated with the life of Winston Churchill and memories of World War II. Filled with deep emotion, the congruence of scenery, royal castles, the silver anniversary of the coronation of the queen, thoughts of Churchill, and the like, Hayford was driven to think of the word *majesty* in relation to the living Christ. He reports, "As Anna and I drove along the narrow highway, the road undulating from one breathtaking view to another, I said to her, 'Take the notebook and write down some words, will you, babe?' I began to dictate the key, the musical notes, the time value of each and the lyrics."[25]

And what was the occasion for the Hayfords being in Scotland and England? They were taking part in the Oxford congress on the relationship of New Song to revivals in the history of the church, the same group Chuck Fromm addressed. The song "Majesty" remains one of the great accomplishments of the new praise-song movement.

> So exalt, lift up on high, the name of Jesus.
> Magnify, come glorify Christ Jesus, the King.
> Majesty, worship His majesty,
> Jesus, who died, now glorified,
> King of all kings.

*Thirteen*

## What about the Hymns?

THAT WINTER SATURDAY was going to be very cold as we drove in an old, unheated taxi to Donyetsk. Demitri and I wore wool hats; Julia wore her cotton scarf, wrapped tightly about her head and face. At the time I was teaching as a guest professor at Svet Evangelia ("Light of the Gospel") Seminary in December 1991. I was among a group of American professors who went for several weeks at a time to teach modular courses through interpreters. Russian-speaking professors were being recruited for this new school, among the first of the Christian schools to open in the Ukraine following the collapse of Russian communism.

An unexpected benefactor had provided the school with sufficient food for the winter months. The former communist commissar of food under the Soviet years still had considerable power in the city. He approached the dean one day the previous summer to attempt to find a common ground. He asked if the school would be resolute in its opposition to vices such as promiscuity, prostitution, and pornography. When he was assured that this was the case, the commissar said, "Then I will see you have food all winter. I am not a Christian, but I will take a stand with you against Western immorality."

We had food, but it was all pretty much the same. We had rice soup, accompanied by onions and barley. Then barley soup with onions and rice. Then onion soup, well, with barley and rice. One day a student rushed out of the kitchen saying, "Chicken!" Some bits of chicken were in the rice that night.

Julia had seen something in my eyes the night before, I am afraid. She looked across the table and said, "Isn't this wonderful?" I smiled, but I did not answer. She went on: "This is the first time in our lives that Demitri and I have not had to worry about food in the winter. Look at this beautiful soup; smell the wonderful onions. We have more than we can eat!"

"But," she said, "we do need some milk. Our little boy has not had milk for a couple of weeks. Would you like to go to the city with us tomorrow?"

So on Saturday we were went to a dairy concession in a large building where varying vendors leased space and the whole affair was called a "supermarket." We moved slowly in the line for over two hours. We were getting near the counter when the people ahead of us all rushed away at once. I did not understand at first. Then Demitri whispered, "The milk must be gone."

Julia went up to the now vacant counter and asked the vender, as Demitri interpreted for me, "Are you sure there is no more milk?" His response was, "None that I can sell." "Then you do have some?" she asked.

He gave her a liter bottle of milk that had lost its paper cap. She smelled it and then passed it to Demitri and me for a whiff. "It doesn't smell too bad, does it?" She bought it and we rushed to the bus and made our way back to the campus.

Julia gave their little boy one small cup after another; finally he said it was enough. Then she made coffee for the three of us, poured a generous amount of milk in each cup, then poured the remainder of the milk in a small pan and put it on the radiator.

With her cup in her hand and leaning back in her chair, Julia's eyes beamed. "Isn't God good?" she said.

I will never forget this.

"Isn't God good?" she repeated. "Not only did our little boy have milk today, but we even have milk for coffee and a little for yogurt in the morning."

Some weeks later when I was back at our home in Oregon, my wife told me late one night that we were out of milk and needed some for breakfast. About midnight I went to our supermarket, about a mile from our home. As I made my way to the dairy case, I realized that I was probably the only customer in the store at the time.

There was no line. The store is open twenty hours a day. And there was a dairy case stocked and "faced" with nearly every kind of milk one can imagine. There was nonfat, 1 percent, 2 percent, full fat. There was chocolate milk, buttermilk, flavored milks. There were creams of varying fat content (or "none"). In that dairy case there were more varieties and quantities of milk and milk products than Julia had probably ever seen in her lifetime.

I stood there and wept. Never had "going to the store" affected me so deeply.

## OUR "STORE" OF MUSIC

When I hear people ask, "What about the hymns?" I sometimes find myself remembering that midnight "milk run." I had been looking at stores of milk of such great variety and abundance as would be nearly unbelievable to many people in the world. In the Western church tradition and in the English language in particular, we have treasures in music for the worship of God nearly beyond belief. We are the heirs of it all. It all belongs to us; or better, it all belongs to God.

Some people are happy with a spot of milk in a coffee cup, and give God gratitude. Rightly so! In their situation that bit of milk is all they have. But we in North America not only live in a land of plenty; we are also heirs of the ages when it comes to music by which to worship the Lord. Among our greatest treasure is the store that lies in the contemporary modern hymnal.

## CONTEMPORARY MODERN HYMNAL

The words *contemporary* and *modern* are not used often enough with the term hymnal. Far too many people think of the hymnal as "old-fashioned." Their ideas about the hymnal may come from some years ago, and they may think that nothing has changed in the publishing of hymnals.[1] They are as misinformed as those who criticize the new praise songs on the basis of the state of the art of twenty years ago.

Hymnals today are better than ever. The great sadness is that some people who lead in worship (especially younger persons) have not developed an appreciation for the hymnal, and others (some older persons) are unaware of the values of the more modern editions. An advertising campaign for an American automobile manufacturer a few years ago reminds me of the task of the hymnal enthusiast. "This is not your father's Oldsmobile," suggested the television pitchman. Well, in a similar way, "This is not your grandmother's hymnal."

Younger readers, give attention here. The modern, contemporary hymnal is a treasure too valuable to ignore and too wonderful to be without in your worship of God; you impoverish yourself and your people when you do not include a loving use of the hymnal in your leading in worship.

Here is an amazing thing. The modern hymnal and the contemporary praise book now hold hands! At the time of this writing, the newest hymnal and the newest edition of the standard praise book in my possession are both filled with surprises.

The hymnal I view as I type these words is titled *The Celebration Hymnal*, with Tom Fettke as senior editor.[2] When I open this beautiful book I am not surprised at the first four hymns that have pride of place. They are as follows:

- "Praise, My Soul, the King of Heaven." The words were written by Henry Francis Lyte (1793–1847), perhaps better known for his hymn "Abide with Me." The music by Mark Andrews (1875–1939) was written in 1930. This lovely song is to be sung in unison, but the melody is more complex than that of many of the more recent praise songs. But like modern praise songs this hymn speaks from the heart of the believer ("my soul") to the praise of God ("the King of heaven"). Along the way there is a full basket of "Alleluias."
- "Holy God, We Praise Thy Name." Here is a treasure from the German church. The words were written by Ignaz Franz (1719–1790), and the English translation was made by Clarence A. Walworth (1820–1900). In eighteenth-century, grand-hymnal style (in which the use of "Thy" is suitable), this very singable hymn (in four-part

harmony) affirms that the singing of God's people here on earth joins with angelic songs in highest heaven in praise of the triune God. The third verse is a singing of a creed; a powerful way to fix solid Christian doctrine in the mind:

> Holy Father, Holy Son, Holy Spirit:
> Three we name Thee
> While in essence only one;
> Undivided God we claim Thee,
> And adoring, bend the knee
> While we sing our praise to Thee.

- "Holy, Holy, Holy! Lord God Almighty." How could there be a Christian hymnal in English lacking this grand musical accomplishment! The powerful, biblical words are by Reginald Heber (1783–1826); the music is by John B. Dykes (1823–1876). In this hymnal there is a powerful new musical arrangement with a choral ending for the last stanza written by Camp Kirkland.
- "Praise the Savior." This hymn by Thomas Kelly (1769–1855) is set to a sprightly three-four time traditional German melody. The words of the fourth stanza can be tongue twisters without practice, but how wonderful they are:

> Then we shall be where we would be,
> Then we shall be what we should be;
> Things that are not now, nor could be,
> Soon shall be our own.

Following these four hymns is the wonderful new praise song "I Sing Praises." Terry MacAlmon is the writer of the words and music, dated 1989. This chorus is given a one-and-one-half-page spread, with an optional musical setting for the last stanza.

How wonderful that this "little chorus" has been perceived as a kind of modern hymn! This contemporary hymnal includes new praise songs along with the rich hymns from German, English, and American traditions.

Beside my new hymnal is the newest printing of the Maranatha! Music *Praise* book. In the last three decades Maranatha!'s *Praise* books have been joining hymnals in the racks of an ever-growing number of churches across the country. I treasured the third edition (the "Red" edition), and the reason was that quotations from my book, *And I Will Praise Him*, adorned both the back cover and the inside front cover. But now we have the "Green" (fourth) edition, and it is larger than ever.[3] On page 1 we do not find a song by Paris, Coomes, Batstone, or Fround. The first entry is by a man named Martin Luther. It is "A Mighty Fortress Is Our God." Hymnists, are you observing this? The principal collection of the new praise songs now includes a number of the greatest hymns of the church. And the new hymnal is replete with the new praise songs.

## BLENDED SERVICES

The "holding of hands" of hymns and the new praise songs ("choruses") in these two publications is an example of a desire on the part of many worship leaders today to bring together these two streams of musical expression. When one stops to think about this a bit, it becomes astonishing. After all, for much of the first decade of the rise of the modern chorus, disdain was expressed in some circles toward "choruses," while people in other circles were completely immersed in them. But gradually the new praise songs became so much a part of the lives of Christian people *in* the churches that the music became a part of the music *of* the churches.

I recall a time many years ago when, as a guest speaker in my home church in Oregon, I had decided to end my sermon by leading the congregation in the singing of a "chorus." Laurie Klein's, "I Love You, Lord," would be, I thought, a vehicle of significant response to the content of my message, which had focused on a psalm of praise. Before the service I had talked this over with the pastor and a few of the elders. None of us knew how this would be received; my own expectation was that few in the congregation would be able to join in on the singing at first. To my knowledge, we had never sung one of the new choruses before in a Sunday morning service. But I was amazed at what happened. It seemed as though everyone knew the song! And those who did not know it learned it quickly.

As I think about this moment in the life of our congregation I am still stunned. The people were way ahead of us. I thought I was doing something rather radical; but they were just waiting to join in on the song. Now, of course, the singing of new praise songs is a fixture in our church's worship, as it is in many other churches.

The desire to use both hymns and the new praise songs sometimes leads to attempts to have what is called "blended" services. In a great number of the churches in which I have ministered across the country I see attempts to bring a blending of these two broad categories of music together.

Ron Man, a strong proponent of blended worship, describes and defends it very well. "Blended worship (also termed 'convergence worship') may be generally defined as a worship service which employs a combination of traditional and contemporary elements (especially music). . . . Some have caricatured blended worship as a service in which one entire portion is made up of contemporary music, and another portion is entirely traditional music. This is not a true blending and would seem to be a formula sure to leave everyone unhappy!"[4]

I have been in a number of churches in which the *pseudo*-blending to which Ron alludes has been done. Often there will be a hymn, a prayer, and then another hymn or two. Then a change of personnel takes place. The worship band members take up their instruments, the worship team members make their way to their mikes, and the worship leader says, "Now let's worship God."

Every time I observe this, I want to shout out, "Haven't we been worshiping God already in singing the hymns?" If the congregational prayer was not worship, what was it? The false idea seems to be that now that we have gotten the hymns out of the way we can really get down to business with God.

Compartmentalizing standard hymns from the singing of the new praise music is not only wrong-headed in terms of the leading of congregational worship; it is a practice that could be the spell of death to hymns, for the singing of hymns is viewed as outside the realm of "true worship."

On the other hand, when a worship leader (along with instrumentalists and vocalists) leads the congregation in a cluster of songs that includes both hymns and praise songs, there can be true blending. This is not something that can be done on the spur of the moment. The songs must be chosen with care, with attention being given to the progress of word ideas as well as compatible musical ideas; modulations need to be planned and practiced, and the leader needs to be able to convey through his hands or voice what the congregation is to do and how they are to do it. The results can be very satisfying indeed.

Ron Man gives this rationale for blended worship: "The main motivation behind blended worship is a conscious decision to bring the entire body of Christ, in all of its diversity, together in corporate worship. Rather than providing separate services to appeal to the tastes of different generations or other subgroupings of the congregation, all are encouraged to make concessions relative to their own personal preferences with the goal of a shared worship experience into which all can enter."[5]

He then gives what I feel to be a splendid biblical validation for this approach. "Quite simply put, the strongest argument for pursuing worship which is blended is the fact that the body of Christ is blended (Gal. 3:28); and it is in corporate worship that the truth of the body's unity (in diversity) can be most effectively lived out (Eph. 4:4–6; 1 Cor. 12:20)."[6]

The ideal of the blended service not only meets the needs of many kinds of people, but it models some of the deeply cherished values of those worshipers. Here is where we can have our spiritual cake and eat it too.

At the early stages of my work on this book I sent my intern Phillipe Willems on a trek throughout the Dallas/Fort Worth area to interview worship leaders on strategies for achieving "blended worship." The results were, in a word, disappointing. We received a lot of fine feedback, and I appreciate many of the reports of these conversations. But the idea of blending, as we will describe later in this book, is not the single solution to the worship wars I had hoped it would be. It is one solution, a solution many would choose, and a solution I prefer. So let's get back to the hymnal.

## VALUES IN THE HYMNALS

These are several obvious values of the modern, contemporary hymnal.
  • Hymnals are a treasury of musical styles. Song leaders, like preachers, tend to have their favorite songs. These well-worn paths can

become a rut—for both pastor and worship leader. The richness of the evangelical tradition in the hymnal is not something to be lost; the wise worship leader looks at new hymns—and at hymns new to him or her, just as the wise pastor preaches from a wider selection of passages than his first comfort zone.

• Hymnals provide the music as well as the words. The sometimes-simple melodies of the new praise songs can be "learned" rather easily in a single hearing; this is a part of the genius of the praise-song movement. But "real" singers miss the richness of four-part harmonies that mark many of the great hymn tunes. It's a fact: Singing in parts, at least from time to time, is a richer experience than singing in unison all the time.

• Hymnals preserve songs from earlier periods for use in our day. We should not think of the hymnal as just an archive; to sing songs from earlier centuries helps believers realize that they are truly part of the church universal. To sing some songs that are hundreds of years old is a valuable part of the special nature, of the true experience, of the Christian faith. We join a train of faith that ultimately is beyond our comprehension.

• Hymnals contain songs of great teaching value. The principal purpose in the singing of a hymn is to join with others in worshiping God. But much can be learned about our faith when we use the hymnal for its riches and not just to find the page for "Amazing Grace." Generally speaking, the lyric in the traditional hymn has a depth and solid grasp of theological content that can't easily be matched in the more simple wording and design of modern praise songs.

• Hymnals present songs of our own day as well. There is much more to contemporary Christian worship music than praise songs. Composers are still writing hymns and sacred songs that are wonderfully contemporary but that will not likely be displayed on the overhead screen. "Seasoned" church musicians love to demonstrate the power and vitality of late twentieth-century hymnody, whereas some younger musicians seem unaware of its existence.

• Hymnals now contain songs from other ethnic communities, as the new ethnic musical styles of God's global church become more known. There is more to African worship music than "Kum Ba Ya." Modern hymnals are beginning to draw on the rich musical traditions of God's global church. For too long, hymnody and church music has all been exported; it is time we in the West become importers as well. I propose that interest in world missions and in global Christian issues could be advanced significantly with the singing of more songs from other ethnic groups of God's people.

- Hymnals contain songs for small children.
- Hymnals arrange songs in topical clusters.
- Hymnals provide valuable information about music.
- Hymnals have indexes of Scripture references, theological ideas, topics, as well as musical categories.
- Hymnals have Scripture readings, responses, and suggestions for special services.
- Hymnals provide a satisfying tactile experience in our worship ritual. There is something very satisfying about holding a beautiful book while singing to the Lord. It is akin to holding a Bible when reading Scripture. We can sing words from an overhead projection, and we can read biblical passages in words copied in the bulletin. Yet something is lost when we don't hold the hymnal and the Bible.
- Hymnals have accompanying materials for church musicians, including director's editions, orchestral scores, historical and musical helps.
- As noted earlier, modern-day hymnals also include a good selection of the new praise songs.

To be a church musician without a love for the hymnal is akin to being a church preacher without a love for the Bible.

## LIMITATIONS IN THE HYMNAL

Yet even with all these values, not all is well with hymnals nor with their continued use in congregations today. Here are six problems to be aware of.

First, while new hymnals are published from time to time, churches are slow in replacing their old ones. The cost factor is significant. Thus many churches use tattered, older hymnals that remind younger people of things in their grandparents' homes. By saving money on the purchase of newer hymnals, however, some churches will pay a significant price—the loss of interest in the hymns as a whole.

Second, singing "with one's nose in the book" is not nearly as much a statement of worship as singing with words projected, and then with eyes closed. Many people tend to sing hymns in a perfunctory manner. However, the problem here is not in the hymnal, but in the patterns people have developed over time as they have sung from hymnals. When a traditional church service is pictured in film or on television, there is a *Little House on the Prairie* approach to the portrayal of hymn singing, even if the context is modern. People do sing, but not very well. They look at the hymnal, but they may not be giving much thought to the words. There is a tendency to be less than fully engaged.

Third, how does one clap hands while holding a hymnal? Is it not interesting that the switch from holding a book to seeing words projected on a screen (in the new praise-song mode) has led to a loosening up of people to use body motions in worship? It is as though the holding of a hymnal was holding them back from certain forms of expression.

Fourth, some people tend to minimize the content of the hymnal as "just songs." For some people who defend the use of hymnals, this idea may seem preposterous, but I have seen it again and again. When the theological gaffes in a line or two of a "great hymn" are pointed out, there is a tendency to excuse things in the hymn that would never be excused in the chorus. One well-known theologian, when challenged on a poor line of a well-known hymn, said: "Well, it is just a song." But I heard this same theologian criticizing a "chorus" for its incomplete statement of a biblical issue.

Fifth, some worshipers tend to sing without appreciation of what they are singing. The poetic imagery found in many hymns is often based on elements of life that have long passed from current experience. Words about sundials are missed by people wearing digital watches; imagery from sailing ships hardly moves those with high frequent-flyer miles.

Sixth, the meaning of some words in older hymns is not always known. I heard that one person thought Martin Luther's words "Lord Sabaoth" in "A Mighty Fortress Is Our God" were the German way of speaking of God as "Lord of the Sabbath."[7]

## OUT OF THE PAST

My favorite bed-and-breakfast inn in east Texas is the Munzesheimer Manor in Mineola, Texas. The home is now over one hundred years old, built in the Princess Anne style by a German immigrant, Gustav Munzesheimer. Bob and Sherry Murray, the innkeepers, have become friends, as we have stayed in rooms or cottages at their wonderful place several times. They have purchased many antique items from the period in which the home was built for decorating their charming rooms. Recently when we were guests there, I saw a 1908 copy of the Sears & Roebuck Catalog![8]

I was hooked. Woolen socks (in lots of twelve) were offered for four cents apiece! A six-hole Steel Range sold for $15.95. Hair tonics, trusses, ladies' hosiery, fans, and lace—each is pictured, described, and priced. These are things from another world. Yet they were being sold less than a century ago. And some of the hymns we sing today were already old when this catalog was new!

Older Christians who have sung hymns in church all their lives do not realize what a cultural distance many of these hymns have from new singers who are new to the faith. In some respects some of the hymns are as quaint and out of date as several items in the old catalog. We do not help them by simply saying, "Deal with it." Chapter 18 includes a number of suggestions on how to help the old hymns regain new vigor.

## HYMNS AND PRAISE SONGS

Some broad contrasts between hymns and new praise songs may be noted. In these contrasts we see some of the strengths of each of these forms of musical expression.

- Hymns may be more doctrinal, with more spiritual "meat." Praise songs may be more personal, with more feeling.
- Hymns may be more instructional, speaking to the people. Praise songs may be more Godward, giving people a sense of speaking more directly to Him.
- Hymns may be more classical in style, rhythmic, but contained. Praise songs may be more fluid, providing more freedom for musical expression.

- Hymnals were thought of in the past as companions to the Bible in instructing people in their faith. Praise songs are often thought of today as companions to the Bible as well, but with this difference: The hymns are compressions of biblical knowledge; the praise songs are vehicles of worship.

## NOT JUST HYMNS ARE AT STAKE

The problem with wars is that they are so hard to evaluate when people are engaged in them. And a war is going on, even though we may hate that idea. The evangelical church is caught up, against its will, in worship wars; the battle is over music. Is this not truly awful?

This war is usually defined in terms of two approaches to music in worship, one army fighting for the new praise songs and the other army dying for the hymns. As the cover story has it in a recent issue of *Christianity Today*, "Triumph of the Praise Songs: How Guitars Beat out the Organ in the Worship Wars."[9]

But the issues are far broader than some think. The new praise songs have taken away the place once given to hymns, and worship teams have replaced choirs. Some churches with a rich heritage of choir, ensemble, and solo sacred music have reconfigured their buildings as well as their music. There is no longer a place for the choir; the organ may have been pushed aside as well.

We are in danger not only of losing hymns, but also of losing a vast literature of sacred music, old and new, that is geared to a higher level of musicianship than is possible from either worship teams or the congregation.

But this is not a new issue, and the praise songs are not the culprits. The issues are broader (and some things are simply not clear to us). I have a theory about musical style and levels of musicianship: *Good attracts good, and bad drives good away.* By this I mean that in a metropolitan area were people have many choices about where they will go to church, people seem to know which congregations excel in sacred music, choirs, ensembles, great masterworks, orchestras, organ recitals, and the like. They also know which churches have praise bands and worship teams. These are not secrets.

Those who love sacred music on a "higher" musical level will be attracted to those few churches that excel in the performance of such music. In Dallas, Texas, for example, I learned early that the music ministry at Park Cities Presbyterian Church is of an entirely different nature from that of many other evangelical churches. The minister of music and the arts at that church is Robert Rucker, an unusually gifted church musician with a love for the rich treasures of sacred music literature. Here is where one might go to be spellbound by Mendelssohn and Bach, as well as by works of modern composers such at John Rutter. Here is a church with a full orchestra and a finely rehearsed choir. And here is a church where one expects the congregation to sing classic hymns in the grand manner.

In Portland, Oregon, Gordon Borror led the citywide Masterworks Choir each spring in performances of long-form sacred art. I had the privilege of singing in Gordon's choir in two of these works, and I will never forget the experience (and blessing). Singing Brahms and Handel under Gordon's leadership will long remain cherished memories. I have often bragged, "Everyone should see Paris, sing Handel, and complete a marathon!" But these experiences, as wonderful as they are, are not realized by many people.

Now I have another theory: Those Christians who have developed a sophisticated musical taste for "classical" sacred repertoire will worship gladly in performances of these great works, particularly when they are performed with excellence. But such Christians are few—and may become fewer![10]

We are not simply in danger of losing the standard hymns. The vast treasures of sacred music in the Western tradition, ranging from organ music to choir anthems, from chorales to cantatas—all are "endangered species" in the current climate.

Yet as in the case of the peregrine falcon, endangered species can be brought back from the edge of extinction if people care sufficiently to see that they do not die out. How does symphony music survive in a rock-and-roll world? How does opera continue to thrive in a Hip Hop age? Great music survives—and thrives—when those who love it continue to support it.

Very few churches will be able to sustain performances of great sacred works over the long haul. But when the friends of sacred music from many churches come to the occasional performances held in that church that can manage to present the great works with full orchestra and choir, then that music will live on.

Music lives as music is played and sung. If the singing of the great chorales were to cease, if the playing of the great cantatas were to end, then that music is dead.

## HYMNS, THE ORGAN, AND THE INSTRUMENTS OF GOD

I suspect that when many people think lovingly of hymns, they also think of the organ. And when they think of the organ, the bigger the better. Years ago Gordon Borror and Richard Unfried were responsible for installing the magnificent pipe organ in the building of the Crystal Cathedral in Southern California. It is said that on a clear day, one can hear that organ all the way to Disneyland. Gordon also installed the pipe organ in the church where he is now pastor, First Baptist Church, Milwaukie, Oregon.

Some of the churches in which I preach have wonderful organs. As I look at the organ pipes—even when they are silent—I think of them as sentinels of praise to God on high.

For many years I have had the privilege of speaking in Bible conferences at Mount Hermon Conference Center near Santa Cruz, California. One of the rare treats there is to attend an organ concert by resident artist David Talbott. He has a phenomenal command of hymnic literature. Both on the piano and on the organ, he is able to weave together a dozen or more hymns into a seamless tapestry, even when the hymn numbers have been called out at random from the audience just before he plays.

I think of other organ concerts where my wife and I have been blessed to listen to this majestic instrument, glorious in the right hands. We visited the Air Force Academy in Colorado Springs a few years ago and were blessed greatly by a concert of sacred music on the organ. We have heard organ concerts in Milwaukee, Manhattan, Washington, D.C., Dallas, and elsewhere. We have been in the St. Thomas Church in Leipzig, Germany, where Johann Bach himself played the organ for many years back in the early 1700s, and we heard an organ concert there. We have also heard an organ concert at Westminster Chapel in London.

So if I say that I love the organ and its sacred literature, I trust you will believe me.

But the organ is on the endangered species list among musical instruments used in worship today. Nancy Hoffman, a long-time church organist in Salinas, California, has noted that fewer and fewer churches are using the organ in their worship services. Older church buildings often have organs that are in need of repair—and that are in need of skilled players. Many newer congregations simply can't afford a pipe organ. Some older congregations have an old Hammond, an instrument fitted for songs of the 1950s but inadequate for the music of today. Newer electronic organs are actually quite wonderful when played with skill; but there are fewer and fewer skilled musicians to play them.

## GUITARS AND DRUMS

Many churches now include guitars, drums, basses, and wind and brass instruments. This raises a question: Is one of these "the devil's instrument"? Before you answer too quickly, let me let you in on a little secret. In ancient Israel, none of the instruments used in worshiping was of Hebrew invention. None. Is that not amazing?

The instruments used in worship in the temple had first been played in pagan shrines in the worship of other gods.[11] Israel was the great adapter when it came to cultural issues. Just as God gave the Israelites cities they had not built and homes they had not constructed, so God gave them the use of musical forms and instruments they did not invent.

David wrote Psalm 8 in praise to God and with a special recognition of God's role in creating the human race. This psalm, which speaks so grandly of the excellence of the name Yahweh in all the earth, was to be performed with accompaniment from an instrument made in Gath,[12] the principal city of the Philistines during David's day (see the superscription to Psalm 8). This is amazing. Goliath, whom David had defeated, was a mercenary soldier from Gath. David had also fled to Gath at a perilous period in his life as he was in flight from Saul, when that king was

160

hounded by the demons of his dementia (1 Sam. 27:1–12). And while at Gath, presumably, David discovered an instrument that years later would be used by the Israelites in worshiping God in Jerusalem.

## SO WHERE DO WE GO FROM HERE?

Chapel services at Dallas Seminary have long been known by students and faculty members alike as great opportunities for singing classic hymns. When Chaplain Bill Bryan leads the singing, often playing his trumpet along with the singing of the student body, hymns are seen to be alive and well. None on the platform sings as strongly, I suspect, as our president. Dr. Swindoll not only sings the hymns; he knows many stanzas of a great many hymns from memory and encourages others to do the same.

Nothing stirs the faculty so much, it would seem, as the wonderful hymn "All Hail the Power of Jesus' Name,"[13] which we call the "seminary hymn." The repetition of the words "crown Him" in the chorus, with the counterpoint of the bass-line punctuation, is unforgettable. Well, it is unforgettable to the professors on the platform. As I look out over the new students gathered at the beginning of a school year, I see some of them singing as lustily as their professors, but others look out of sorts. This is not a "with-it" tune for them. Some will learn to like it, even to cherish it. But for others, it is a different musical and worship language.

Admittedly the singing of hymns is an acquired taste. We who have learned to love singing hymns have done so because we have been singing them for a long time and have done so in contexts that were positive in nature. In a chapel message a few years ago I focused on the great hymn "Holy, Holy, Holy." Along the way I said something I had not planned to say: "After all," I said, "I have been singing this hymn for fifty years." Gasp! What did that do to win friends of this hymn among people who measure the life span of music by such things as clothing fads?

At the same time we on the platform cannot expect new students to love singing older hymns any more than we can expect new students to leap in joy at the thought of learning the principal parts of the Greek verb. We have hopes for both, but we do not always have success.

So here are some ideas for consideration:

- As much as older Christians love hymns, they should not expect all younger believers to share their joy in these older musical forms.
- German-English-American hymns are a historical development of musical style in the Western tradition; these hymns are not the whole of the musical experience of the church.
- We live in a world of change in musical styles and notions. Hymns can be preserved in a variety of ways.
- Music in the church should be more global in nature as we recognize more and more the reality of the body of Christ worldwide.
- Musical styles are multiple; no one style is "the right style" for worshiping our Lord.
- The best of all traditions, old and modern, may be used by the people of God—and these varied types of music will enrich the taste and experiences of the people who sing, play, and hear them.

In the same issue of *Christianity Today* that heralded the victory of guitars over organs and praise songs over hymns, Mark Noll celebrates the enduring values of evangelical hymns.[14] There is no question in my mind whatever that he is correct in his assessment.

Remember the picture of Julia, leaning back with her cup of milk? It was all she had, but she was delighted and praised God.

We have a lot more. We can enjoy a cup of milk, or we can open the whole dairy case.

*Part 4*

TRANSITIONAL ISSUES

# Interlude

⟨⟨⟨⟩⟩⟩

## A Change of Pace

I WOULD LIKE TO BELIEVE that there is a best approach for a congregation to take in its desire to enhance its worship of God. The superior approach would be for the whole church to move as a unit in their experience of ever-broader circles of style and form. I would love to see a church that is able to have a formal service of dedication of missionaries on one Sunday and to have a country-and-western theme on the next. I would love to see a church that gladly performs the masterworks of sacred repertoire and is also free to feature a full praise band.

Not long ago in a service in which I participated at Grace Community Church in Auburn, Washington, the program began with a stage band. On another Sunday there might be a church orchestra and on another a praise band. Why, I ask, as the people of God, may we not celebrate diversity of gifts, talent, experience, culture, and styles in music and worship patterns, as we say we wish to celebrate the diversity of peoples that comprise the church of God? Would not a diversity of musical and formal styles, in unexpected patterns, portray the church universal better than any set, expected style and form? Why not black gospel on one Sunday and standard hymns on another? And why not have some blondes singing in the black Gospel choir, and African-American women and men leading hymns on the following Sunday?

I love the worship ideals presented for many years at the First Baptist Church of West Los Angeles under its pastor, Paul Edwards. The service might open with organ music, include a setting of hymns, and involve a praise band with lively congregational singing. The choir was led by a splendid musician who was born in Mexico City, and the members of the choir and the congregation had faces reflecting multiple people groups across the planet. Students from UCLA sat beside investment bankers; Santa Monica artists joined voices with people in the film industry. As I sat in the congregation and then stood behind the pulpit in this church each spring, I would feel like I was looking out at a meeting of the United Nations. Better, it was the church of God.

Not all churches can easily draw on such diversity of people. Churches are drawn from people in communities; not all communities are so diverse as that of West Los Angeles. But with some sadness I suspect not all congregations would desire such diversity of people or of style.

Some white congregations don't welcome people of color. Many established congregations are even more resistant to changing the "colors" of their worship patterns. When we attempt to achieve a blend in style and form, we find that what looks good on paper rarely works so well in the congregation. Some people do not stretch as much as we might hope. Just as there are those who resist using a new translation of the Bible, so there are many people who resist new elements in worship styles and forms.

The problem we face in many churches in attempting to achieve a blend of style and form is that we are limited in the range of choices we can actually make. Some hymns will lose the young crowd before their charm has its effect; offbeat clapping loses some of the older set altogether. "Worship wars" occur. And as some people are coming in the front doors, others are leaving through the side, and not all leave quietly.

So, while the ideal may be blended worship, many leaders conclude that various styles of worship are necessary. Here we need a younger voice than mine, and a mind and heart more attuned to the minds and hearts of younger believers and more keenly directed to the minds and hearts of those who have not yet come to Christ for salvation.

Chapters 14–19 are written by my son, Craig H. Allen, with a few of my own observations thrown in. Some of the ideas he presents differ slightly from those I have advanced. But he is in a local church *doing* the leading of worship, not just flitting about from church to church, observing and participating, as I am.

But I also wish to echo a word of warning from an "older" writer. We make a mistake if we attempt to make too much of the distinction between contemporary participatory worship and older, traditional forms, if we attempt to estimate the level of true worship that is actually taking place. Warren W. Wiersbe rightly observes that it is possible in God's eyes that more true worship may be happening in the hearts of people in a quiet meeting of fifty people than in the din of a couple of thousand clapping, singing people. Only God really knows. And that is all that matters.[1]

## *Fourteen*

༺❦༻

# Those Seeker-Sensitive Services

## OUR NEW SERVICES

IN THE FALL OF 1998 the church where I (Craig) serve began a new direction in our planning of worship services. We moved from having two blended services to one blended service and one with a more contemporary flavor. For the second Sunday of each month we also developed a seeker-sensitive service. In this chapter I seek to clarify the differences and the rationale for the changes we have made at Laurelwood Baptist Church in Vancouver, Washington.

## THE "TRADITIONAL" WORSHIP SERVICE

The free-church Anglo-Protestant tradition has long been "sermon-centered."[1] Everything leading up to the sermon was regarded as preparatory (even "preliminary"). The sermon was regarded as the main event. The meeting room was called "the auditorium," the place where people come to listen. It was also called "the house of God," so disciplines of reverence, quiet moments, reflection, and silent prayer were valued. Music was used primarily to buttress these ideals. Cavalier attitudes were not permitted. Jokes from the pulpit were not tolerated.

Worship was serious business, with attentiveness to the sermon being the highest goal.

In these traditional settings the principal function of music was presentational. Music was for the edification of believers. Hymn tunes were drawn from styles of the eighteenth and nineteenth centuries. The lyrics were designed to inculcate doctrine into the lives of the singers. Hymns were not sung so much to God as to one another. The choir was thought to have a "priestly" role in singing prepared music to God *on behalf* of the people, as well as a "prophetic" role in singing God's Word *to* the people.

A strength of the traditional service is that it helps us to sense a connection with the riches of our historic tradition. The church did not begin with last week's newest song craze; Christians have been singing God's praises for nearly two thousand years.

The traditional service elements also help us to maintain contact with the content of our historic beliefs. While people have had Bibles in their homes and pews for many generations, it has been a function of the worship service to help them understand what the Bible teaches and how biblical faith should mark their lives. The preaching was done to indoctrinate the congregation; that is, the content of the sermon was a divine direction in what to believe and how to act. The tone of the preacher was that of a prophet, a spokesman for God. His words were presented as God's message. The music that preceded the sermon acted as a buttress to the sermon. When the hymns were selected intentionally and with the theme of the service in view, the music and the sermon were "on the same page," and they reached the heart with the same powerful ideas.

Along the way, congregational responses in traditional worship patterns have been somewhat cerebral. The goal was assent in heart and mind to the teaching of the text, both in the sermon and in the song. The tone of hymns tends to be solemn and triumphant; solemn, because the truths are important, and triumphant, because truth will one day overcome error.

A fixture in traditional services has been dress style. Women would wear full dresses and men would be in suit and tie. Children would be in their "Sunday best." Commonly the argument would be presented that if one would dress up to meet with the president of the United States or to appear before the queen of England, would one not also dress one's best to meet with God?

These values are still found in many churches in settings around the globe. Chinese believers dress up for church services, as do African believers; the slots for hymns are found in liturgical services as well as in "free" services.

One thing seems obvious, however. These days the crowds are smaller and grayer in many services of this type. (I, Ron, recall visiting a church service with Beverly in Jönköping, Sweden, one Sunday morning. We were in an immense, beautiful building. We had to search for the congregation. At last we discovered where a small section of the apse was roped off for the gray-headed band of worshipers; the rest of the great cathedral was still, empty, and sad.)

## THE "CONTEMPORARY" WORSHIP SERVICE

Changes in worship styles in white American churches began in the late 1960s, particularly in charismatic circles. Today the extent of change has crossed nearly all denominational lines, and the lines of many nations as well.

The major feature of the "new" worship style is not only music. It also includes a more active sense of participation by the congregation in their worship of God. The musical style gives opportunity for this new dimension, but that sense of participation is the more important issue. New expressions are based on the idea of the wholeness of human personality, with an emphasis on heart and body rather than just in intellectual assent and volitional commitment. The newer worship style includes an emotional level that was rarely seen, and sometimes discouraged, in the patterns of American (and European) formalism. Emotion had been a part of frontier revivalism but was stilled somewhat in the Sunday services of the redeemed. Laughter and weeping—both suspicious actions in some traditional services—were now commonly expressed by people who were led to be a bit more free to be "themselves" before God and with each other.

The black worship tradition in America differs from that of the traditional white church. I (Ron) have black Christian friends who are somewhat puzzled when I speak of the concept of emotion and joy in our newer worship services. One woman told me, "Well, it's about time. What took you so long?" A sense of participation has always permeated the African-American worship patterns. Music was never done in the "slot" pattern. The congregation and the preacher interact with one another in a most lively manner. It is not unusual for a white Christian who visits a black church for the first time to come away astonished ... and exhausted.[2]

## THE FOCUS IN THE CONTEMPORARY SERVICE

The focus of contemporary worship is on using several means of helping people relate to God in ways that are thought to be more culturally relevant. This is the pattern of today, not yesterday. Worship leaders now question why contemporary forms may not be used with the same sense of God's blessing as earlier forms were used in earlier days. Do we drive 1940s cars or wear 1880s clothing? If we are living in the twenty-first century, should we not worship God in styles appropriate to our own time?

The most obvious aspect of change in these services is in the music. But again, the reason for the change is to provide a platform for a more active participation by ordinary people. The model uses the singing of new songs in popular rather than in classical styles. The words are designed, on the one hand, to be fresh expressions, and on the other hand, to be very biblical (often quoting words from the Book of Psalms). The musical instruments are often guitars, drums, and synthesizers, played in ever-changing styles.

Contemporary music fosters more congregational response than does traditional hymn-singing in our present culture. One reason is found in the attitude of the new praise songs. They are not so much conveyers of doctrinal truth (edification) or stanzas of ultimate victory (assurance); these newer songs are now prayers and praises sung directly to God. Short songs joined in medleys allow songs to build on one another. In the older "hymn-in-a-slot" pattern, there was rarely a sense of building of thematic ideas in music. One simply sang one hymn, all stanzas, and then moved to something else. Now leaders of worship weave ideas from one song to another over an extended period of time (fifteen to twenty minutes is not uncommon) for a profound emotional, personal impact.

Along the way, some outward elements have changed as well. Among these is dropping the expectation of formal Sunday dress codes. People tend to dress in a more casual manner in these services, believing that the dress of the heart is far more important than that of the outer man (or woman). Also gone are hymnals, organs, choirs—even crosses! Little attempt is given to link today's believers with believers in the past; the focus is on the methods and musical styles of today.

The service is now seen as an interaction in which people hear *from* God in the Word and respond *to* God in the music. The uses of visual aids, drama, and other multimedia elements are all perceived as helps for both impact and retention. Celebration is central. We worship Christ for His victory at the cross and the empty tomb, and we anticipate His coming kingdom.

## THE "BLENDED" WORSHIP SERVICE

For the past decade the church in which I serve had been in transition from a mildly progressive traditional service to a more blended service. In a blended service the ideal is to preserve the best of the past and to use the best of the new in our worship services. To achieve this goal we have sought to find guidance on worship from the whole of the Bible. More recently we have become more contemporary in tone and in music style and have added an emphasis on visual and relational communication. We also recognize that what is viewed as "contemporary" is continually changing.

We have sought in our blended services to be inclusive, using worship teams *and* choir, piano and organ *and* synthesizers and guitars. We use violins *and* we use drums. We have responsive readings *and* feature dramatic sketches. We encourage clapping to new praise songs as well as the raising of hands in the context of intimate worship songs, as well as when singing great hymns of deep theology. We continue to emphasize expository preaching, but we also have laughter and we use many visual aids. A blended approach may not continue to be the best answer for every church, but our goal is to worship God through Jesus Christ, empowered by the Holy Spirit.

## THE CONTROVERSY

What might seem to be a clear idea to some is not clear at all to others. The term "blended" seems to some people to be a reasonable strategy. To others the idea smacks of compromise.

There are strengths in both the traditional and contemporary approaches, and the blend helps preserve both in balance. But not everyone appreciates this blended idea. The one-size-fits-all service has limitations. Some people feel we are not contemporary enough for their taste; others find their comfort zones stretched too far. Moreover, we continue to ask what approach will be a means of attracting the lost.

More and more church leaders are asking if they should develop different kinds of services. Our task is not to attempt to copy the model of other growing churches.[3] Rather, we must seek God's will for *our* church and seek prayerfully to discover what He wants for *us*. Our goal is the worship of God, not the defining of a label of how that worship may be achieved.

## CONTEMPORARY WORSHIP (BOOMERS)

Contemporary worship began to burst across denominational lines in the early 1980s. With "Boomers" (people born between 1946 and 1964) in mind, services were designed to be fast-paced, visually stimulating, bright and energetic musically, emphasizing positive and practical messages. While seeker services generally target *unbelievers,* true contemporary worship services are designed for *believers* who desire to worship God in current and meaningful forms. As they see believers genuinely worshiping God, unbelievers discover something they do not see anywhere else in life. As in Acts 2, worship is the focus of these services, but a bonus comes in conversions.

## CONTEMPORARY WORSHIP (BUSTERS)

In recent years a new contemporary worship approach has emerged among "Busters" (people born between 1964 and 1982). It features still *more* interaction of the worshipers. The focus is on being authentic, not polished.

There is less concern about efficiency and more about relationships—with people and with God. The music tends to be harsher and louder, paralleling modern life. Teaching emphasizes personal experience stories rather than information. Doctrine is appreciated more if seen lived out than just discussed as a concept. Rather than "attend a service," these Busters want to "meet with God."

## SEEKER-SENSITIVE WORSHIP

If "contemporary" was the buzzword of the 1980s, "seeker sensitive" was the logo for the 1990s (and, we expect, for the early years of the twenty-first century). A "seeker" is an unbeliever. But this unbeliever is regarded by the people of the church as one whom God may be drawing to Himself.[4] (Obviously, not all lost people are seeking God. Yet if an unsaved person has decided to attend a service, that may be an indication that God is working in his or her heart.)

In our seeker-sensitive service on Thanksgiving Day a few years ago we considered how things would be perceived by a nonchurched person whom the Lord was drawing to Himself. Might songs including archaic English verb and pronoun forms ("didst," "Thou," "camest," and so forth) be barriers to a seeker? Does our theological vocabulary communicate relevantly? Do we explain the concepts behind our terms? Do such elements as our building, dress, bulletin, service style, and the like, draw unbelievers in or repel them? Being seeker sensitive means that every element of the worship service is sifted through a grid that asks, How will this likely be received by Joe and Mary Unbeliever who visit this morning? When we are sensitive to seekers, we attempt to remove those unnecessary obstacles or barriers that may hinder our nonbelieving neighbors from trusting in Christ.

## SEEKER-DRIVEN SERVICES

The distinction between seeker-sensitive services and seeker-driven services is that the latter are designed from the ground up for unchurched people. No attempt is made to stimulate worship, because unbelievers cannot worship God.[5] The validity of the Bible and the deity of Christ are not assumed; a case must be made for any belief that we wish to present. Everything done in the service is to cause the "audience" to look to God. Effort is made to earn people's trust, to connect with their views of life, and to help them see their need for a Savior. This exclusively evangelistic focus has resulted in many conversions for Christ in newly planted churches. But it is a difficult approach for established churches to use.

We would issue a gentle warning. Change should not be sought just because it is in fashion. Any change in worship style and form should proceed from the conviction that such changes will be pleasing to God and adaptable to the congregation. A worship leader is no leader if no one is willing to follow.

# *Fifteen*

## Leading the Church toward Contemporary Worship

EACH JUNE LISA AND I (CRAIG) are caught up in the Portland Rose Festival Treasure Hunt. Clues are given each day in the sponsoring newspaper, *The Oregonian*. Recently in our annual quest we had driven to a rural Oregon town of just over seventeen hundred people. We had learned that 150 years ago this little town had been the county seat and had been one of the most influential towns in the emerging state. Numerous buildings displayed signs that boasted of historic importance. Among these buildings were a few churches. But some buildings were no longer used by churches; they were now museums. We looked with sadness on buildings that had maximized their impact for Christ generations ago and are now simply old buildings. Then we thought of another church that has grown from less than two hundred people to well over a thousand in just ten years. It is located in a nearby town as small as the one we were visiting.

### IS THE GOSPEL OLD-FASHIONED?

One sign in the small town we visited attracted my attention. The sign was new but the words prompted a sense of discord: "We preach Christ-crucified," and "Old-fashioned." Some must have felt that in this small town the joining of these words was a positive draw. The underlying assumption seems to equate spiritual vitality (a focus on the atonement of our Lord) with older worship styles ("old-fashioned"). One does not have to have a sign on a building to project a similar viewpoint.

One of the most daunting challenges of worship leaders today is to lead an established congregation through significant change. It is a mistake to think that an effective transition is a one-time fix. Our approach to ministry should pursue an ongoing, cyclical process of growth. This cycle might look something like this:

Careful evaluation prayer ➤for God's leading ➤appropriate change ➤ careful evaluation➤prayer for God's leading➤and so forth.

## CHANGE, CHANGE, CHANGE

Life is about change. There is little escape from the constant change in modern life. A radio commercial tells us that more information has been generated in the last thirty years than in the previous five thousand! No town is too rural these days to escape the impact of unrelenting society transformation. Even little "Dancer, Tex., pop. 81," the fictional town in a recent film, depicts people impacted by the lure of California, television, the Internet, and music. We may prefer the cane chair on the front porch, but most pass by in fast cars.

Changes abound in popular culture, especially in the means of delivery. I think there will always be magazines and papers, but many people today get their news (what little they get) on headline services, some over their computers. Newspapers themselves have changed. *The Times* of London may finally stand alone in its resistance to the redoing of the look of newspapers that followed the advent of *USA Today*. Newspapers now feature pictures, color, and short articles.

Participation and visual image are the marks of contemporary communication. People listen to and take part in talk shows and chat rooms. Movies and images fill their lives. Music is visceral, not just background sound. People these days come to church services with different expectations than the saints of earlier generations.

Again, there is nothing spiritual about engaging in change, if it is just change. But when change is motivated by a love for God and a desire for His worship to be more effective among the changing needs of people, then it may be wonderfully led and blessed by the Holy Spirit.

Our ongoing goal should be to continue to keep the church unified in purpose. We must be uncompromising as we pursue the mission of the church. We must be driven by His Word and compelled by His love to exalt Christ as community, to present the gospel to the lost in our own community and abroad, and to build up each other through the gifts of God's Spirit. We must adapt ministry forms and approaches to the increasingly diverse people groups we find in our rapidly changing culture.

## A PROCESS

I propose to use the word *contemporary* to describe the sense of *present effectiveness* in worship ministry. What is contemporary at the time of the writing of this book may have changed by the time you are reading it! As we write, we think of contemporary worship services as having some elements in common. These include popular music styles, visual stimulation, celebrative atmospheres, much singing and participation by the laity. But as the process continues, these elements may shift.

Here are questions we may ask as we evaluate the use of "new" ideas on our worship of God:
- Is the idea taught in Scripture as a normative act or behavior?
- Is it modeled positively by biblical example?
- Is it at least consistent with or derived from a clear principle, goal, or example of biblical worship?[1]

For example, we fulfill the first criterion as we focus on glorifying God through exalting Jesus Christ and remembering His death and resurrection in word, song, and sacred ceremony. When we bring glory to God through the use of performance choirs and spontaneous songs of the people, we fulfill the second criterion. As we use pianos and drum sets for the musical accompaniment in corporate praise, we fulfill the third criterion.

If, however, we were to suggest that people "bark in the Spirit," we would be adrift in a rudderless boat. Think of all the nonsense we hear about what passes for Christian worship in some places. Charming of snakes. "Holy" laughter. Slaying in the Spirit. Playing drums! Oops—this is one we like! Drums (percussion instruments) in worship serve in a biblical pattern; the other ideas do not.[2]

Whether a particular approach to worship of God originated in the time of King David in Israel, through Paul in his ministry in churches in Asia Minor, through Martin Luther in Reformation Germany, through a congregation a hundred years ago in Texas or last month in Australia—the question we must ask is this: *Is God accomplishing His purpose in our midst through this approach today, with the people we have now in this setting?*

In established churches the usual response to a new idea about ministry style is the well-worn adage, "We haven't done it that way before." But special pleading by new-ministry promoters is no more convincing when they simply say, "This is current."

Possibly some of the ways we have done things in the past are not the best today. It is also possible that some of the ways we have done things in the past were not the best back then either, but they were unquestioned. Some new ideas were not desirable in the past and aren't in the present. But perhaps some of the richest means of true worship are waiting to be developed in congregations today.

We explore some of these ideas in the next three chapters.

# Sixteen

## Why Pursue Contemporary Worship?

MANY PEOPLE IN PASTORAL LEADERSHIP yearn longingly for "the good old days." There was a time in some golden age when everyone read from the same version of the Bible. All knew the same hymns. Services in one church were virtually the same as in another. There was no such idea back then as "worship wars," except as a reminder of the conflict during the days of the Reformation. But those were the very olden days.

Things were far more simple when people read from the same page, sang from the same page, even prayed from the same page. Today, many do not even know where the books may be.

Distasteful as change may be to some pastors, all pastors confront it constantly. People in worship leadership may confront change differently from each other, but none can escape it.

### THE RISE OF CONTEMPORARY APPROACHES

At the time of this writing, what has become known as the worship renewal is about three decades old. It was all so unexpected! What started among unlikely groups of believers has spread nearly everywhere. From the beginnings of the early Jesus People in southern California,[1] these ideas were pursued by groups as diverse as Pentecostals, Baptists, and Mennonites. The new modes have spread across North America like a western wildfire, transcending most denominational and association lines. Indeed, the sweep today is global.

Along the way was the great discovery of the biblical priority of worship in the life of the church. Though it would seem to be obvious, people were now learning that the church is primarily about people responding rightly to God. This has not always been the case.[2]

Believers have always worshiped God, of course, but worship was not necessarily regarded as the principal task of the church. Often it was felt to be ancillary. Even though a number of older church leaders in more traditional churches have been caught sleeping through the revolution, the worship renewal movement has brought the priority of the worship of God into focus in the lives of many people.

Many church groups that had been influenced by frontier Christianity were focused primarily on evangelism. Others maintained the tradition of revivalism; the annual week of revival services defined the high point of church life. Rural congregations have typically focused on fellowship, with the church building serving as the central focus of the community as well as the home of the congregation. Many churches had long treasured teaching and preaching as their central ministry. Numerous churches have had a wonderful focus on world missions, with the annual week of global-focused conference as their spiritual high point. Other churches have aggressively pursued social concerns, both for the good of their community and for the world. But worship remained an elusive focus in many of these churches. It was there, but it was not central. American Christianity has often been centered on the individual, as our most prominent evangelistic approaches reveal.[3]

## BRINGING BALANCE TO OUR VIEW OF GOD

In traditional worship patterns the emphasis has tended to focus on the transcendence of God. The great "objective" hymns such as "Holy, Holy, Holy," and "Immortal, Invisible, God Only Wise" served as a lovely means of instilling in people the notions of God's great attributes of holiness and wonder, and instructing them in attitudes of reverence.

Newer contemporary worship songs have had an uncanny ability to help people voice statements of need and dependency on God, as well as giving them words to express their love for God. Think, for example, of the songs, "Shout to the Lord," and "Knowing You." Now, instead of singing *about* God, people are also learning to sing *to* God. Instead of speaking "objectively," they voice their "subjective" responses to His wonder.[4]

Along these lines I have thought of the hymn "How Great Thou Art" as one of the first contemporary worship songs, though it dates from 1953 and uses older language.[5] It emphasizes so beautifully the transcendence of God, whose "power [is] throughout the universe displayed." Yet God is personal—He is "my God," and I am affected by Him. I am caught in "awesome wonder" when I "consider" what He has made. The hymn demands a worship response from the singer at every chorus: "Then sings my soul, my Savior God, to Thee." The last verse describes worship responses, including the words "shout," "joy," "bow in humble adoration," and "proclaim . . . how great Thou art."

The reason this song has been so well loved for half a century is because it speaks to our minds and hearts about who God is and the sacrifice Jesus has made for us, but it does not end there. This hymn also inspires us to respond to God with an overflowing heart of love and gratitude. This is a worship song! More recent examples of songs effective in teaching about God and encouraging believers to respond to Him in love include "Lord, I Lift Your Name on High," "Give Thanks," and "Jesus, You Are My Life."

## RECLAIMING THE POWER OF SINGING TOGETHER

Other contributions of the contemporary worship renewal include a reclaiming of the power of congregational singing in directing people's hearts to God. Before the coming of the worship renewal, certainly many believers sang wonderful hymns with praise to the living God. But the usual approach to the singing of the congregation was what may be called the "slot" mentality.

Each week one of the responsibilities of the pastor was to choose three hymns for the "hymn slots" in the worship service. Typically there would be an opening hymn, a hymn before the sermon, and a hymn after the sermon.[6]

God created music to be a powerful vehicle. Unsaved, depraved people use this God-designed tool for their own destruction. Believers use it for the praise of God. David calmed Saul's evil spirit with his harp, the Israelites played trumpets and the walls of Jericho fell down, and angels sing in praise to God. We can thank the contemporary worship movement for helping to restore the significant place for music in worship as God has ordained.

In the assembly of believers who join to sing to God, the unity of the Spirit can be expressed and experienced by those present. Psalm 33 calls the righteous to "Rejoice in the Lord" (musically). Moreover—and how wonderful this is—"praise from the upright is beautiful" (Ps. 33:1).[7] Psalm 34:3 calls us to "exalt His Name together," and verse 5 states that those who look to Him in the context of community worship are "radiant." Believers are to speak to each other in "psalms and hymns and spiritual songs" (Eph. 5:19; Col. 3:16). All of these Scriptures make the point that singing is not something reserved for musicians, nor is it just for private enjoyment or public performance. Rather, singing is something God has called all believers to participate in as a means of expressing the praise of our hearts, edifying one another, and communicating truth about God. In the process of singing together, our hearts are transformed. The contemporary worship movement has helped to highlight these centuries-old truths of Scripture.

## RESTORING THE EMPHASIS ON THE HOLY SPIRIT IN WORSHIP

God the Father is seeking for and desires to look with favor on those who worship Him in spirit and truth (John 4:23–24). Sometimes more traditional worship services have come under criticism for focusing only on the "truth" aspect of worship and neglecting the aspect of worshiping in "spirit."

It seems reasonable that what the Father desires is a true "spiritual" connection between the "breath" of God and the "breath" of the believer.[8] While the phrase "spirit and truth" certainly includes our mind, heart, and emotions, I believe this is referring to a dynamic interaction in which the true worshiper is so deeply moved by truth about God that there is a stirring of the Holy Spirit within him or her that then elicits a worshiping response (Rom. 8:14–16; Gal. 4:6). In worship we don't focus on the Holy Spirit as such; we worship the Father through Jesus the Son. But we cannot truly worship God apart from the Holy Spirit. He is the "breath" that is our "connection" with the Father! Believers are to respond to God by being sensitive to the Holy Spirit who connects our life to the Father.

Worshipers are to approach God with true motives and a genuine heart before Him. But that genuineness of heart and purity of motives come as divine gifts from the Holy Spirit, who actually empowers true worship within us.

The One true worshiper of the Father is the Son; the living Christ is our High Priest before the Father. When we worship in spirit and in truth our worship becomes a part of the Son's worship of the Father. The One who empowers Him, empowers us—the Spirit of God. So the Spirit is at work in us to enable us to bring true worship to the Father in concert with the living, resurrected Son. This is the heart of true biblical worship.[9]

## ENCOURAGING SPONTANEITY, CELEBRATION, AND EXPRESSIVE WORSHIP

"Latino worship is a fiesta. It is a celebration of the mighty deeds of God." So writes Justo L. González in describing an aspect of the worship of Hispanic Christians.[10] Contemporary worship services have typically allowed for more spontaneity in services. This does not mean that planning should be deemphasized. Instead, the idea is that we should be aware that God, who can work through the worship pastor and teaching pastor in their offices during their midweek preparation, is also able to work through them in real-time at any point in any service.[11] An understanding of the Holy Spirit who "blows wherever He pleases" (John 3:8, NIV) can help bring a bit of healthy flexibility and spiritual sensitivity to an otherwise decent and orderly service.

While it may be a bit much to call the weekly service a "celebration service," or to have celebration as the singular theme every week, celebrating our salvation is among the highest callings of the believer in Christ.

Many people from traditional church backgrounds like to claim Psalm 46:10 as a theme verse for the mood of true worship: "Be still, and know that I am God." Worship, they say, is done best in silence, not in song—and especially not in loud song. Of course, silence can be a very effective tool at given points in worship services, providing times for personal reflection, silent prayer, or even for a simple spiritual "pause." However, this verse in Psalm 46 is misused when it is said to call for silence.

Psalm 46 is a psalm of trust,[12] but verse 10 is given in a context of warfare and violence (46:1, 6), leading to the prophecy of an outpouring of God's wrath against the enemies of the faith (46:8). The call to "Hush!" in verse 10 is not a call for quiet reflection; it is a stern setting for the impending horror of divine judgment![13] The prophetic Armageddon scene of Psalm 46:10 might be a potential service theme somewhere along the way in the life of your church, but it is certainly not a standard context from which to model a weekly worship service.

What we need to do is to read just a bit further to see the opening of Psalm 47, a psalm that *is* concerned with appropriate behavior for believers in divine worship. "Oh, clap your hands, all you peoples! Shout to God with the voice of triumph! For the LORD Most High is awesome; He is a great King over all the earth" (47:1–2).

Psalm 47 calls for the nations to worship God enthusiastically and joyfully for His awesome wonder. Further, God's ultimate victory through Christ is the very substance of New Testament Christian worship. The call in this psalm to "sing praises to Him" is based on God's reign. "God has gone up with a shout, the LORD with the sound of a trumpet. Sing praises to God, sing praises! Sing praises to our King, sing praises! For God is the King of all the earth; Sing praises with understanding" (47:5–7).

As to the charge that praise choruses are repetitive, did you notice that the words "sing praises" are found five times in two verses?[14]

To see the Father reigning as the Creator King and to await the triumphant millennial reign of Jesus in Jerusalem is the essence of Christian worship. Certainly there is a place in public worship for confessing sin, being contemplative, meditating on Scripture, interceding in silent prayer, and taking sermon notes. These more private and restrained acts of worship are biblically valid. But the restoration for redeemed people of the high priority of celebration and allowing them freedom to express exuberant joy to their King are hallmarks of the contemporary worship renewal.

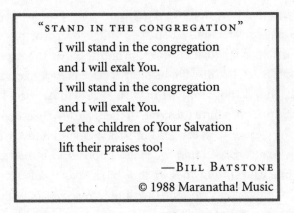

"STAND IN THE CONGREGATION"
I will stand in the congregation
and I will exalt You.
I will stand in the congregation
and I will exalt You.
Let the children of Your Salvation
lift their praises too!
—BILL BATSTONE
© 1988 Maranatha! Music

## THE REALITY OF MUSICAL LANGUAGES
## AND TRANSITIONAL TIMES

Missionaries have long known that they must learn to understand a culture and become fluent in speaking a foreign language to have significant impact in another cultural setting. The leaders of the Roman Catholic Church decided at Vatican II that they would seek to be more effective in reaching and retaining Americans for Catholicism by allowing Mass to be presented in English rather than in the Latin language. Looking back, these approaches seem to be so obvious that resistance to them would be pointless. But the transition to something obvious can still be difficult. Effective contemporary churches have recognized that there are advantages in taking a missiological approach to establishing the tone, elements, and musical style of a worship service. We simply must know the cultures of the people in our church and in our neighborhood, and also to be aware of the gaps between them.

I like to speak in terms of "worship languages." This notion includes but is greater than the issue of musical styles. This idea refers to all the elements that help direct a person's attention to God and then to inspire this person to respond worshipfully toward God. This includes the way the Word of God is presented, the tone of the service, the degree of formality, the personality of the service, the songs chosen, the musicality of the singing, prayer for God's blessing, and the style of music.

All these can be designed or determined by the pastor and worship planner, with the exception of programming the power of God; for His power we may pray fervently. Usually conflicts over worship styles erupt when a particular language is given prominence at the expense of another. People react, because it is as if the service is no longer in "English," so to speak. They do not recognize the structure of the service. The "sound" of the music does not have meaning to them and to their experience.

A worship leader who can lead musical worship fluently in a variety of worship languages will find much less opposition from the congregation than one who simply does what he or she personally likes. One way to love a congregation is to take the time to discover how they are best stimulated to worship God. That is why they have come! Good worship leaders commit both to stretching themselves to learn the language of the people and to stretching the people so that they learn to expand their worship-language fluency.

We may illustrate these ideas using the letters of the alphabet. Let's say that one group in a church happily worships God only in dialects A through D, another group in M through P, and still another in dialects X through Z. Here we wind up with three congregations in one building. We are ripe for conflict over worship styles.

Now the problem is exacerbated if the worship leader naturally leads only in a worship language of, say, R through V. The worship leader may seek a two-part remedy. First, he or she may seek to learn to lead in the center of each of the worship languages, seeking for the strengths in each. Second, the worship leader may then begin to seek to stretch each of the groups. He or she may seek to stretch the first group to, say, A through T, the second group to F through V, and the third group to J through Z. Now there would be unity, at least in J through T!

The concept of worship languages is helpful when one approaches newer and younger believers. If the standard musical fare of these people is alternative music, the gap to the standard hymnal is immense. The use of more contemporary praise music can help to bridge the gap for them. This will also include the use of newer instruments in the congregation.

Introducing new instruments might be done in this order: synthesizer/keyboard, electric bass, acoustic guitar, solo orchestra instruments (flutes, trumpets, violins, saxophones), light percussion (tambourines, shakers, congas), electric guitar, full drum set. This progression is simply a way to think of moving people gradually from the known and familiar to the less known and/or less appreciated.

Perspective matters. We help our people gain the long view when we help them understand that musical styles often have a shelf life. A look through any standard hymnal will reveal that perhaps up to 95 percent of the songs included have been written in the past two or three hundred years. Somewhere along the way we have dropped almost everything the church had ever sung for the first seventeen hundred years or so.[15] Was this because the songs were not theological or biblical? Hardly. When Isaac Watts began the modern hymn movement, church people had been used to singing metrical psalms—straight off the pages of the Bible, whether these settings worked musically or not! It was purely for aesthetic and style reasons that metrical psalm singing died away in all but some Reformed churches. In most of our churches we sing virtually nothing from the days of the early church. Cultures and styles have changed and changed again too many times to hang on to the older musical languages.

We need to remind our people that the hymnal is not the Bible. We use it as long as it is effective for stirring people's hearts toward God. Thousands of hymns that were once sung by God's people are no longer in our hymnals. Isaac Watts is considered by many authorities to be the greatest English hymn writer.[16] He wrote about eight hundred hymns, though the hymnal of the church I serve contains only fifteen. Fanny Crosby wrote around seven thousand hymns, sixteen of which are in our hymnal. Many of the older hymns originally had between eight and fifteen stanzas. I have seen hymns in old hymnbooks with as many as twenty-four stanzas. There is nothing sacred about singing "all" the verses. Editors have already edited out many verses they did not consider appropriate for general usage in our day.

A contemporary approach should include the use of the hymnal for what it is, a rich treasury of songs that have ministered to saints over the years, many of which continue to have ongoing impact. And if the Lord tarries His return, possibly in a few hundred years from now, very little of anything we presently sing will still be sung. That means they will have been replaced by new songs written by the new songwriters who have been led in their worship of God to write songs that were worthy of being embraced by the church at large.

The change in music sung for church gatherings in contemporary centers mirrors what has happened with Bible translations. Except for "King-James-Version-only" circles, most of America has moved beyond the archaisms of the Authorized Version to one of many modern translations. There are multiple reasons for this change, to be sure. But for most believers the transition has been a choice of language style. They simply prefer how the new translation of choice reads for them, and it is therefore more meaningful to them. This is the primary reason many younger people express disinterest in the hymns. They feel that it is too much for them to learn a new language, especially when they know that this particular language is archaic. They know that Old English is not the future, and they are not terribly interested in going in a direction they think is backward. Contemporary songs written in "today's" language do not have this initial barrier for the uninitiated.

If your church is struggling with the idea of moving away from traditional hymns and embracing newer songs, try to separate the substance of the hymns you love from the form in which they appear. Try to think through what is enduring of the hymns. Then look for (or compose!) newer songs that meet the same kind of need. This might include factors such as rich theological truth, a variety of doctrinal content and emphasis, biblical themes, wording fresh enough to make repetition desirable, singable and memorable melody, impressionable harmonies that heighten the lyrics, and in forms suitable for the congregation—not just the music majors on the platform. As we choose new songs, we can still look for some of the elements that made the great hymns great. Then in future eras people will be seeking to replace worthy aspects of songs we now sing.

## ESTABLISHING A CONTEMPORARY CLIMATE

"Have you driven a Ford *lately?*"

"Corn Flakes—Try them again for the *first time.*"

These ads strive to encourage people to look afresh at what they thought they already knew. This encouragement to look anew at the familiar is great advice for church leaders who desire to see their churches move forward. When I visit another church, my eyes take in everything. I notice the architecture of the building, the paint, the lighting, the cleanliness, the kind of piano, the friendliness of the people, the typeset of the bulletin, the clarity of signs to get me where I want to go, the interior colors of the sanctuary, the carpet stains, and other elements. It is amazing how attuned I become to details in a strange setting.

It is helpful for church leaders to try to look at their church through new eyes—to see things again for the first time. As we look at things through "visitor's eyes," we can begin to evaluate whether our church is communicating what we desire. Though the buildings are silent, they are communicating. And people who visit are listening.

Every church has a "look" to it. From this look people make value judgments as to whether this church is likely to "fit" them. The architecture of the sanctuary, the condition of the buildings, the look of the stage, and the color of the carpets will all contribute to people's initial judgments about a church that they visit.

Similarly every church service has a "feel." The lighting, the volume of the music, the participation of the congregation, the level of formality, the sense of flow and progression—all these are factors that contribute to how a person feels about a service. From this feel people will determine whether they want to return and whether they will be comfortable inviting others. Ideally the look and feel of your worship environment will be consistent with your vision for your worship services. On each of these issues it is good to think through the question, Are we communicating what we want to communicate?

Our congregation has met for worship services the last ten years in our gymnasium. Some have aptly called this combination a "sanctuasium" or a "gymnatorium." We have had numerous people visit us over the years who have told us they would not choose to worship here, because it "doesn't look like a church." Three years ago we completed a remodel of our gymnatorium. What a difference new paint, new carpet, and new woodwork make! Our formerly orange and dark brown colorings had communicated a "lost in the 1970s" message that caused us to start every service in a bit of a deficit—roughly twenty-five years behind the times. As we are situated in a community of largely new home construction, our meeting place was communicating a conflict with our community.

Now, our blue, purple, and sand tones offer an inviting welcome and an appropriate aesthetic appearance that is consistent with the look of the community we are trying to reach. People do not seem to comment on our basketball hoops anymore. Their eyes are drawn to the woodwork, stage, and cross up front. Before we launched our facility upgrade, some people opposed spending money on this remodeling. But since it has been completed, complaints have ceased. Some people had to see the value with their eyes before they could realize what a difference it would make. Since the change, the only question has been, "Why did we take so long to do this?"

There is nothing spiritual about having a beautiful building in and of itself. Many cathedrals in Europe and performing arts halls in American cities have beauty to them without necessarily inspiring genuine godliness or true worship. The purpose for improving facilities needs to be to honor God by reflecting His character, excellence, and beauty.

To say from the pulpit, "God is awesome, and He does everything beautifully and excellently," is weakened if people look around and sense that everything we do is cheap, rundown, and messy. If we want to communicate that we care about people, we need to pay attention to the kind of things they care about. A strong case can be made that in addition to the worship center, the most important areas to invest in are the nursery, the young children's classrooms, and the rest rooms (particularly the women's rooms). If these are not appropriate, we had better not advertise ourselves as "a church that ministers to people."

Often the manner in which something is said speaks more loudly of the essence we desire to communicate. If the person in opening the service speaks very formally, for example, people may tend to stiffen, sit back, and consider themselves as part of a quiet audience at a formal event like a graduation or memorial service. If the goal is to have a participative service where people are free to respond to God with a range of emotions, it might be helpful to have a less formal approach to starting a service. A warm greeting, a gracious smile, and an opportunity for people to stand up and meet one another can bring a sense of openness to the service that helps people to be more willing to participate.

Similarly, praying in "King James English" can communicate things about God that we may not intend, especially to children in the service. Is God old-fashioned? Is He an Elizabethan? Can't I just speak to Him with my normal vocabulary? Or how about "Christianese"? When speakers use "insider" language, referring to biblical concepts that have meaning only to the initiated, we run the risk of putting up unnecessary barriers to those who are not yet "in the know." Of course, any term can be used if it is explained rather than assumed. But some preachers move out of their normal voice and into "preacher's voice" when they step behind the pulpit. Unfortunately this can communicate to people that the pastor is now moving into "performance mode," which may actually reduce the impact of his message because it may seem to lack genuineness. One mark of contemporary preaching is that the preacher is speaking to real people as a real person. Without showmanship a genuineness is communicated that can be powerful.

An opposite but equally unfortunate message can be sent to people if the worship leaders are so casual and lackadaisical as to communicate that worship is not a serious affair. Some begin with words like these: "OK, guys, let's get going and worship the Lord." Trivial language does not serve such a grand task!

It is possible to relate to people without excessive formality but still to maintain an appropriate reverence and to communicate significance for the purpose of the gathering. Well-chosen words can direct people's attention away from themselves and the demands of their week and toward the glory of God.

We are most vulnerable in the leading of congregational prayer. There is no excuse for thoughtlessly meandering through a public conversation with God in which people are expected to join in with their hearts. What are we communicating about prayer and about God when we do this? Alone at home, anyone can pray spontaneously (and mean-deringly!), as thoughts come in real time. However, if one is praying on behalf of the congregation, there should be a purpose to the prayer that helps direct the service. Our public prayers should result from private preparation.

The balance here is that worship needs to be genuine—neither overly formal nor sloppy and haphazard. Leading in worship should neither be put-on nor unprepared.

Other issues besides buildings and words can contribute to the climate of a worship service and can communicate relevance. What do we want to communicate about God and the gospel? Do we want to communicate a message about the gospel that says, "To come to Christ you must clean yourself up and put on your very best?" Or do we want to communicate, "Come to God as you are, and He will clean you up from the inside out. The 'robes of righteousness' He provides for you are what is important."

In an upscale urban setting the best choice for church leaders may be to match their community by dressing like the real estate agent and the banker. However, if most people in your community tend to dress in Dockers and sport shirts (or jeans and sweatshirts), there may be occa-sions where an informal look communicates more consistently with your spoken message of how to relate to God.

Are we the source of cultural barriers that hinder people from seeing Christ? Or are we making efforts to remove all such barriers so that we might continue to build bridges to more people? It is true that people will stumble on Christ who is the "stumbling block" (1 Cor. 1:23). As we approach issues of worship, we want to make sure that people don't stumble on *us* on their way to Him and end up missing Him. We want to be like Paul, who wrote, "We put no stumbling block in anyone's path" (2 Cor. 6:3 NIV).

## AN INCARNATIONAL APPROACH

One of the most difficult barriers in moving toward a more contempo-rary form of worship is getting past a felt concern about compromising, "dumbing down," or cheapening what "church" is supposed to be. Yet we need to remember that the look of the early church gatherings hardly resembled any of our church meetings today. So what we are changing from is usually not a biblical prescription, but simply a cultural model that has had an effective life span. We want to make sure that the scriptural priorities for public worship are being implemented and arranged in meaningful forms. But the forms can be adapted for the good of the people. The best example of this is Jesus.

When Jesus came to minister to people, He did not demand that they mature themselves, aspire to lofty doctrine, and then once perfected, come to Him. Rather, He modeled a ministry approach of condescension. He went to where people were, and He adapted Himself to them. He actually became one of them. He learned their language and culture, and He lived among them. And He did all this in order to present the love of God to them firsthand. Ultimately this love was expressed as He looked down from being suspended on the cross. Jesus revealed that incarnational ministry is costly. It is humbling and time-consuming. But its impact is powerful.

An incarnational ministry can be one of the strengths of directing a church toward a more contemporary model. For church leaders, modeling an incarnational approach means letting go of an expectation that the people will worship as you do at your level. It means that the leaders are willing to learn the songs, styles, and cultures of the common people. Yes, we want to raise them up. But we move them by first coming down, living among them, and then walking forward with them. By forgetting our preferences, rights, and backgrounds, we show love to the people, thereby building credibility in their eyes.

We open doors rather than build walls to newer and younger believers. In so doing, we increase our outreach options. An incarnational approach to ministry considers how people will see Christ and inspires leaders to go to whatever distance necessary to bridge the gap to make sure they really do.

## DISCOVER WHAT GOD IS BLESSING
## IN THE UNIVERSAL CHURCH

Another strength of many contemporary church ministries is the new freedom to reach beyond previous denominational limitations and borrow from other traditions what God appears to be blessing in ministry approaches. Though the current "no more walls" campaign has its share of problems— for example, the tendency for doctrinal discernment to be sacrificed for an alleged new "unity"—there is a positive point in this movement. People are discovering that no denomination or church has a lock on the power of God or on the correct approach to congregational worship.

Riches are not just in our circles; the riches are also "out there." Rather than looking only within one's own circle of churches to see what God is doing, many churches are using various media resources—CDs, videos, books, the Internet, audiotapes, faxes, e-mail, television, and others—to see ministry impact that they would miss by their eyes alone. Similarly, we are not confined to reading about what God did in generations past, but we can find out what God is doing around the world right now! This is a very exciting aspect of ministry today.

I encourage worship leaders to "swim in other streams." When I go on vacation, I try to go to churches that are different from my own. I find it healthy to experience some cross-fertilization of Christian movements. Recently I attended a conference in Seattle for people in music and worship ministry. I sat in several seminar sessions and a worship service led by Bob Fitts. This leader of a Youth with a Mission (YWAM) school in Kona, Hawaii, ministers in circles different from mine, but God used him to bless me greatly. He helped refresh my spirit and refocus my heart on such basics as loving my Savior, seeing God's goodness, and modeling God's grace as a worship leader.

My Baptist upbringing has given me a solid reverence for and devotion to the Word of God. Reformed writers have largely shaped my daily faith and trust in the sovereignty of God. My ability to express affection for God lovingly and to adore Him intimately has been primarily inspired by charismatic influences. Serious-minded academicians have often spurred my pursuit of the knowledge of God and discernment in doctrinal areas. Influences from mature, older brothers and writers from various denominations and eras have stimulated my appreciation for the beauty and excellence of God and the desire to emulate those traits in life as an aspect of godliness. The ability simply to enjoy God and His goodness has largely come from my time in youth ministry and spent with my wife and twin preschoolers. My love for the Psalms and desire to integrate music with theology to express my worship has been inspired most strongly by my father.

The point in mentioning these diverse influences is to reveal the value of immersing ourselves in a broad spectrum of influences where God is at work. It is possible to say without apology, "I belong to this church and that denomination because of its emphases, but I am also eager to learn what God is doing in and through other Christian streams." So go visit other churches on your vacation time. Learn from them and remember why you do things differently.

A fine recent book describes the variety of expressions of worship in the current setting. *Experience God in Worship* is a series of essays by George Barna, Jack W. Hayford, Bruce H. Leafblad, and others.[18]

# Seventeen

## How to Lead in Transition—Pastoral Issues

GORDON BORROR often challenged his seminary students by saying, "A choir will never rise above its director." He also said of choirs, "They can sing anything you can teach them." In these encouragements Borror emphasized the overarching importance of effective leadership.

Choir directors are prone to common frustrations. "Where will we find more good tenors?" "How can we help those altos to sing in tune?" When my grandfather was discouraged with musicians, he used to say, "The white is the paper, the black stuff is the notes. Sing and play the black." Directors tend to feel that the limitations of their volunteer musicians place low ceilings on their musical goals. Borror would argue that the onus is on the director; he or she simply needs to learn to lead on another level.

As with the musical directors, so with the other pastoral staff—especially the senior pastor. A church cannot rise above its pastor. A church cannot pursue a translation to a new model of worship ministry unless the pastor—the shepherd with appropriate authority—is truly leading the way.

## LEAD WITH A VISION

Some leaders are occasionally tempted to look at the booming numerical growth of some churches and then attempt to copy their techniques in the hope of having similar results at home. Only rarely does this work. Years ago many young pastors wanted to be another John MacArthur or Robert Thieme. Many pastors have wanted to be Billy Graham. Others wanted to be Chuck Smith. Still others attempted to be Charles Swindoll, and Howard Hendricks has innumerable clones.

Today I find myself somewhat appalled by the Willow Creek "wanna-be's" who are confident they can use some formula to replicate the success of the ministry in South Barrington, Illinois. Here is news: Bill Hybels is unique. So are MacArthur, Thieme, Smith, Swindoll, and Hendricks. And, of course, so are you. The effective ministry of one person is not a transferable entity. One can learn principles of ministry from these and other individuals, but one cannot *be* one of these, or any other.

God calls His servants to be those unique persons He has made them to be. Nothing is more important in this area than in seeking direction from the Spirit of God for one's own growth and leadership direction. Deciding to emphasize a new approach in ministry simply because it is reported to "work" in another church is a poor strategy. New ideas in ministry need to be addressed in terms of the present mix of factors that face a given congregation.

Not long ago the worship team in our church discussed the possibility of adding a Saturday night service that would focus primarily on high-school and college-age youth and young parents. As we began the discussion, we were excited about the potential advantages. We also knew of a number of churches that have done this with splendid results.

But the more we discussed the matter, the more we realized that this was not the right time for this move for our church. We simply concluded that God was not leading us on this path yet. We did not have the number of musicians and leaders that this would take to do well; to move ahead with our present resources would greatly strain the ministries we were doing well.

So was our decision a lack of vision? A lack of faith? A lack of belief that God could work in our midst? No. The more we looked at this, the more we realized that we had made the right decision for our situation.

## SHAPING A VISION

Shortly after our current pastor, Mike Wilde, came to our church, our elders commissioned an all-church survey. A church consultant did the evaluation. The survey results demonstrated that we had historic strengths as a congregation in the areas of teaching and worship. We were comparatively weak in evangelism. Our consultant helped us conclude that we needed to strengthen this area if we were to avoid congregational stagnation. But the means of growth for us was not to become a "seeker" congregation. We knew what we were—a twenty-five-year-old, well-established church family.

We also learned that the demographics of our congregation were no longer mirroring the community where God had placed us. Our ministry approaches were also not suitable for reaching the unsaved people in our neighborhood. What we needed was to develop an attitude in our members that went beyond "going to church." We needed the notion of "being the church."

Our pastor and elders developed a vision statement for our congregation. They did this in the context of much prayer and deliberation. The simple statement, now a filter for decisions and congregational goals, read, "To glorify God by making a community of disciples in East Clark County through ministries of the Word, worship, and witness."

We now have direction as a church. Everything we put energy into, from staffing to funding, should advance in some clear manner this purpose of making a "community of disciples." Evangelism now shares with Bible teaching and worship an important place in our church.

If God is glorified by our equipping believers to reach the lost, then we have a direction for the way we structure our ministries, including our worship services and our music program. We seek to achieve a balance in helping people grow in God's Word, encouraging people to worship God gladly, and giving the support needed for our people to be active in reaching the lost.

The implementation of the evangelism goal has impacted our planning for our Christmas season. In the past we have presented Christmas cantatas, but our Christmas program is now designed as an outreach event.

As the worship pastor I can now consider what role the choir, ensembles, soloists, instrumentalists, and dramatists will have, in the context of the church vision that includes reaching out to lost people. I have new questions to ask: Why would an unbeliever in my neighborhood want to come to this event? What music or storytelling approach will they likely respond to the best? Will a flier attract them? Would a personal invitation be more effective? I even ask questions about the most appropriate use of sound as I plan the worship and outreach goals.

The idea of a clear church vision can help to direct the congregation in the choices they may make concerning the tone and atmosphere of the worship services. A church that is near a retirement village may be called of God to minister to mature people who have a long history of church ties. This awareness may call for a more formal type of service, with use of the hymnal and even using the King James Version for Scripture reading.

Our church is located in a community of starter homes and young families. We want to encourage our thirty-somethings to bring their unchurched neighbors with them. Our leaders are now committed to operating in a way that communicates that the ministry of the gospel is more important than holding on to traditions of the past. We have had to help our older members understand why our church cannot stay the same. We need to help them connect their burden for their children and grandchildren to the ministry goals of the church. Similarly we need to help our younger people understand the tremendous scope of change our seniors have endured in their lifetimes and to be sensitive not to push them in areas that are not demanded by our vision.

## TEACH AS YOU LEAD

Probably no lasting change happens in our churches apart from effective pastoral leadership. Also it is unlikely that effective leadership will happen apart from good teaching. There is a place for modeling God's Word clearly and a place for teaching it effectively. The teaching and preaching ministry of the Word of God should be a part of the pastor's work in worship leadership.

First, the pastor should begin to think of his preaching as itself an act of worship. By the way he speaks of God, in the values he communicates concerning the Lord, in the manner in which he elevates the living Christ— the pastor is modeling the attitudes of true worship. Moreover, when he preaches, it should be in a personal sense of dependence on God's Spirit at work in him for the good of the people. The sermon is not something done *after* the people worship; the sermon itself is *an act of worship on the part of the minister.*[1]

Second, the pastor who wishes to lead the church in the worship of God should plan to preach often on the subject of worship. He should focus from time to time on the diversity of worship patterns found in the Bible. Too often we find that certain clusters of people in a church have their own familiar worship turf issues; rarely does a congregation have a full, biblical input on the wonder of our worship of God.

Here is an overview of some significant passages that represent the diversity of worship themes in the Bible. The effective worshiping pastor will be even more effective in leading the church in worship as he brings sermon attention to these diverse texts in his congregation.

*Genesis 1* is a worship passage for it puts the attention of all creation squarely on God the Creator. The words "In the beginning God" inform a worshiper's view of the Bible. He exists from all eternity. Everything exists by Him and for Him. Nothing finds its purpose apart from Him. All beauty comes from Him. Everything that is good is sourced in Him. Nothing originated with Satan; he merely perverts for evil purposes what God has pronounced good. We as people are God's highest creation, with the noble calling of responding to Him in gratitude, obedience, service, and love.

*Exodus 15* is the first psalm recorded in the Bible (see chapter 7, "The Beauty of Praise"). Here Moses modeled an exuberant form of worship that focused on God's having delivered the people of Israel from their Egyptian oppressors. This Old Testament salvation story prefigures our redemption in Christ. This was the Old Testament salvation event to which

Jewish believers looked back, much as we Christians look back to Jesus' victory on the cross. Moses' joyful exuberance expressed here is a model of the godly response of the saved to our Savior.

*Psalm 34* emphasizes public worship: "Oh, magnify the LORD with me, and let us exalt His name together" (34:3). Public worship is directed not only toward God; it also benefits other believers. As one person boasts in the Lord, others become transformed and they too rejoice in Him.

*Psalms 27, 84,* and *Matthew 22* present the intimate aspects and priority of worship. Worshiping God is the "one thing" to seek (Ps. 27:4). Being a believer rightly involves crying out "for the living God" (84:2). Food for the soul is found in worshiping God intimately and passionately. To love God with one's entire being (Matt. 22:37) is the truest and simplest understanding of genuine worship—given by Jesus Himself.

*Psalms 145–150* (the *hallēl* psalms) connect the heart of vocal worship—praise—to singing. In the Bible the reason believers sing is always to exalt the greatness of God. Singing is not limited to musicians; it is for the godly, the upright, the righteous, the saints. Young and old alike are called to sing "a new song" (149:1) because God continually refreshes us in new ways. We sing not because we are musical, but because it is a beautiful way to praise Him (149:4). We include instruments of artisanship of various kinds of sounds (150:3–5) to respond to a multiresplendent God. God is to be praised musically through vocal singing and accompaniment from every available musical instrument (see chapter 13, "What about the Hymns?").

*Nehemiah 7–12* details the priority given to worship in God's eyes. The first order of the day, once the walls were built, was to appoint worship leaders. Physical worship responses are modeled here, including standing, shouting "Amen," and bowing down. An appropriate connection is made here between celebrating God and the place of food and feasting. Also fasting, mourning, and public confession were included in the midst of an otherwise celebrative event. Time limits hardly existed as the various worship activities continued on for hours at a time. Percussion, brass, and stringed instruments were played, and men's, women's, and children's choirs sang. (Also see the emphasis on musical worship and worship leadership in numerous passages in 1 and 2 Chronicles.)

*Isaiah 1, 29,* and *58* describe the kinds of worship services God detests. God takes no pleasure in meaningless ritual. He wants hearts to be aflame, justice pursued, mercy poured out, and salvation received. Those who "worship" with their lips but not their hearts receive a just and fierce condemnation. There is a kind of fasting that God appreciates, but He abhors false worship.

*Isaiah 6* is a powerful look at personal worship before the throne of God in the midst of God's angels (see chapter 5, "The God We Worship"). Of course, this setting is not reproducible! However, being awestruck by the indescribable holiness of God and having an overwhelming sense of being forgiven—a sense that fuels a life of willing service—is presented here more powerfully than possibly in any other Scripture passage.

*Acts 2* emphasizes believers' devotion to Scripture, fellowship, breaking of bread, and prayer among believers (2:42). These functions enabled believers to experience the awe of God among them. The power of God working in the midst of people who are meeting each other's needs in tangible ways and praising God together fueled effective evangelism (2:43–47).

*Romans 12 and Galatians 5* present a lifestyle of worship that transforms one's entire being. Worship is far more than singing songs on Sunday. It is a life of sacrificing our wills to God's, of seeking to be transformed by the truth of God's Word, of living daily by grace through faith, and of manifesting a life of love toward others (Rom. 12:1–21). Ultimately a life of worship can be viewed as living by the power of the Holy Spirit—keeping in step with Him and manifesting His traits (Gal. 5:16–25).

*Ephesians 5:19* and *Colossians 3:16* emphasize the important role of musical worship in the life of the church. Music is presented as one of the means by which "the word of Christ [may] dwell in you richly." The inclusion of a wide variety of musical expressions is presented as a chief way to give thanks to God through Christ. Of interest is the fact that the sentence in Ephesians 5:19 that refers to styles of music precedes the section on submitting "to one another out of reverence for Christ" (5:21, NIV).

*Revelation 4–5* presents reverent heavenly worship that focuses on the holiness of the Father and the worthiness of the Son. These heavenly previews give us focal points for the subject of our worship, namely, God the Father and Jesus our Redeemer, and they emphasize that our worship of God will endure into eternity.

*Revelation 19* presents a different kind of heavenly worship experience. Here the great multitude is unrestrained in its thunderous shouting of "Hallelujah" for God's acts of salvation over His enemies (19:1, 3, 4, 6). Isaiah 12:6 also gives a picture from the earthly perspective of unrestrained celebration for the day when God will establish His kingdom on earth: "Shout aloud and sing for joy . . . for great is the Holy One of Israel among you" (NIV).

These passages do not cover all the aspects of worship emphasized in Scripture, but they serve as a broad foundation for teaching believers what God's Word says about the role of worship. Any church that understands and accepts these emphases of worship will be diverse in expression, tolerant of variety, and fervent in its desire to worship God passionately.

If people in one's congregation truly grasp Nehemiah 7–12, Ephesians 5, and Colossians 3, can they really continue to argue that musical worship is not important?

If they accept Exodus, the Psalms, and Revelation as God's Word, can anyone persist with a point of view that sees exuberant celebration of God as worldly or inappropriate for public worship?

If they understand the holiness of God and His condemnation of false pretenses of worship as presented in Isaiah 1, 29, and 58, can they help being compelled to take the worship of God seriously and avoid stooping to mindless repetition or meaningless ritual?

If believers are brought face to face with the psalmist's passion for deep intimacy with God and take to heart Jesus' command to pursue a love relationship with Him, can a community of believers continue in apathy?

If a church grasps these aspects of worship and takes to heart the priority of public gathering to praise, sing, and be transformed by God's Word, can the unbelieving community continue to be unaffected? How important, then, that pastors teach their congregations what the Bible says about worship.

Other issues could also be addressed by the pastor or in various other arenas in a church from time to time. It is important to attempt to correct unfortunate teaching influences that your church may have inherited from divisive, legalistic, or underinformed "authorities." Those who come to your church from an experience-focused background need to receive some serious grounding on what it means to walk with God and grow in truth. Those who pride themselves on being "mature" and are condescending toward "lower" art forms and less familiar forms of worship expression need to be challenged to live a life of love and acceptance.

Sponsoring a worship conference is a wonderful thing for churches to plan together. Include a choir festival, a praise band, or a series of biblical worship teachings. Offer a course on worship as an adult Sunday school elective. Encourage small groups to pursue brief studies on worship with a particular focus. Prioritize the concept of worshiping God in everything your church does. Do not allow worship to be relegated to some inferior rung of church purpose. And don't stop at simply teaching concepts of worship; instead, strive to model them for your church, assuming that more will be caught than taught.

## LEAD WITH LOVE AND PATIENCE

Transition often breeds resistance. Characteristics such as love, patience, kindness, and gentleness are so important in leading other people through change—especially if the idea of change did not necessarily originate with them. It has been helpful for me to remember to *guide* rather than *drive* people.

A wise pastor or worship leader will honor people by recognizing their preferences and the power of tradition. People hold to their traditions because somewhere along the way these traditions have gotten hold of them. God has touched their hearts and lives in the past through a particular vehicle, and the impact has continued to the present. To change a church's direction does not mean we are making those meaningful vehicles invalid. It just means we are pursuing different goals through different means in the present. The hope we have is that these new forms will have a similar impact—and might later become the focus of someone else's tradition-buster campaign! I have seen colleagues who model a respectful, worshiping heart get much further with the cantankerous than I have by my debating, arguing, or trying to score theological points. In times of tension, especially, it is important to reveal a worshiper's heart. One who challenges people to expand their understanding of worship while appearing not to be living by the Spirit could be mistaken for a heretic. When stretching people on issues related to worship, it is crucial to express your personal joy in worshiping the Lord. The genuineness of a worshiper's heart in action can move more mightily than words alone.

Part of loving a congregation lies in knowing when to deal with an individual who is causing dissension in the church. Probably few subjects in the church today raise as many passions and stubbornness as the issue of worship. Pastors and elders must love the church enough to deal appropriately with dissension among members. Well-intentioned people often need to be listened to, given consideration, and loved. The unity of the church as a reflection of the unity of the Godhead is far more important to protect than the overly zealous convictions of individuals who use dangerous tactics to divide a congregation over worship-style issues.

Change is always difficult to accept. Good leaders give people time to understand and accept the changes being made before they are completely implemented. It helps to explain *why* this particular change is beneficial to the church at large (or to particular people groups within the church or community), and how this will affect them personally. An effective transition process for something as significant as adding a new service, changing service times, or changing worship styles may take six months to three years of focused attention.

One possible schedule for effective change could look like this:
- For two to six months confirm the Lord's leading by seeking to arrive at unity among the staff, the lay worship leaders, elders, and deacons.
- Spend an additional three to nine months gaining congregational support through teaching and preaching presentations, dialogue, responding to initial concerns, planning and strategizing with affected ministries and individuals, and praying for transition.
- This might be followed by six to twelve weeks from the initial announcement of confirmation until the actual date for launching the new event. It is helpful to communicate often in word and writing, and not to assume that people "got it the first time." It is crucial to ask the entire church, as well as particular groups, to pray specifically for God's leading and direction through the transition. If God can direct the leaders, He can also persuade the followers.

- During the first six weeks of implementation listen to people's comments and concerns and be willing to adjust and adapt, as necessary, to problems that arise.
- During the first six months of implementation monitor the situation and evaluate ways to improve.

We have used a similar approach to what is described above to move from one service to two, from two services separated by Sunday school to two "tandem" services, and from two identical services to two different styles of services. I have found that by following these steps we gained greater unity. Wherever we slacked, divisiveness tended to rear its head. If a move or transition was sensed by the people and the church leaders to be God's prompting and leading, it will not be regarded as an "experiment." Moving forward will not be a trial; it will be an act of faith and obedience.

This is similar to a church plant or a new ministry launch—only the foolish move ahead in the flesh. Instead, churches should move forward boldly in vision as the Spirit of God leads them. Be sensitive to the people as they acclimate to the new idea. If you are uncertain about God's leading, then by all means, *wait* for His timing. Making this move without the Holy Spirit preparing the way can be very destructive to a congregation. A false start may also deter the ability to make a true start for many years. And then the naysayers will be right when they accuse the leaders of not listening to God's will.

## LEAD BY BUILDING BRIDGES

It is always a good practice to lead by building bridges, but it is particularly necessary for those churches with people whose ages span from the nursery to the nursing home. When retirees see teenagers as "grandchildren," they do not think of them as "punks" anymore. We have seen God break down barriers during testimony-sharing times in services where people's ages have spanned many years. When "Gramps" sees God break through to the heart of a fifteen-year-old, suddenly the spiked hair does not look so bad anymore.

Our pastor has encouraged our senior saints to share testimonies at hymn-sing "favorites" nights about why a song is so meaningful to them.

Now younger people to whom the song previously meant nothing are drawn to consider the words. One advantage of staying in a church a few years is to see teens who once said they hated hymns later raise their hands and request favorites, and then tell why a particular hymn is their favorite. Anything that can be done to help younger people understand why we do what we do can encourage them to accept the idea. If we don't have a good answer as to why we are doing a certain thing, they actually have good reason to question it.

We have had good success over the years in bringing youth "highlight" services out of the youth building and into the main auditorium as part of a regular evening service. They bring their alternative music into the "sanctuary" and put together their slide shows to their heavy music, and it builds bridges to the congregation. In some services we've had, anyone could tell the music was initially pressing some borders. Yet thirty minutes later there was not a dry eye in the house because a young person just rededicated his life to the Lord and told how God got hold of him. These are priceless moments when bridges are built and credibility covers the chasm.

*Eighteen*

※

# How to Lead in Transition—Musical Issues

WHENEVER A DISCUSSION on contemporary worship or worship styles arises, the focus of conversation tends immediately to shift toward issues of music. I (Craig) hope that by saving the musical issues for last, some consideration has been given to the other significant issues relating to a worship service. A worship service can honor God if it faithfully presents truths about Him, is led in a manner that is spiritually sensitive to the moment, and strives to exalt Christ and point people to Him. A service can be considered current and effective in its appeal to people if the flow is logical and uplifting, the style is appropriate to the congregation, the facilities are clean and well maintained, the platform people are well prepared and sensitive to God's Spirit, and the sermon expounds the Word of God and relates it to people's lives. In all, a service that is empowered by the Holy Spirit, that focuses on the character of God, and that encourages personal refreshment in Christ will impact lives and promote true worship.

Issues of music should be discussed in this context. Music should be understood as a tool to help further the worshipers' fellowship with God. Ideally a worship service includes elements of "conversation" going both directions. In any loving human relationship both parties make opportunities to listen and to speak, and in healthy dialogue one interacts with communication from the other person. Applied to a worship service, this means our response to God (in attitude, heart, words, and actions) should be affected by the revelation we hear from God in His Word. "Worship" is our response of heart and mind to God who has revealed Himself. As Gordon Borror puts it, this is a dialogue of "revelation and response."

Rather than thinking of the music in church services as being merely preliminary to or preparatory for the "main event" of preaching, we should think of the music as a means of worship dialogue. Music can teach truths from God's Word, and it can provide opportunity for desirable responses (for example, change of heart, confession, increased love, gratitude, renewed commitment to action).

Teaching need not be limited to the sermons, and worshipful responses need not be confined to the singing time. We should stop calling the congregational singing time "the worship," and especially stop calling a sequence of songs a "worship package" or a "worship set."

Worship transcends singing!

Singing, in and of itself, may or may not serve the specific role of worship. Ideally the entire worship service should be a mix of elements that communicate truths about God (teaching), in which unbelievers are presented with truths of the gospel (witness), and believers are encouraged to grow in grace and knowledge of God (edification), and in their love and reverence for God (worship). As a communication vehicle, music can play a role in each of these areas.

Worship can be offered to God through music as well as through other means. And music can encourage worship, edification, and witness.

From one direction in the dialogue of worship (revelation), music can serve as an instrument to communicate truths *from* God's Word *through* musicians *to* the hearts of the people. This can occur through lyrics sung by vocal soloists, ensembles, choirs, or worship team performances in which the words are presented to the congregation for people to hear and take to heart. This can also be accomplished by instrumental music that accompanies and enhances Scripture readings, visual images of video, mime, banners, paintings, and so forth, or by the playing of familiar melodies that bring meaningful lyrics to mind. In any of these roles music can help present God's Word to people, thus serving the same purposes as preaching and teaching.

The goal of communicating God's truth is the same; however, the media form is music (or other art) rather than just monologue prose. Probably the most powerful means of communicating biblical truth to people musically is by involving them in the process. This is why the congregation is the most important choir or singing group! Teaching a biblical truth by having the congregation sing it is a most effective route to helping people "own" that truth. This is a strong case for seeking to increase the appetite for and the amount of congregational singing in your services. Also it should spur us to raise the proportion of teaching that we try to accomplish through congregational singing. In short, if a pastor wants to be more effective at helping his congregation own scriptural truth, he might be wise to encourage the congregation (and worship leader) to sing more!

From the opposite direction in the dialogue of worship (response), music can serve as a means by which believers respond to the revelation they have received. In a public service, worship is a response that begins in the heart of the worshiper and is offered to the heart of God. This can take a variety of forms, including tears of conviction, songs of joy, determination to change, feelings of intimacy, giving of finances, commitment to serve, and words of praise.

Think of revelation as extending downward from God to us, and of our heart and vocal participation as extending vertically upward. In edification, music can be a means by which we hear God's Word and then internalize it by singing it back to Him. In worship, believers are offering their heart response to God. As a witness, music can be performed for the benefit of unbelievers to receive truths about God. Also believers can speak to one another in musical edification (horizontal arrow on the left) and to unbelievers in musical evangelism (horizontal arrow on the right).

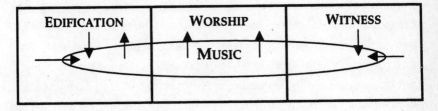

Music is a God-designed, effective means by which worship responses can be expressed in the assembly. When music is composed, performed, and received as an offering to the Lord, God is glorified. If the musical styles or approaches are divorced from the comfort zone or worship language through which your congregation can respond, then your musical worship is not contemporary to your church and probably ought not be used. A worship leader needs to determine whether it is worth the effort it takes to lead a congregation in learning or expanding into an unfamiliar musical genre or worship language. The answer might be yes, when it is an art form worth rising to (for example, Handel's *The Messiah*), a tradition worth continuing (for example, a heritage of great hymns), a current "sound" worth exploring (newly published music), or a neglected biblical approach worth reclaiming (intercessory prayer or kneeling). Whatever is added should initially be pursued sparingly, yet consistently, and increased to the degree that your people become fluent in it and accept it.

New styles of music might stretch all of a church's resources, including the congregation, musicians, and finances. Adding new styles of music will probably necessitate expanding preparation time, recruitment and training of new musicians, new funding, and perhaps new services.

## STRETCHING, GROWING, AND RECRUITING MUSICIANS

Like many pianists, I was trained exclusively in classical music throughout my formative years. By the time I graduated from high school I had given several piano classical recitals, won prize money in a handful of competitions, completed the highest level of syllabus examinations, performed in two of Oregon's three performing arts centers, and won a piano scholarship to the music school of a private liberal arts college. I mention this only to point out a contrast. At that time I could perform advanced pieces by Chopin, Brahms, and Beethoven from memory but I didn't know how to play or figure out three-chord songs like "Seek Ye First," "Amazing Grace," or, to my family's embarrassment on one occasion, "Happy Birthday"! I did not know how to follow a vocalist as an accompanist, lead a congregation in hymn singing, modulate between two songs in different keys, sight-read well enough to play for choir, or improvise in any way for "fill" music. In short, after ten years of serious piano study I was well on my way to being a classical music major and virtually unprepared to contribute to church worship music except in artistic performance.

During my four years of college piano study I continued training as a performance artist, usually practicing classical music more than four hours a day. Ironically, it was during this time that I began to develop a new set of skills independently of my classical teacher. I began to add to my classical music theory some jazz training, some self-study "pop" music, a bit of imitation of other versatile pianists, a tour with a Christian rock band for a summer in Europe, and a new hobby of writing songs in a variety of pop styles. In college I began to pursue singing, more formal composing and arranging, and accompanying and choral directing. While at seminary, I pursued and honed these skills to a greater degree while seeking to incorporate them specifically into church worship and ministry settings.

While these collegiate ventures were great, they were also largely on my own. Having come out the other side, I can look back and wonder what it might have been like had things been different. I had no worship leader to work with me as I was growing up. My classical pursuits were entirely "secular," except for those occasions when I played classical pieces for offertories at church. There was no model of music-for-ministry integration nor a built-in training opportunity for me to learn to play for youth groups, children's choirs, or church bands along the way. I was essentially on my own as a musician, pursuing technique from largely non-Christian sources on how to grow as a versatile musician.

My experience in working with church musicians confirms this pattern. Many pianists come with some amount of classical soloist background, with little experience in accompanying or ensemble playing. They tend to have great blank stares when asked to play anything that is not written in the music. By contrast, most guitarists, bass players, and drummers have come from the "street" school, neither knowing how to read music (notes or time), nor understanding the music theory structure behind the chord patterns or rhythm they have memorized. A typical "church pianist" has three or four keys in which he or she is comfortable playing, usually all flat keys in addition to C. Meanwhile typical youth group guitarists play in only three or four keys, all sharp keys in addition to C. A worship leader who tries to pull together these musicians from such diverse backgrounds and limitations has quite a challenge.

Among the best contributions a worship leader can make in the ministry of his church is to invest in teachable musicians. Even if progress seems to be a stagnant dream and musician resources are thin, it is worth the effort to build now for your church's future. As I write, we have just finished a week of vacation Bible school for children ages four through eleven. For the third year in a row I used this as an opportunity to train young, budding musicians. The ages of our players (guitars, bass, drums) ranged from twelve to eighteen. It was a great time of growth for each of them.

For years I prayed that God would send us additional musicians. I have a friend who was called to a church the same size as mine who basically inherited an all-star band of experienced musicians. I was able to play with them once, and, since then, I have had to confess my envy more than once. I have prayed specifically for God to send us a skilled drummer, a saxophone player, guitarists, and bass players, in addition to more versatile keyboardists. But rather than God answering those prayers, He has given us remarkable opportunities to help young musicians grow "in house," and in many cases to send them off to serve in other churches.

We have a sister church whose primary music leadership grew up through our ranks. We now have more guitarists than I can schedule, most of them under twenty-five years old. Our weekly drummer is sixteen, and he gets better every week. I have been investing in my adult keyboardists (who fit the previous descriptions) for many years. They can now play modern "praise" music somewhat comfortably, accompany our choir and ensembles, play basic synthesizer/keyboard parts, double as (keyboard) bass players once in a while, and occasionally even modulate. In addition, I have had the opportunity to teach keyboard lessons for a few years to two of their sons, who are now contributing to our music ministry regularly. I have learned the value of investing in the training of the teachable and of staying in one place long enough to begin to harvest the fruit of their gains.

As each musician tends to be either a "note-reader" who has taken music lessons or a "feel" player who has learned on his own, it is helpful for the worship leader to know how the different musicians think about and approach music. Each has strengths that can be used and limitations that can be gently nudged. In general, you probably want to stretch your "legitimate" players rhythmically and stylistically, and expand the musical knowledge, available keys, and extent of playable chords of the self-taught musicians.

We have found that rotating the musicians—each playing once or twice a month—keeps people fresh and eager, and keeps people on the music team for years without reaching "burnout." For special events it can be a great boost to hire highly capable musicians to play parts that the regulars are not capable of doing well. This can inspire them to move to the next level in their abilities and to appreciate the goal toward which you are attempting to develop them. The best tool for recruiting musicians tends to be great music. Musicians like to belong to a group in which they can use their skills and gifts. Musicians will draw musicians.

New styles of music demand new approaches to singing, different harmonies, different rhythmic "feels" on instruments, and generally a different "sound" or "mix." To lead an ensemble of vocalists and instrumentalists, the music leader must be familiar with how to achieve desired sounds and an appropriate "mix." This demands a willingness to listen intently with "new ears," and to adapt to new approaches. As new musical styles are introduced, chordal patterns and harmonic sounds become dated. It takes intentional effort to stay fresh.

If a worship leader desires to stretch his or her musical bounds, he can do so by listening to a wide variety of music, including newly produced worship songs. Listening to secular radio can help a player keep abreast of style changes, new uses of instruments, and the radio "mix" that listeners' ears are becoming accustomed to. We can be sure that today's Christian high schoolers as well as last month's new adult converts have not been listening to the church music of ten to twenty years ago. If they are part of the community of worshipers whom we desire to respond to God in our services, we want to be sure that at least part of our musical spectrum includes them.

In the last couple of years I have had to renege on promises to myself regarding stylistic lines that I was not willing to cross. Being a trained musician from the Northwest meant I felt I could never stoop to worshiping God by using "country" music. Well, our congregation has now embraced "God Is Good All the Time" as one of its favorite songs. Similarly I had long thought that "alternative" music was on the fringe and was too rough and harsh for church use. Now it is clear that alternative music is becoming mainstream, particularly among the under-twenty-five crowd, and that guitar and drum-based music has virtually reduced acoustic piano to a secondary role. As I stretch my ears, I am increasingly finding treasures from sources that I previously thought were out of bounds. It can be tempting to fight these kinds of sweeping changes while clinging to comfort zones and personal taste preferences. However, I am finding it both wise and rewarding to use these changing times as an opportunity for me to continue to grow and stretch, and even to see my personal tastes and worship languages expand significantly.

## CONTRASTING SERVICES NEED NOT BE DIVISIVE

Perhaps you have heard the refrain, "If we have two different kinds of services, we'll split the church." Perhaps you have even said it yourself. I used to believe that, but not anymore. If there is a concern that by offering two services you will then create "two churches," this concern probably reveals that you already have "two churches" present—just within the *same* service. If there is obvious tension in your congregation over worship style, it is likely an indication that people's preferences are not being honored sufficiently and people are struggling to respond to the Lord in ways they find comfortable. In this case having somewhat different services could potentially be a *unifying* move.

Imagine a person who has felt that his or her comfort zones have been assaulted week after week on Sunday mornings. Now if there is a service that is more conducive to his or her worship background and personality, that person will probably be more supportive of the church and less anxious about the services. The higher the percentage of your people who feel, "This is my church," the less tension will be manifest and the more energy will be available for worship. For better or worse, this area of worship style is one of the chief determinants of people taking ownership of their church. If people love your service, they will be freed to respond to God and eager to invite others to do the same.

For years we pursued an effective "one-size-fits-all" approach to worship at our church. Our two services were identical and we were quite committed to the "blended" approach of mixing traditional and newer worship elements in a balanced way.[1] Eventually, though, we progressed to a crisis where our services could stretch no further without snapping. We had to ask legitimate questions, such as these: How much ground can one service cover? How far can we stretch our senior saints with new sounds and styles before the service ceases to be worshipful for them? How long will our ministry be effective to the younger third of our church if we do not continue to utilize newer music styles? How much variety can we offer in one service to meet everyone's stylistic preferences before our worship service is reduced to a variety show? In our attempts to make sure there was "something for everyone," we soon had something for everyone—to dislike!

Churches that are ministering to multigenerational congregations in one service or in identical services eventually have to make one of three compromising decisions on worship style issues:

- "Aim for the middle" and minimize the traditional and progressive extremes. Musically this might be represented by a Peterson-Gaither-early Maranatha combination.
- Focus on either the traditional or progressive aspects to the minimizing of the other. This may please the older or younger set, but definitely not both. Many stagnant churches have stuck to traditional forms, and many young booming churches have only contemporary services. But both approaches deny the church an opportunity to benefit from strengths of the opposite approach.
- Try to include a variety of music forms, realizing though that this may not please very many people. If you take this approach, have a contemporary celebration one week, a gospel-sing service another week, and a hymns focus the third week. Over time your congregation may come to appreciate the variety.

Each of these options becomes increasingly less promising as time moves forward because of two realities: What is traditional changes slowly (those who love hymns move more slowly in their taste changes than others do), and what is new changes rapidly and constantly. What was traditional a generation ago differs from what is considered traditional today, but the gap between the two is not nearly so marked as the changes from what was considered contemporary in the 1980s and what is considered contemporary today. This means that annually the gap between traditional and progressive styles gets wider, and the balancing act becomes increasingly difficult. Twenty years ago it was probably somewhat easy to maintain unity in a service that still introduced new elements. Ten years ago this had become difficult to sustain musically. Now the gulf is so wide, new music styles are being introduced so frequently, and the speed of change has come so fast, that trying to keep pace with the new and to maintain the old has become a staggering challenge, particularly for one service.

## EFFECTIVELY ADDING A NEW SERVICE

The idea that contrasting services are divisive probably results most often from one of two actions: (1) Moving too quickly. A sign that the leaders are moving too quickly is when people begin to react against the stark changes rather than embrace gradual newness. (2) Pitting one service against the other. This can reveal itself when a spirit of superiority is communicated, where one service is said to be "alive" (versus "dead") or one is seen as "compromising" where the other is thought to be "keeping the faith." If the speed of change is paced sensitively to the congregation, and if both services are equally celebrated for their strengths, then two contrasting services ought not split the church.

If your services are quite traditional in format, it might be good to consider moving one to a more blended approach by adding newer music, different instrumentation, and less formal styling. If you are offering two "blended" services, consider stretching one slightly toward the traditional direction, and stretching the other slightly toward the new and progressive, while maintaining significant continuity between them. Over time, the amount of distinction between the services can be increased as your congregation accepts and appreciates the changes.

If you are considering expanding from one service or from two identical services, here are some suggestions to consider.

- Strive to introduce new elements gradually into your existing format. Perhaps this means more singing, or introducing a physical expression of worship, or adding drums. Go slowly enough to gain credibility but steadily enough to make progress.

- Offer contrasting services *occasionally* (once a month or once a quarter) with strong communication in advance to prepare your people for the changes. Give cautious people the assurance that the following week will be "back to normal." Give the progressive element the assurance that this was one step and more will follow.

- Offer two contrasting services. Either add a new service or change one of them. Keep one service the same and at the same time slot in order to maintain continuity. In the church I serve we found it an advantage to continue one blended service where we could relax the speed of change and actually celebrate much of our worship heritage. And in the new service we pursued the contemporary approach with a strategic plan to accelerate our speed of change.

- Offer multiple services with clearly different identities and different target attendees. This can be dangerous as it can feed the "churches within a church" syndrome that you may not desire. On the other hand, this gives you opportunity to target services for particular needs. A successful church in California has targeted services (all significantly different) for builders, boomers, and busters. Other churches are using Saturday nights as a new service opportunity to reach people who would not normally attend on Sunday morning. In particular, many churches are finding that Saturday night services are in demand by high-school students, college-age people, and younger singles because they like to stay out late and sleep in, and by young families because of the difficulties associated with getting young children ready on Sunday mornings.

The following are tips you might consider if your church desires to pursue changing to contrasting services or adding a new distinctive service.

- Skip a traditional service. Offer the distinctions of contemporary and blended (rather than traditional) unless your church is in a rural, historic, or liturgical setting, or your church draws heavily from retirement-age people or people from "high-church" backgrounds. Consider creatively naming your services to avoid the traditional/contemporary monikers.

- Deliver what you promote. Do not call it contemporary if your younger people tell you it really is not. On the other hand, ask yourself, To whom is it contemporary? Recognize the difficulty in pleasing everyone, particularly in defining the word "contemporary." A friend of mine recently described contemporary music as "changing every three weeks." You might poll youth, college, young singles, and young married couples to find out what range of current music style matches their interests.

- Champion both services. Pursue each service with excellence and without favoritism. Ideally the people who attend each service should think that one is your favorite.

- Pursue an overlap between your services rather than a gulf. Significant overlap allows people to vacillate between services and still feel this is their church. Too wide a gulf between service options can contribute to the establishment of a divided congregation.

- Make the differences clear. Have enough distinction between the services to give people a real choice. Distinctions can be in areas of song choices, musical style, instrumentation, volume levels, amount of music, degree of formality, lighting level, opportunity for congregational interaction, use of video or drama, and dress.

- Stay fresh. Recognize that a contemporary service must continue to develop and change, or it will soon cease to be progressive and lose its reason for being.

- Do not wait too long. Everything will never be perfectly in place. Start when God's leading seems clear and trust Him to grow your resources and your congregation as you seek Him. Ask your people for grace and patience as you transition together.

- Do wait long enough. Wait for a strong grass-roots desire for change. Trial services can be helpful here to let people see what the future could look like. Follow these up with much discussion with and preparation of your people.

- Coordinate your plans with other ministries in the church. Work closely with Sunday school leaders (and other affected ministry leaders), because the times when the classes meet will determine which service people attend.
- Listen intently. Pursue feedback, particularly regarding your pace of change. Listen to people of all ages. (In Israel there was wisdom in not allowing Levites to lead in musical worship for the nation until they were thirty.) Consider the opinions of mature adults.
- Keep things positive. Keep criticism from going underground. Do offer a variety of appropriate opportunities for people to express concerns, whether in writing, in appointments or phone calls with leadership personnel, or in smaller gatherings. When publicly seeking feedback (in town hall or business meetings), make it a ground rule that views be stated "positively." Do not allow a critical spirit to take over. Hear from many voices to balance out the few who might choose to dominate the meetings.
- Count the cost and consider the gain. You may lose some people, but you will probably gain others. Things will change. Don't take this lightly and don't be surprised by it.
- Secure the necessary resources. You may need to rent or buy new equipment, and/or you may need to hire certain musicians, at least temporarily.
- Seek the Lord. Do not add a service simply because you read about it in a book. Be sure the Lord is leading and preparing the church leaders and the congregation for this kind of move. If God is leading and you are following obediently, His blessing will be evident.

## FUNDING FOR CONTEMPORARY WORSHIP

Some churches have determined to hire a music and worship pastor as the second staff position after the senior pastor, because of the importance of Sunday morning worship. It is helpful for the senior pastor to be freed to focus on preaching, teaching, casting a vision, counseling, and other ministerial roles, and to let an associate do the music and worship programming and administration. Do not hire a great musician and expect him to be a pastor, any more than you would hire a pastor and expect him to be a musician. Hire or invest in the training of someone dually gifted in directing people's attention toward God and working with and inspiring other musicians.

In past decades it was considered standard for a church to purchase an organ and a piano. Larger churches might purchase a pipe organ and a grand piano. In today's dollars, prices might range between $10,000 and $250,000 for an organ, and between $5,000 and $40,000 for a piano, depending on the size of the church and the quality and newness of the instruments. Some churches today find it difficult to fund more contemporary instruments, even when they are typically far more affordable than a piano and organ. If the piano and organ purchased by the church are to be used primarily in one service, it makes sense to have the church purchase quality keyboard(s), drums, mixer, amplifiers, speakers, monitors, microphones, and other needed sound equipment to make everything work effectively for the other service. Guitars and basses tend to be more player-specific, like trumpets or flutes, and are cared for by the player, who will carry their portable instruments back and forth from home to church. But the larger (difficult to transport) instruments and the equipment used by everyone should be budgeted for and funded by the church.

For churches planning to purchase some of this equipment, it is wise to obtain the services of an audio consultant. Even if your expenditures need to be spread out over a series of years, a good consultant can help you plan what you need at various stages of growth. Once you have a plan marked out and have prioritized your purchases, you can prepare budgets or special giving campaigns. Sometimes approaching donors for one-of-a-kind special items can be an effective way of securing what is needed and bypassing budgeting issues. If you are short on money, someone knowledgeable can do research on new equipment (via the Internet and music-equipment magazines) and then pursue the used market (via newspaper ads, the Internet, word of mouth, equipment-rental places, local music stores) for those same items.

Also hire an acoustical engineer at the earliest stages of any building program where acoustics may be a factor. Hire an architect who is willing to work hand in hand with an acoustician and to adjust aesthetic design for acoustical reasons. Churches have built multimillion-dollar facilities and then had to turn around and pay exorbitant fees to attempt too late to have their building "fixed" so that their worship center is both intelligible for speech and conducive to musical worship.

In addition to money for equipment and personnel, monies will need to be budgeted to fund ongoing ministries. The present going rate on choral anthems is between $1.25 and $1.75 per anthem per copy. So if a choir of twenty-five singers purchases fifteen new songs to add to their repertoire each season, this will total about five hundred dollars. If the choir includes one or two seasonal cantatas with accompaniment tracks and rehearsal tapes, you can immediately double this amount. Children's choirs and special-event programs will require funding as well. CCLI licensing needs funding each year. New songbooks for worship musicians, music for accompanists, soloists, and ensembles need to be purchased from time to time. Rehearsal rooms will need a keyboard and some kind of basic sound system. Any arranging or in-house production or recording of music may be very expensive, involving high-powered computers, mixers, monitors, and an extensive assortment of specialized music equipment. Pursuing computerized data/video projection (highly recommended!) requires a good amount of money. Drama materials are another item to budget. Sending your worship leader and other key musicians or sound technicians to training seminars or conferences can be wise annual investments.

A rule of thumb used for the last couple of decades in churches with effective music/worship programs is to designate at least 10 percent of the church's ministry budget (not counting salaries, rent, or mortgage, and similar items) for music and worship. Most people who visit a Sunday service will decide after one or two visits whether to come back. So if you want effective ministry in the lives of people, fund your weekly worship service. Unfortunately a quality ministry of music costs money. But it can more than "pay its way" in meaningful ministry.

# *Nineteen*

# Extending the Life of Hymns

## THE ROLE OF HYMNS

MANY CONGREGATIONS WRONGLY ASSUME that contemporary music excludes hymns. There are valid reasons for this common way of thinking. First, the wording of so many hymns involves out-of-style poetry and includes archaic words and phrasing. Even great biblical concepts stated in odd ways can be difficult for many to latch on to and to embrace. Second, the rhythmic structure of most hymnal songs is limited. Typical hymns composed mainly of quarter notes and eighth notes in straight beats lack the creativity and variety of much of today's modern and syncopated rhythm patterns. Third, the harmonic vocabulary of most hymns sounds dated to modern ears and the constant chord changes of hymnic chorale style (typically every sung syllable) is quite at odds with guitar-based pop music that seeks to establish a rhythmic groove over slower chord changes. For people not raised on hymns these are significant hurdles to overcome.

However, people who were raised on hymns know them and love them, and can vouch for the significance of their ongoing use. The question is, How do we continue to benefit from the strengths that hymns offer our worship times? One easy answer is to continue to use the best of the hymns done in their traditional style, simply acknowledging their continued importance. For hymn lovers, this will be well appreciated. But what about contemporary services in which traditional hymns, sung with original words, rhythms, harmonies, and organ, may not be attractive? Should we abandon the hymns, or is there a way to help them to endure?

A balanced approach presumes two understandings. First, the goal is not to canonize our hymns. Hymns should never be confused with or placed on the same rung as Scripture. They are not "inspired" like the Word of God, nor are they inerrant, or authoritative for doctrine. The Lord has enabled godly poets and songwriters to bless the church with songs that have been ministering to people for many years. To question the continued usage of these venerable hymns does not in any way demean their significance in ministry in the past. But we shouldn't continue to use any ministry mode simply because it was effective in earlier years. The hymns we choose to keep alive should be maintained because they continue to stimulate true worship in the hearts of their present singers.

Second, to extend the life of many of our hymns we would be wise to find creative ways to dress them for modern use. We can keep hymns alive through new musical adaptation. It is possible to keep the same familiar melody but to reharmonize a hymn in a way that makes it sound as if it were written last week. Similarly, some subtle or significant rhythm changes can add tremendous life to older hymns and give them an entirely new feel. However, there is a danger in changing hymns too much for congregational use. Arrangers can be much freer when writing for ensembles or instrumentalists. And simply rephrasing a few, carefully selected words can often make an enormous difference in the singability and meaningfulness of still potent hymns.

Hymns can be used in a number of effective ways in contemporary or blended services. A hymn can be intermingled in a set of new songs and provide a refreshing depth in the middle of lighter fare. The contrast of an objective song about who God is can be helpful in stimulating informed worship in the midst of subjective songs about our love for God. Singing hymns with full praise-band instrumentation (drums, guitars, bass, synthesizers, and others) can be very powerful. In singing hymns our church often includes piano and organ, praise band, choir, and worship team vocalists—and it is wonderful!

Certain hymns, of course, do not go out of style. I have probably heard a dozen high schoolers tell me in the last couple years that they just love "Amazing Grace." And nothing compares with a high-powered singing of "How Great Thou Art." Some songs are just timeless. Maranatha! and the Promise Keeper's Promise Band have been particularly effective at bringing new life to wonderful hymns through creative arranging of hymns for praise bands. Some of the arranging I have done in our church to contemporize hymns rhythmically and chordally has been well received. Additional techniques to make hymns live can include the following guidelines.

- Carefully choose only thematically relevant verses. (You don't have to sing all the verses; they have already been edited down by publishers in many cases.)
- Have a soloist sing a particularly poignant stanza; use choir or worship team vocalists to alternate with the congregation.
- Sing during communion. (some of our best hymns relate to the Cross, and many of the new songs are severely lacking here.)
- Use creative instrumental arrangements.
- Sing a capella; this works great on older songs that everyone knows.
- Feature a men's quartet and have an old-time hymn sing.
- Offer special hymn-sing services several times a year and have people share why certain hymns are meaningful to them.

## TIPS FOR EFFECTIVE HYMN PLAYING

The accompanist's role (usually the pianist) is critical for helping make hymns live. Often, when people say they do not like hymns, they are actually referring to the stodgy, unmusical manner in which they have so often experienced hymns. But hymns need not be played in a boring way. My wife and I have good friends who recently moved out of the area to a rural town and were searching for a church. This is an excerpt of an e-mail they sent me regarding their church search and the music at one church they visited. (Maybe you too have visited a church like this.)

The worship team (I use the term loosely) got up to start. The pianist began playing. The one man on the team seemed as if he was the one who
was supposed to lead. But the pianist was the one who really led. We were
singing along and all of a sudden, she would slow way down—for no apparent reason. And the worship team didn't know any more than we did
that she had changed the tempo or decided to linger on that particular
section of music. Often the worship team seemed to be surprised when we
would start or stop or linger. . . . Some of the songs were familiar, so we
sang out. We found out that they sing some songs "differently" than we
were used to. When we held a note—and everyone else stopped, we just
looked at each other and laughed quietly.

At a worship seminar at Western Seminary a few years ago, Paul Oakley
presented a workshop on ways to accompany hymns. My keyboard approach to playing hymns was transformed. For people who thought hymns
all sound the same, Mr. Oakley showed us in unforgettable ways the range
of music that can be expressed in hymns from different eras. He performed "O Come, O Come, Emmanuel" as it was originally written (as
plainsong, probably to bell choir accompaniment) to a single chord played
at the top of the piano and sung in unison. It was stunning! He played "A
Mighty Fortress Is Our God" on the organ with as much ferocity and
power as any praise band I've ever heard. The level of organ virtuosity he
demonstrated has not gone out of style. He brought a silky flow to hymns
like "My Jesus, I Love Thee" that made one truly want to love Jesus more.
His overall point was that hymns were written from an enormous range
of musical genres. We make them impotent when we put them all through
the same musical mold.

Here are a few tips related to hymn playing that might help energize
your congregation's singing and increase their appreciation of hymns.

- Realize that the notes on the page of the hymnal are *not* piano parts!
  This chorale style arranging and printing dates back to the time of
  Bach and is conceived *vocally*. The notes on the page are for soprano
  melody and alto, tenor, and bass harmony. So the pianist should not
  play what is on the page! Leading a congregation by playing the four
  vocal parts as written is a sure recipe for killing congregational sing-

ing. (By contrast, an organist can play off the page, doubling the bass line with pedals, as a support to the piano, because of the "sustain" of the organ sound.)

- Fill out the written harmonies to adapt to a keyboard playing style. Think in terms of chords, rather than notes, that can be played in a variety of ways (inversions, octave doubling of bass, right hand playing one or two octaves higher while expanding to full three-and-four note chords).

- Study music theory. Learn enough music theory to know where to place substitute chords, where to add seconds, suspensions, and sevenths. It is worth learning how to play "fills" at the ends of phrases; you may utilize notes from the scale of the key you are in and the notes of the chord you are currently on.

- Play the lyrics. This can be called "word painting" at the piano. Try never to play two verses of a hymn in an identical way. Strive to make the voicing, rhythm, power, volume, sensitivity, and phrasing match the words and mood that people are singing. This is a tremendous aid to congregational singing.

- Listen to other ensemble musicians. As you play with other instrumentalists, focus on listening to them at least as much as you listen to yourself. Adapt to their playing. Approach the music as an ensemble that works together, not as several soloists who are each doing their own thing.

- Utilize accompanying and arranging techniques. These include using variety in chord thickness, varying your rhythm (play sixteenth-note arpeggios, play one-half note solid chords, two hands playing offset rhythm), varying your left hand (octave bass, flowing arpeggios, playing in treble clef), laying out completely (a capella), playing very softly (nearly a capella but with enough volume to keep the singers in tune), changing keys, altering tempo (have an appropriate lyrical or climactic reason for this), reharmonizing, and punctuating rhythms where singers do not sing.

- If you are playing a synthesizer keyboard, do not play like a pianist. Strive to emulate the style and technique of the instrument family or sound you are trying to reproduce. A string section, a full orchestra, a trumpet, a synth lead, or electric piano should all be played differently. It is best for electronic instruments to supplement acoustic instruments (rather than lead) because they tend not to "cut through" clearly enough for a congregation to follow well.

## CONCLUSION

Most of this discussion on transition relates to areas of progressive musical worship for churches desiring to move into contemporary circles. What seems contemporary today may be outdated within a short time if it is not led and empowered by the Spirit of God. It is just as troublesome for churches to put "Contemporary Worship" on their signs today, if genuine Spirit-empowered worship is not happening, as it is for churches to celebrate that they are old-fashioned. The stakes are too high to play a trendy game of follow-the-leader with some megachurch. Worship is about the glory of God. Worship should transform the believing fellowship into a ministering community.

Heart-worship by believers serves as a witness to the lost. True worship revives and refreshes the soul. As leaders in worship, we need to seek God's clear leading about His purposes for our congregations with the resources He has provided, and then boldly and cautiously lead our people on that course.

# Part 4

CONCLUDING ISSUES

# Twenty

## No More Idle Worship

IN 1985 ROBERT WEBBER wrote a book appropriately titled *Worship Is a Verb*. We may speak about and discuss worship as a subject (a noun), but it is not until we actually worship (a verb) that we are where God wants us to be.

One time as I (Ron) was preparing to speak in the Dallas Seminary chapel service, a number of items seemed to converge in my life—something that is often the case in preparation for preaching. It seems that in God's providence, the preacher's mind—never far from the sermon moment that is approaching with an unrelenting pace—is directed to one experience after another that relates to the topic and the text.[1] Three items that came to mind on that occasion were a paragraph in a novel, a news report, and a music review.

### HUBERT AT CHURCH

The British writer P. D. James is more than a crafter of mysteries; she is a significant novelist who has chosen the mystery format for her considerable art. In a recent book she describes one of her characters, an old barrister, as a person beset by routine, regimen, and ritual. These rugged bits of ruination affect not only his workaday world, but also his weekends. Here is how she describes Sunday mornings:

> Hubert smiles, remembering, sitting still and silent as if he, too, were carved in stone.... The simplicity and ordered beauty of the service, the splendour of the music had seemed to him to represent the profession into which he had been born. He still attended every Sunday. It was as much a part of his routine as buying the same two Sunday newspapers at the same stall on his way home, the luncheon taken from the fridge and heated up in obedience to Erik's [his helper] written instructions, the short afternoon walk through the park, then the hour of sleep and the evening of television. The practice of his religion, which, it seemed to him now, had never been more than a formal affirmation of a received set of values, was now little more than a pointless exercise designed to give shape to the week. The wonder, the mystery, the sense of history—all had gone.[2]

I found this description to be deeply disturbing. I could not easily dismiss the picture of Hubert. I think there are Huberts in lots of churches.

Then I was reminded of an article about a poll conducted by the George Barna research group. The article had this headline: "Many Attend Church Services, but Few Worship."[3] The research project, as reported in this article, suggests that fewer than a third of the people who attend Christian worship services in American churches believe that they have actually worshiped God.

It would seem that the aging lawyer in James's novel is not unique among churchgoers. But is this not sad? She describes a person who is surrounded each Sunday by symbols, songs, and signs of our faith, but is unmoved by mercy, untouched by grace, unafraid before God's majesty. The fictional Hubert and countless real people like him are a very sad lot.

## WHEN WORSHIP IS IDLE

Then in the same few days I saw a headline in the *Dallas Morning News* that arrested my attention. The headline said, "Idle Worship." This great phrase led into a very caustic review of the lackluster performance of a rock group.

The reviewer argued that the lead singer received adulation that was not deserved and spoke of the lead singer as lacking in any qualities that might lead young girls to scream so deliriously about him. Of course, some would ask, Why do they scream for *any* rock singers? But in this case the reviewer felt he was really on to something. For him, the adulation directed toward the poorly performing singer was *idle* worship, because the one to whom the screams were directed seemed most unworthy.[4]

## IDLE OR IDOL?

Frequently the Bible condemns in the strongest possible terms the worship of *idols*. Idol worship is clearly a sin. But what if people are "idle" in their worship? I suggest that idle worship is a sham.

The worship of idols is a sin; to be idle in worshiping God is a sham.

Worst of all is when the senior pastor is not himself engaged in the worship that he is ostensibly leading. As stated earlier, the one who leads in God's worship must become the lead worshiper.

## THE SENIOR PASTOR AS THE WORSHIP LEADER

A church will not grow as a worshiping body beyond the worship of the real worship leader—the senior pastor. The official "worship leader" is not the true leader of worship. What the pastor models or does not model in his personal worship among the congregation, what he teaches or does not teach on worship theology and expression, and what he validates or ignores during the service—all of these have enormous ramifications on how far the congregation will follow the designated worship leader.

## THE PASTOR AT WORSHIP

The senior pastor with whom my son Craig now serves has a worshiper's heart and a worshiping lifestyle. He sits in the front row of the congregation—which makes quite a statement in itself. He is not a "professional clergyman" who sits dignified and expressionless on a lofty platform; rather, he is part of the congregation. But he sits in the front as a means of exercising leadership and availability. If you stand next to him, you probably can't outsing him! He is generally the first person in the congregation to stand and, when appropriate, to start clapping on fast, lively songs. He may be seen to weep during prayer, to close his eyes during beautiful instrumental music, to respond with a hearty amen after a well-performed choir anthem, to be impacted by Scripture as it is read, to follow up a spontaneous testimony from a member with an unplanned prayer. Higher on his priority list than "scoring" on his message is being sensitive to the Spirit of God in the midst of the worshiping community.

Though we have two services (currently with different worship tones and music), he participates in both of them, with equal fervor. He sings the older doctrinal hymns with as much joy and fervency as the newest praise songs. For anyone in the congregation who is noticing, it is apparent that the issue with him is not the song, the style, the speed, or the volume, but our great Lord to whom he is singing. To this Lord, our pastor gives his whole heart. You won't see him ruffling papers, reviewing his notes, or rehashing his sermon introduction during the song service, choir anthem, or special music. As the leader in worship, he takes everything in as it comes, and trusts his message preparation—which has been thorough—to the Lord.

## WORSHIP AND THE SERVICE

A pastor can make or break a worship leader's job by the way he responds to the non-sermon elements in a service. If the pastor views his thirty-five minutes of presenting the sermon as the substance of the service, with other elements as the preliminaries or the warmup,[5] the congregation will surely pick up this same attitude. After a while the people will begin to show up late, criticize the length of the music and other elements, and begin talking about the sermon as being more important than the music.

Ideally a pastor can model to the congregation that a worship service is a dialogue between them and their God. The worshiping pastor sees all elements of the service—congregational songs, special music, Scripture reading, even announcements—as opportunities to connect people with

God, and to spur ministry to one another and to the lost. A worshiping pastor can take a ministry promotion announcement and turn it into a time of pursuing the direction of the Holy Spirit and seeking the blessing of God. A missionary's presentation can lead to a time of praise and intercessory prayer.

A worshiping pastor can appreciate how songs can prepare people's hearts to receive the Word of God, as well as give people appropriate words and emotions to respond to the preached Word. Also he can see how songs can often be significant in themselves; that their ministry to the believer as well as their ministry *from* the worshiper to the heart of God can be powerful. A pastor who is focused on helping his people connect with God will be pleased whenever that connection is made in a service, even if he gets up ten minutes late to speak. In fact the pastor's response to that situation can either make everyone else feel at ease or encourage them to become stiff clock-watchers. We plan our services to be between seventy-five and eighty minutes in length. But we have found that if we go over that time, people are not concerned if they have met with the Lord and have been refreshed spiritually.

Another way the senior pastor reveals himself as the worship leader is by how much time and attention he gives to educating the congregation on worship theology and practice. For a congregation to grow in its ability to worship God publicly, there needs to be positive modeling, permission for the people to experiment and grow, and as much teaching as possible from the senior pastor. Though my son Craig as a worship leader gives a variety of prompts during a given service, sometimes taking a few minutes to prepare the people on a worship concept that may be new, there is no substitute for the senior pastor expounding (or briefly commenting on) worship Scripture passages with "pulpit" authority.

## LEADING IN UNDERSTANDING

To guide a traditional church into a worshiping model of responding to God demonstratively, from the heart, takes more than a sermon here or there. It takes developing a theology of praise, adoration, prayer, serving, singing, thanksgiving, giving, and declaring God's glory publicly.

Churches need carefully reasoned, biblically expounded presentations on how to grow as a worshiping community. A congregation needs to hear from the senior pastor that growing as a worshiper is like growing as a disciple.

Coming to Christ for salvation does not make one a mature worshiper; it means someone has begun as a worshiper. People need to be encouraged to study Exodus, Psalms, Colossians, Hebrews, and Revelation and see the priority—the preeminence—that God's Word places on people exalting God and giving Him the glory that is due Him. When a pastor prioritizes his preaching themes around strategic worship passages, the worship elements in a service surrounding the sermon begin to make sense. The sermon now has a context, as it is in a pursuit that is consistent with the rest of the service, namely, pointing people toward a passionate relationship with their Lord.

## LEADING THE LEADERS

Another element that shows the senior pastor is the key worship leader is how he invests in his platform worship leaders. If a pastor has an associate who is the worship leader or a minister of music, the pastor does well to disciple this individual. If the platform musicians are rotating volunteers, this may be more difficult, but the principle remains: the greater the investment in worship leadership, the greater the return of congregational response.

The pastor can help the worship leader be much more effective by giving sermon plans and themes weeks in advance. This can help the worship leader prepare music and personnel resources that help make a service flow together and make the impact of the service stronger. Like the analogy of focused light versus diffused light, a service in which the pastor and worship leader are focused together will generally have more impact on the congregation than one that flits in various directions.

To rephrase an old adage, "The pastoral staff that prays together stays together." A pastor who prays for and with his worship leaders(s) will benefit from camaraderie, united vision, and reduction in "fire fighting." A pastor who models his private devotional life to his worship leaders will inspire admiration and help develop spiritually healthy disciples.

Many musician-artist types have melancholic and perfectionistic tendencies. Hence encouragement can never be overdone. Probably it is fair to say that most musicians can be challenged to the degree that their efforts are acknowledged and appreciated. It is always time well spent for a pastor to evaluate the effectiveness of a service with the primary worship leader in a positive, constructive manner, emphasizing what went well. Inspire musicians and worship leaders to grow with their strengths.

## THE LEADER IN HIS HEART

Seldom will a church outpace the senior pastor's personal life of worship. Does the pastor seek the Lord from a pure heart? Does he have what the psalmist describes as an "undivided heart"? Is his life with his wife and children consistent with his life before people at church events? Does he study God's Word to feed his own soul and then share the overflow with the congregation? Or does he merely prepare "messages"? Is he constantly seeking to renew his mind by the transforming of God's Word (Rom. 12:2)? Are his mind and heart set "on things above" (Col. 3:2)? Does he seek to grow in loving the Lord with all his heart, soul, mind, and strength? A church where the pastor is not pursuing these things will probably not grow significantly as a worshiping body. But a pastor who is pursuing these things places himself in a position of usability before the Father, who may lovingly choose to pour out His blessing on a faithful servant.

So . . . no more idle worship. Let's "worship the LORD in the beauty of holiness!" (Ps. 96:9).

# Twenty-One

## So Let's Worship the Triune God

D. G. KEHL writes the following: "The act of worship without actual worship is a miserable, hypocritical experience. So if worship wearies you, you aren't really worshiping."[1] A. W. Tozer asks, "What kind of a Christian should be considered a normal Christian?" This is under the heading, "The Normal Christian Worships God."[2]

### THE WOW FACTOR

"Oh, pastor, you really made that passage live!" By God's grace there have been numerous times when someone has come up to me after a worship service and has said something along these lines. I smile, shake the person's hand, express appreciation—and I have a wonderful glow within.

Over the past forty years God has given me many opportunities to preach His Word. I began preaching when I was still in my teens. With only one year of Bible school under my belt, I preached in both large churches and migrant farm workers' camps. Through my college years I often preached, and at Dallas Seminary I learned the art of exposition, and this has marked my life.

When someone comes up to me after a service and says something about the power of the message, the persuasion of the Spirit, the wonder of God's grace through His Word, I soar. I walk away from events such as this with thoughts of appreciation for my great teachers, for the privilege God has given me in the ministry of His Word, and with prayers for continued blessing in the ministry of preaching and teaching the Scriptures.

But I know that the words of these people are not quite accurate. A good sermon does not "make the Bible live." The Bible has life apart from any sermon, explanation, lecture, or message that a mere person might make. The Bible lives (Heb. 4:12). But what these people mean when they say such warm words is that the Scriptures were shown to relate to their lives. The preacher has, in a sense, not gotten in the way of God's message, but has been a vehicle to take the text from an age different from our own, and by God's grace has shown how that old message can still touch lives today.

So again, the words, "You made the Scriptures live," or wording to that effect, are among the most wonderful compliments a preacher can receive. Less often, however, do preachers hear words such as these, "Oh, pastor, how you led us in the worship of God today."

Occasionally I have received words such as these, but not very often. More often I have received words (and I say this respectfully) that speak of my "wowing" the congregation with a powerful message.

Now, this is not a little thing! It only comes when the text has first so powerfully been used in my own life by God's Spirit that I am overflowing with its wonder and grace. To "wow" a people with the wonders of God's Word is a worthy goal![3]

But how much better not only to lead people to an appreciative response to Scripture, but also to share with one another in worship of God through an understanding of God's Word.

Tozer preached a series of messages on the worship of God at Avenue Road Church in Toronto in 1962. He had planned to write a book on the theme, but he died before he was able to complete it. These sermons have been published as the book he might have written, under the title *Whatever Happened to Worship?*[4]

In one of these sermons, "Born to Worship God," Tozer said this about the resurrection of Jesus and its purpose in relation to worship:

On the third day, Jesus rose from the dead. Since then He has been at God's right hand. God has been busy redeeming people back to Himself, back to the original purpose of their being mirrors of His glory.

Yes, worship of the loving God is man's whole reason for existence. That is why we are born and that is why we are born again from above. That is why we were created and that is why we have been recreated. That is why there was a genesis at the beginning, and that is why there is a re-genesis, called regeneration.

That is also why there is a church. The Christian church exists to worship God first of all. Everything else must come second or third or fourth or fifth.[5]

As we have stressed in this book, nothing is more important in the life of the believer than the worship of God. It is for His worship that we have been created. It is for His worship that we have been redeemed. It will be for His worship that we will be taken to heaven.

In the broadest sense worshiping God is fulfilled as we are refreshed each day with the sense of being in the presence of God. In this sense the love of one's neighbor is an act of God's worship, as are faithful actions in work, home, and community.

I love the title of Marva Dawn's newest book. She calls worship a "royal 'waste' of time."[6] In her tongue-in-cheek title, she scores a nice double entendre. For some people worship might be thought of as a "waste of time." But for the people who have learned to draw near to God, to bask in His glory, and to praise His wonder the subtitle will speak to them: "The Splendor of Worshiping God and Being Church for the World."

The Bible emphasizes the need for private, inner worship from a pure heart. But it also emphasizes the need for corporate worship, those times when we focus on and respond to our God with other believers.

Think of all the things we may do or have when we gather for worship: prayer, confession, giving, celebration, remorse, repentance, praise, song, hymn, liturgy, litany, laughter, touch, clapping, baptism, the Lord's Supper, kneeling, preaching, reflection, study, learning, thinking, silence, solo, choir anthem, organ prelude, orchestra, worship team, ensembles, and others.

When done in spirit and truth, worship brings beauty to God and a smile on His people.

## THE PASTOR AS LEAD WORSHIPER

Some years ago James Houston, founding principal of Regent College in Vancouver, British Columbia, edited and abridged some classic books on the spiritual life. His treatment of Richard Baxter's book, *The Reformed Pastor* (first published in 1656), is a splendid contribution to a new generation of pastors. Baxter wrote this about the pastor and his worship: "Take heed, therefore, to yourselves first. See to it that *you* be the worshiper which you persuade your hearers to be. Make sure first that you believe what you persuade others daily to believe. Make sure you have heartily entertained Christ and the Holy Spirit in your own soul before you offer Him to others. He that bids you love your neighbor as yourself implied that you should love yourself instead of hating and destroying yourself—and others too."[7]

The true minister of God is first a worshiper of God. He does not just lead in worship; he is the *lead worshiper!* The praise song by Wayne and Cathy Perrins, "When I Look into Your Holiness," includes this chorus:

> I worship You, I worship You;
> The reason I live is to worship You.
> I worship You, I worship You;
> The reason I live is to worship You.

> © 1981 Integrity's Hosanna! Music/ASCAP.
> All rights reserved. International copyright secured. Used by permission.

Yes, this chorus is simple and repetitive, but its words are true. May we commit our lives, as this song suggests, to worshiping God wholeheartedly "in spirit and truth."

# *Endnotes*

## CHAPTER 1
## LEADING IN WORSHIP

1. This is not to encourage doing any of these actions "politely." None of them is appropriate for people on the platform in a worship service. It is my observation that some of the finest ministers of God's Word are at their worst when they are seated on the platform during congregational worship. The major issue is that these people tend to view congregational worship as something others do; they are "on" only when they begin to preach.

2. Gordon Borror and I describe the wrongheadedness of the idea of "preliminaries" and "main event" in our book *Worship: Rediscovering the Missing Jewel* (Portland, Oreg.: Multnomah, 1982), 137. The ordinary use of the term "preliminaries" should be excised from the vocabulary of a worshiping leader. When used of the actions of the congregation that take place before the sermon, this word conveys everything that was wrong in earlier approaches before worship renewal began in our circles in the last quarter-century. The only legitimate use of this word, it would seem, would be for actions of the

worship leader *before* the service begins. Once the service has begun, preliminaries are done.

3. Peter E. Gillquist, *The Physical Side of Being Spiritual* (Grand Rapids: Zondervan, 1979). Gillquist has told his story in his more recent book, *Becoming Orthodox: A Journey to the Ancient Christian Faith* (Brentwood, Tenn.: Wolgemuth Hyatt, 1989).

4. Robert E. Webber, *Common Roots: A Call to Evangelical Maturity* (Grand Rapids: Zondervan, 1978). Webber has written a number of books on worship; four of them are listed in the bibliography. While he is principally known for his interest in historic liturgy, Webber is also a proponent of blended worship services.

5. Robert G. Rayburn, *O Come, Let Us Worship: Corporate Worship in the Evangelical Church* (Grand Rapids: Baker, 1980). Much of the material in this book is helpful, but he is simply too strong in his condemnation of the beloved gospel song "I Come to the Garden Alone." I suspect he did not really understand it as the imagined voice, the testimony, of Mary at the garden tomb. I cherish this song as one of the few that speaks from the point of view of a woman of faith. Far too many hymns are the calls of men, such as "Rise up, O Men of God."

6. See Anne Ortlund, *Up with Worship* (Glendale, Calif.: Regal, 1975). This is a small but powerful book. Anne and Ray Ortlund have been in the forefront of the evangelical renaissance of biblical worship.

7. See A. W. Tozer, *Worship: The Missing Jewel of the Evangelical Church* (Harrisburg, Pa.: Christian, n.d.). Tozer's messages to a group of pastors in Canada more than twenty-five years ago may be to evangelical worship renewal what Betty Friedan's book *The Feminine Mystique* (New York: Norton, 1963) was to the modern women's movement. Were he to "visit" our churches today, the late Tozer would simply be amazed (and, one hopes, very pleased) to see that the jewel of worship is no longer missing!

8. See Donald P. Hustad, *Jubilate! Church Music in the Evangelical Tradition* (Carol Stream, Ill.: Hope, 1980). This is a wonderful volume. It should be essential reading for church musicians—and their pas-

tors. Hustad has been among the strongest proponents of hymns in Protestant worship. See the bibliography for other volumes by Hustad.

9. See Ralph P. Martin, *Worship in the Early Church*, rev. ed. (Grand Rapids: Eerdmans, 1974). Martin was a pioneer in evangelical circles in encouraging churches to focus on worship themes both in the New Testament and in the early church.

10. Our book was published in the "Critical Concern" series by Multnomah Press. We were thrilled to be a part of this series but were also aware that the series dealt with controversial issues. The subject of worship was not considered a common or usual topic in our circles in the early 1980s. Robert Webber told me that on several occasions he has been challenged by various scholars as to whether the subject of worship is a suitable topic for a serious theologian. God, sin, salvation—these are the classic ideas for theology. But worship was felt to be an inferior topic. We should be grateful to God that these attitudes are changing, though slowly.

11. John M. Frame, *Worship in Spirit and Truth* (Phillipsburg, N.J.: Presbyterian & Reformed, 1996).

12. Ibid., xiv.

## CHAPTER 2
### GETTING READY FOR WORSHIP

1. When Isaiah saw the elevated throne and the Lord seated there, he responded "Woe is me; I am undone" (Isa. 6:5).

2. The Hebrew *ṣôʾîm*, translated "filthy" in Zechariah 3:3–4, is an adjective from a root meaning "human excrement." Unger writes, "The participles of the verse, *attired* (*labhush*, 'clothed,' 'dressed') and *standing*, stress a continued state of moral and spiritual filthiness of one who should have been conspicuous for holiness and emphasize how utterly incongruous Joshua's condition was, the longer it lasted. In delineating Joshua's vile attire and thus Israel's sin and culpability, since he is representative of the nation in its priestly role, the Hebrew language could have employed no more trenchant term.

The word commonly rendered 'filthy' actually means 'excrement-covered' and hence not only vilely dirty but offensively smelly. The word appears only here as an adjective in the Old Testament" (Merrill F. Unger, *Unger's Bible Commentary: Zechariah* [Grand Rapids: Zondervan, 1963], 59).

3. While standard translations render "Satan" as a proper name here, it is better to understand the term "satan" as a descriptive title in texts such as this. The Hebrew word is given with the definite article (*ha-sātān*); the idea is "the Accuser." From this idea, the title later became the principal name for the enemy, as, for example, in Revelation 20:1–6.

4. Not all agree, of course, but I believe that the phrase "the Angel of the Lord" is a powerful way of referring to the second member of the Trinity, an appearance of Christ before the Incarnation. It is from this point of view that in some English translations the term "Angel" is spelled with a capital "A" (see, for example, Gen. 22:15).

5. Modesty is especially important for women who are part of worship teams in more contemporary services. There are times when I find myself rather embarrassed at the sloppy and even immodest dress of some women in these situations, especially younger women and older girls. Yes, they have a warm heart for God, but they still need to give attention to appropriateness in dress. Youth pastors are not likely the ones to help here; no offense intended, but many youth pastors rarely exhibit neatness themselves. I recommend that a woman who is respected in the congregation, perhaps a pastor's wife, give talks from time to time to worship team members on the issue of appropriate dress on the platform.

## CHAPTER 3
## THE BIBLICAL ROLE OF WORSHIP

1. I recall with great fondness first hearing this emphasis on the glory of God rather than on redemption in my first class in theology when I was a beginning student at Dallas Theological Seminary in 1964. The professor of that course was Dr. John F. Walvoord, now chancellor of the school.

2. The New King James Version (as well as the King James Version) uses italics for words that are supplied by translators. Thus in this verse the term *places* is an insertion; one could read more literally, "who has blessed us with every spiritual blessing in the heavenlies in Christ."

3. See chapter 5, "Praise—The Center of the Psalms," in my book *And I Will Praise Him: A Guide to Worship in the Psalms* (reprint, Grand Rapids: Kregel, 1999). In that chapter I deal with a variety of Hebrew words for praise in the Book of Psalms. The words differ, but they all have two things in common: biblical praise is public, and biblical praise is vocal. See also chapter 7 in this present book, "The Beauty of Praise."

4. See Earl D. Radmacher, Ronald B. Allen, and H. Wayne House, eds., *The Nelson Study Bible* (Nashville: Nelson, 1997), 1197.

5. The word *hendiadys* comes from two Greek words meaning "one (idea) through two (words)." My invented word *hendiatris* could mean "one (idea) through three (words)."

6. The meaning of the word *seraphim* in Isaiah 6:2 is "burning ones," from the Hebrew verb *śārap*, "to burn."

7. We will return to Isaiah 6 in chapter 5, "The God We Worship."

8. These words are from "Praise to the Lord, the Almighty," composed by Joachim Neander (1650–1680), translated by Catherine Winkworth (1827–1878).

9. Frame, *Worship in Spirit and Truth*, 11.

10. Craig H. Allen, "To Your Throne," ©1992 Craig H. Allen (ALLENMUSIC).

11. Allen and Borror, *Worship! Rediscovering the Missing Jewel*, 23.

## CHAPTER 4
### MERE RITUAL OR TRUE WORSHIP?

1. A recent poll was taken by the MIDUS (Midlife Development in the United States) Foundation. As reported in *USA Today*, the picture is very sad. "Religion is endorsed by most people in the USA, but the trend is toward an eclectic faith that doesn't demand firm convictions or frequent attendance at services, the MIDUS findings

suggest." David Kinnaman of the Barna Research Group in Ventura, California, agrees: "Spirituality in the U.S. is a mile wide and an inch deep." Both quotes are from the article by Marilyn Elias, "Word, Sex and Prayer in America," *USA Today*, 9 February 1999, 6D. See George Gallup, Jr., and D. Michael Lindsay, *Surveying the Religious Landscape: Trends in U.S. Beliefs* (Harrisburg, Pa.: Morehouse, 1999).

2. Dick Francis, *Wild Horses* (New York: Putnam's Sons, 1994), 33.

3. Ibid., 34.

4. "*A molded calf* was an ominous worship symbol. Not only were the cow and the bull worshiped in Egypt, but the bull was a familiar embodiment of Baal seen in Canaan. *This is your god* can be rendered 'these are your gods,' suggesting that the worship of the Lord had been blended with the symbols of Baal and other fertility gods. Aaron thus had led the people in breaking the first three commandments: They had bowed to another god beside the Lord; they had made a graven image; and they used the Lord's name in false worship (see v. 5). God had said repeatedly that it was He and only He who had brought the Israelites out of Egypt (20:2; 29:45–46), an event they had all witnessed" (*The Nelson Study Bible*, 157).

5. One of the most shocking elements in the story is the report concerning stolen silver. Micah had stolen 1,100 talents of silver from his mother. When he returned it and confessed his crime, his mother forgave him and blessed him in the name of God (Judg. 17:1–2). So far, so good. But then with the blessing of his mother he had the silver made into household idols, and then made them central symbols in his household shrine with his son as priest. Later Micah upgraded his shrine by consecrating the wandering Levite as his new house priest. All this was done in the name of the Lord. Micah said, "Now I know that the LORD will be good to me, since I have a Levite as priest!" (17:13). The sardonic comment in this satirical report is given in the words of the narrator: "In those days there was no king in Israel; everyone did what was right in his own eyes" (17:6).

6. Micah's ministry was contemporary with that of Isaiah, the great prophet whose prophetic call came in 740 B.C. with the death of King Uzziah. Micah here anticipated that the Assyrians would de-

stroy Jerusalem even as he predicted they would destroy Samaria (Mic. 1:6–7). The destruction of Samaria took place in 722 B.C. His prophecy concerning Zion/Jerusalem in 3:8–12 actually did *not* take place then! This is an amazing fact: In this case the true prophecy of a genuine prophet of God did not eventuate in the predicted result until many years later. The reason is that Micah and Isaiah, along with the godly king Hezekiah, in partnering with God's Spirit, were able to lead the people to a series of events that precluded God's judgement in their lifetime (see Isa. 36–37). Later in the ministry of Jeremiah, the prophecy of Micah 3:12 was recounted as an example of a dire threat of divine judgment that was averted because of the intended response among the people (Jer. 26:18–19). In Jeremiah's day (the late seventh century and early sixth century B.C.) there was no such reprieve. Jerusalem was destroyed in 586 B.C., not by Assyria, but by Babylon.

## CHAPTER 5
## THE GOD WE WORSHIP

1. J. Carl Laney, *God: Who He Is, What He Does, How to Know Him Better*, Swindoll Leadership Library (Nashville: Word, 1999).

2. The Hebrew word translated "temple" is the same as the word for "palace." It is simply the translator's choice as to how to render the word in English. The word (*hêkāl*) has a long history, going all the way back to Sumerian, in which the ideogram *E.Gal* meant "big house." The use of the term "altar" in verse 6 likely refers to an incense altar in the heavenly palace rather than to the sacrificial altar in a temple. Everything about this passage is royal rather than priestly. Isaiah saw *the* King (Yahweh) on a throne; what better place on earth for Isaiah to have been at the onset of the vision than in the throne room of the earthly king when heaven's King made Himself known to him?

3. Uzziah in 2 Chronicles 26 is the same figure as Azariah in 2 Kings 15 (see *The Nelson Study Bible*, 636). I follow the Jewish tradition that holds that Isaiah was a member of the extended royal family and a confidant of the king in the last years of the monarch's life.

4.  I discovered this significant connotation of the Hebrew word for "smoke" (*'âson*) years ago when writing on this word for the *Theological Wordbook of the Old Testament*, ed. R. Laird Harris, Gleason L. Archer, Jr., and Bruce K. Waltke (Chicago: Moody, 1980), 2:705.

5.  The translation "The whole earth is full of His glory" (the second line of the seraphim's words in Isa. 6:3) fails to show the power of this statement. The word order and emphasis of the original is this: "The fullness of all the earth is His glory." Seen in this way, this line balances the first line. The emphasis on God's holiness speaks of His transcendence, and the emphasis on His manifested glory in the earth speaks of His immanence. This is both a wonderful pairing of ideas and also the basis for a significant, but usually neglected, biblical concern, namely, biblical ecology.

    If the earth is the manifestation of the glory of God (as this verse surely affirms), then an attack on the earth is in some manner an attack on the glory of God. None would say that the earth exhausts the glory of God (!), but few of us realize that the earth is a true expression of His glory. Gale Heide has written a fine book advocating an evangelical Christian concern for the environment (*This Is My Father's World: A Unique Perspective on Environmental Ethics* [Fountain Valley, Calif.: Joy, 1998]).

6.  The traditional translation, "The LORD [Yahweh] is one," is deficient for the context of the Book of Deuteronomy in particular and the history of Israel in general. Israel never struggled with the notion "Is God many or is He one?" Israel constantly struggled with the idea "Is God, God alone?" or "Is God one among many?" The Hebrew term traditionally translated "one" is better rendered "alone" in this great verse. See also *The Nelson Study Bible*, 304.

7.  Another use of a word in a "triple" form is in Jeremiah's lament over the impending Babylonian destruction of the land of Judah. He was so overcome that he said, "O land, land, land" (Jer. 22:29; the rendering "earth" here misses the point). See Ronald B. Allen, "The Land of Israel," in *Israel: The Land and the People*, ed. H. Wayne House (Grand Rapids: Kregel, 1998), 17–33.

8.  This truth is wonderful to contemplate. The Hebrew verbs in this

verse for "taken away" and "purged" are the technical words for the actions of God on the Day of Atonement by means of the two goats (Lev. 23:26–32). The one goat was driven away into the wilderness as a picture of God "taking away" the sin of the people. The second goat was killed and the blood was sprinkled in the Most Holy Place to make an "atonement," the meaning of the term translated "purged" (better, "covered").

9. In the New King James Version the opening words of Exodus 34:6 read, "And the LORD passed before him and proclaimed, 'The LORD, the LORD God. . . .'"

   The first occurrence of God's name Yahweh (conventionally rendered by "the LORD") in the quoted words is separated from the second use of that term, and the second is joined with the word "God." But this is an error. In the Hebrew text the accents are very clear. The two uses of the divine name Yahweh are joined by the strongest conjunctive accent and the pair of words is separated from the term "God" by a very strong disjunctive accent. This distinction, which has often been overlooked, has enormous significance in our understanding of what God says in these words. The doubling of the divine name ("Yahweh Yahweh") may be unique in Scripture. From time to time we have the long form followed by the short form ("Yahweh Yah") or the short form followed by the long form ("Yah Yahweh"), but this is a very rare use of the long form twice in the same unit. The significance is patent: Here is a deeper expression of the meaning of the divine name (which is the expression of God's character) than has been revealed up to this point in the Scriptures. See Ronald B. Allen, "What Is in a Name?" in *God: What Is He Like?* ed. William F. Kerr (Wheaton, Ill.: Tyndale, 1977), 107–27.

10. It is remarkable that in the Hebrew text of this verse (Exod. 33:9) the "Pillar Cloud" is the subject for each of the three verbs, "descended," "stood," and "talked." The New King James Version and other English versions have added the words "The LORD" as the subject of the verb "talked." Verse 11 confirms that Yahweh was the One who was speaking to Moses, but inserting "the LORD" obscures the astounding reality that the Pillar Cloud spoke. The Pillar Cloud is

the Lord. The term "Pillar Cloud" takes us forward to the Mount of Transfiguration in the New Testament (Matt. 17:2), where the Savior stood upright (like a "pillar"), but whose face shone like the sun and whose clothes were as white as light (as a "cloud"). See Ronald B. Allen, "The Pillar of the Cloud," *Bibliotheca Sacra* 153 (October–December 1996): 387–95.

11. Samuel Terrien, *The Elusive Presence: Toward a New Biblical Theology* (San Francisco: Harper & Row, 1978).

12. In my first book on the Psalms I make very much of the *ḥesed*, "loyal love" (Allen, *And I Will Praise Him*).

13. See Jonah 4:1–3 and *The Nelson Study Bible*, 1498. The Book of Psalms and the prophets have many references to Exodus 34:5–6.

14. This is true of each of the terms, including "word," "dwelt," "glory," and "only-begotten" (Ronald B. Allen, "Affirming Our Right-of-Way on Ancient Paths," *Bibliotheca Sacra* 153 [January–March 1996]: 3–11).


## CHAPTER 6
## WORSHIP AS RESPONSE TO GOD

1. Laney, *God*, 187–200.

2. It is becoming more generally known that the traditional English rendering, "the LORD is one," is deficient in this verse. The Hebrew word for one can also be rendered "alone." As I mentioned earlier, Israel never questioned the unity of God. However, the constant challenge to the faith of the people of Israel was the issue of "other gods." The first and second commandments (to have no other gods and no graven images) both relate to this central issue.

3. The original setting of these words, which Jesus quoted, is in a group of "woe oracles" that Isaiah directed to false religious leaders of Judah in his day (Isa. 29:13). Perhaps the more familiar setting of these words is Jesus' use of them in His condemnation of the Pharisees (Mark 7:6). In both cases the parties addressed in these words of judgment thought they were doing all the right things. But they had added their own requirements to the commands of God and wound

up giving more importance to their human additions than to the divine command. And in the process they had lost their love for the Lord—the most essential command of all!

4. An example is seen in the case of Issac, who loved (*'āhab*) his wife Rebekah (Gen. 24:67).

5. To choose God is parallel to loving Him, and to serve God is parallel to worshiping Him. This parallel of "choose" and "love" also helps us understand the troublesome words of God's love and hatred in Malachi 1:2–3: "Jacob I have loved, but Esau I hated." These words do not describe warm and loathing feelings, but God's determination of choice. He had made His choice in the one and not in the other. In many occasions the word "hate" in the Old Testament has this notion of "not to choose." This meaning in Malachi must be carried over into the New Testament, where the verse is quoted in Romans 9:13. That is, the basic meaning of the Hebrew verbs translated "to love" and "to hate" takes precedence over the meaning of the Greek words into which they are translated. This is a subtlety not often realized by readers of the Greek New Testament.

6. Phylacteries are small leather boxes with leather cords to bind them on one's head and hand. The boxes contained small scrolls with the words of this central section of Deuteronomy as well as some verses from Deuteronomy 11.

7. The term *mezûzôt* refers to the small containers that are used to hold the words of these texts (Deut. 6:11) and that are attached to doors and gates. Christian visitors to Israel in our day are aware of these small boxes attached to the frame of each entry door in their hotels.

8. These three words are not the only terms the Old Testament uses to describe the Lord's gracious Law. In Psalm 119, an alphabetical acrostic, the psalmist uses eight terms to describe the Law of God: "law," "testimonies," "way," "precepts," "statutes," "commandments," "judgments," and "word." See *The Nelson Study Bible*, 1003, for a discussion of the use, meaning, and "key verse" for each of these terms.

9. After the introduction and setting in Nehemiah 9:1–4, this magnificent psalm has four parts: (a) the glorification of Yahweh's name (9:5–6), (b) a recital of God's faithfulness to His people despite their

checkered history (9:7–31), (c) an acknowledgment of God's righteousness (9:32–35), and (d) a confession of the renewal of God's
covenant, with glad response in obedience (9:36–38). See *The Nelson
Study Bible*, 799.

10. The true contrast is between *legalism* and *grace*. By *legalism* I mean
those changes and additions that Jewish people had developed in
the intertestamental period. They had lost the notion of biblical
grace, much as the early church soon lost the biblical concept of
grace a few hundred years later. The Jewish people moved from understanding that the Law was a *gracious* gift given to a redeemed
community by a holy, merciful, and *ḥesed* God to thinking that the
Law was given as a means of earning salvation from a "god" who
keeps records of deeds and misdeeds, and then adds up the parallel
columns. This is postbiblical Judaism. It is not biblical faith. This
misunderstanding led to viewing the Law as a burden, a severe task-
master. Any system of religion that presents a set of rules to keep as
a means of achieving salvation is a perversion of grace, a falling into
works. Further, any system that adds a list of requirements that go
beyond Scripture becomes legalistic, and as such, is also a perversion of grace.

God is a God of grace. His salvation can never be earned, mer-
ited, or achieved; it is solely of His bestowal.

11. I have written elsewhere on the topic of God's call of Abram, arguing that it was all of grace (Ronald B. Allen, "When God Reached
Out to Abraham," *Moody* [November 1989]: 36–40).

12. There are two things that I am *not* saying here. First, I am not saying
that every single individual believed; surely some were just "along
for the ride." But the larger number was saved, for "Israel believed."
Second, I am not saying that future generations of Israelites are saved;
this act of faith was noted only of the first generation. In each generation people must come to belief in their own time. The salvation
of one's parents does not assure the salvation of the child. But this is
truly significant: The same Hebrew construction used of the faith
of Abram in Genesis 15:6 is used here in Exodus 14:31, except that
the verb is here in the plural.

13. As Robert H. Wilkin writes, "Saving faith means believing the gospel, believing in Christ alone for eternal life. Nothing else is saving faith. Not only is believing the gospel enough, but it is the only way to salvation. Jesus guarantees eternal life to all who believe in Him for it" (*Confident in Christ: Living by Faith Really Works* [Irving, Tex.: Grace Evangelical Society, 1999], 15). I am also strongly convinced that saving faith in Old Testament times was also simply believing in God for salvation; nothing could be added to simple belief. Throughout the long period leading from God's first promise of a Savior to Eve in the Garden of Eden (Gen. 3:15), to the arrival of Jesus Christ, people of faith would have had a growing awareness of God's plans for a coming One. But the principal content of their faith was not in the death and resurrection of Jesus—not before these grand events had transpired! Like Abram, they believed in Yahweh. Like Abram, God counted their faith as righteousness. And like Abram, they were saved!

14. Laney, *God*, 187–200.

## CHAPTER 7
## THE BEAUTY OF PRAISE

1. F. Duane Lindsey wrote on the concept years ago (see "God Is Beautiful: Part 1 of Essays toward a Theology of Beauty," *Bibliotheca Sacra* 131 [April–June 1974]: 120–36.

2. This point is developed more fully in chapter 8.

3. This is not to say that Exodus 15 is the first instance of poetry in the Bible. The Book of Genesis has an unexpected richness in Hebrew poetry. In addition to the long prophetic poem of Jacob's blessing on his sons (Gen. 49), there are numerous shorter poems throughout Genesis. The very first poetry in Genesis is in chapter 1, in celebration of God's creation of man (1:26–28). Verses 26 and 28 are highly elevated prose; verse 27 is pure poetry. I have developed the significance of this point in my study of Psalm 8 (Ronald B. Allen, *The Majesty of Man: The Dignity of Being Human* [reprint, Grand Rapids: Kregel, 1999]).

4. Moses, the great prophet of God, wrote other psalms; one is the wonderfully prophetic psalm in Deuteronomy 32; another is Psalm 90, a lament of old age. On the latter see *The Nelson Study Bible*, 973. There have been many scholarly studies of the psalm of praise in Exodus 15; a splendid recent study is by Richard D. Patterson, "The Song of Redemption," *Westminster Theological Journal* 57 (spring 1997): 453–61.

5. I recall hearing lectures years ago by Perry Yoder on a theory of spontaneous oral composition as against planned, written composition of Hebrew poetry. His theory was based on the percentage of regularly recurring "stock-in-trade" parallel words, common to both Ugaritic and Hebrew poets. The reading of the psalm in Exodus 15 shows that it is very specific in topic and creative and original in presentation. This is a labored work of art, not a hastily contrived piece, written "on the spur of the moment."

6. I recall one of the years I participated in the Masterworks Choir under the leadership of Gordon Borror when we were singing selections from Handel's great oratorio *The Messiah*. One of the less known pieces is Chorus 37, "The Lord Gave the Word." The chorus includes the words, "Great was the company of the preachers" (based on Ps. 68:11), and repeats these two lines throughout the piece. I was assigned to augment my singing in the bass section by giving devotionals to the choir on the texts that we were singing. When I turned to the Hebrew text of this verse, I was astonished to see that the term translated "preachers" is a *feminine* participle, indicating *women* as the "preachers." The setting of the verse is clearly the Exodus from Egypt (68:7–10). Thus this verse celebrates the *women* who led in the praise of the Lord in the aftermath of His great work in the Exodus. How fascinating to see that centuries after the event, the women who led Israel in the worship of God in the aftermath of the Exodus were still remembered in this psalm. Then centuries later the singing by the women was commemorated in one of the greatest musical accomplishments of our faith, Handel's *Messiah*.

7. See Walter C. Kaiser, Jr., "Exodus," in *The Expositor's Bible Commentary* (Grand Rapids: Zondervan, 1990), 2:392–97.

8. Indeed, Kaiser proposes a meaning for the Hebrew word translated *song* as a word for *power* that simply has not yet been recognized (ibid., 397, n. 2).

9. The Old Testament writers loved to pair words together in both common and unusual combinations; in this manner words were sharpened as they colored one another.

10. It should not be troubling for the men among us to find that from time to time we are led in our celebrative music by gifted, talented women! For after all, it is the Lord who is the center of worship; all eyes are to be directed toward Him. Frankly, I would observe that if women may not lead the church in worship of God, then it would seem to follow that they should not sing solos in the congregation either, for that is a way of leading in worship. And if not solos, should women sing in the choir? Or lead a choir? Should they play the piano or organ? Once one begins on this path, the course becomes ever more slippery. Whatever one's convictions may be about the role of women in church leadership, it appears that there is ample biblical precedence for women (and men!) to be a part of the music ministry of a congregation, and indeed to lead it to the praise of God. In those churches in which males are responsible for the leadership of the congregation, surely there is room for women to serve God in music ministry, under the blessing of and in response to the designated male leaders. We might remember that some of the psalms were written by women; think of the psalm of Deborah in Judges 5, the psalm of Hannah in 1 Samuel 2, and the psalm of Mary in Luke 1. Miriam was not the only gifted woman musician in the Bible.

11. House, ed., *Israel: The Land and the People.*

12. Psalms 113 and 114 are read or sung before the Passover feast; Psalms 115–118 are read or sung after the Passover feast. The wording of Psalm 118 is the most intensely prophetic and messianic of the whole set; it speaks powerfully of death and resurrection of the Coming One. This is one of those texts that demonstrates that both the death and resurrection of Jesus were "according to the Scriptures" (1 Cor. 15:3–5).

13. See Ronald B. Allen, *Lord of Song: The Messiah Revealed in the Psalms*

(Portland, Oreg.: Multnomah, 1985), for a development of this highly prophetic psalm.

14. Chapter 13 begins a new division of the Book of Isaiah, "Woe Oracles on the Nations" (Isa. 13–27).

15. The context suggests "sing" instead of "say." In Hebrew the verb "to sing" has the same spelling as the verb "to say"; the homonym is not sufficiently recognized in our translations. The verb in verse 1 is in the singular; in verse 4 it is in the plural.

16. I discuss many of these words in *And I Will Praise Him*, chapter 5, "Praise—The Center of the Psalms." Each of these words calls for *public, vocal acts.*

17. David's words in Psalm 22:3 tie in wonderfully with the idea of God's holiness and the worship of His people. "But You are holy, enthroned on the praises of Israel." If we think again of the biblical notion of the holiness of God, the second line of this verse is quite unexpected. It seems that God received the praises of His people as the cushion under His throne. The Hebrew participle *yôšēb* suggests an ongoing act of "sitting" on or over these praises.

18. The Hebrew term translated "Most High" is ʿelyôn, a word that is often used by the poets of the Bible to describe the supreme glory, majesty, and sovereignty of God, when viewed over the nations and over their "gods."

19. I love the new praise song of Pete Sanchez, Jr., "I Exalt Thee," and a companion song by Brent Chambers, "Be Exalted, O God." I regret, however, their use of the King James Version of the verses from the psalms with the archaic pronouns "Thee," "Thou," and "Thy." I speak of this anomaly in chapter 12. Archaic pronouns may seem to "belong" in the older hymns; they seem to me to be quite out of place in the new praise songs.

20. Psalm 147 has no superscription, but the rebuilding of Jerusalem and the regathering of its exiles (see 147:2) suggests that it was composed in the period following the return from Babylon in the sixth century B.C.

## CHAPTER 8
## WORSHIP IN SPIRIT AND TRUTH

1.  I have developed the analogy of the rose in a video series called *The Bible as a Rose* (Portland, Oreg.: Western Seminary, 1990). The series has nine installments, of about thirty minutes each, along with a workbook.

2.  The term "Teacher of Righteousness" was used of the founder of the sect we call the Qumram community, usually associated with the writing of the so-called Dead Sea Scrolls. What is not so well known is that the phrase comes from an alternate reading in Joel 2:23 (Ronald B. Allen, *Joel* [Grand Rapids: Zondervan, 1988], 85–96). I believe that Joel 2:23 may include a double entendre, referring both to *faithful rain* and to the *teacher of righteousness*; the latter is a messianic title that is rightly applied not to the founder of the Qumram community, but to Jesus of Nazareth.

3.  See the discussion in chapter 6 on John 1:17, "For the law was given through Moses."

4.  The Book of Leviticus, for example, does not begin with the words, "Moses arose and commanded the people, saying. . . ." Rather, the beginning of this book may be rendered this way: "Then the LORD proclaimed to Moses, even He spoke to him from the Tent of Meeting, saying, 'Speak to the Israelites, and say to them'" (Lev. 1:1). In Exodus, Leviticus, Numbers, and Deuteronomy Moses often wrote (in several ways) that his message was *from* the LORD *through* him.

5.  The Greek *amēn* transliterates the Hebrew word *'âmēn* ("truly"). The point is that Jesus spoke with a level of authority never before known. He did not quote God; He spoke as God, for He *is* God.

6.  Cain's name is an example of paronomasia. The sound of his name (*qayin*, which means a "craftsman" of some sort) is similar to the Hebrew verbal form translated "I have acquired" (*qānîtî*). It is significant that there is no similar word play on the name Abel (*hebel*). The reason is most likely found in the fact that Abel means "vapor." Probably this was not the name his parents gave him at his birth; only later, as they grieved inconsolably at his bloody body, would

they have said in sadness, "His life was like a vapor!"

7. Possibly Eve believed that her first son was the fulfillment of God's promise in Genesis 3:15. This verse could be read this way: "I have acquired a man, even the Lord" (Walter C. Kaiser, Jr., *Toward an Old Testament Theology* [Grand Rapids: Zondervan, 1978], 79). Whether or not this is correct, one thing is sure: Eve's faith in God was deep. Even if we take a "minimal" approach, her words about receiving a man from the Lord show that she was putting her faith in God's promise and His provision.

8. The first readers of this text, however, knew full well what God's demands were concerning His holy worship in sacrificial acts. Leviticus was a part of their instruction; the godly among them would have heard and read this story with great attention to detail, for they knew that they themselves would be facing similar issues.

9. Actually, "of the fattest" would be clearer. That is, Abel brought not only the "firstborn" to the Lord, but the best (the healthiest, "fattest") ones.

10. We have no idea what his offering really was, of course.

11. *The Nelson Study Bible*, 177.

12. The same word "offering" (*minḥâ*) is used of both sons' sacrifices (Gen. 4:4–5). A technical term for animal sacrifice was not used of Abel's offering, and a broad word was used of Cain's offering. Yet we read nothing about sin as the prompting for these sacrifices; sin was strongly in the aftermath!

13. We may observe here the aptness of John's description of Cain: "not as Cain, who was of the wicked one and murdered his brother. And why did he murder him? Because his works were evil and his brother's righteous" (1 John 3:12). John attributed three things to Cain: wicked works, Satan's power in his life, and his murder of his brother.

14. See, for example, Jeremiah's strong condemnation of paganism in Judah in Jeremiah 1:15, 16; 2:7–13, 17–25; 3:1–5; and especially in 7:28–31.

15. The term Samuel used here is a part of a play on words in which the writer of 1 Samuel contrasted Saul and David. The Hebrew word he used, *sākal*, "done foolishly," sounds almost exactly like the word *sakal*, "acted wisely," the word that describes David in 1 Samuel 18:30.

16. The traditional translation is "Be quiet," but I suspect the words were a bit more forceful than that. A reader of this verse naturally compares the response of David to his accusing prophet, Nathan (2 Sam. 12:13). David was a "man after God's own heart" (1 Sam. 13:14), not because his sins were less serious than those of Saul, but because his response was what it should have been when accused of wickedness by God's prophet.

17. It is sometimes asserted that Saul had no heart for God; in my judgment this is far too strong an assertion. It is more likely that Saul is an example of a person who does have a heart for God, but who is not faithful in his behavior or careful about his attitudes toward God. He is a picture of a wandering saint and as such has many kin among the people of God.

18. *I Worship You Almighty God* by Sondra Corbett Wood, © 1983. Integrity's Hosanna! Music/ASCAP. All rights reserved. International Copyright secured. Used by permission.

19. A recent study on the life of David is Charles R. Swindoll, *David* (Nashville: Word, 1998).

20. Of course, there is one sacrifice that did bring pleasure to God—the death of His own Son. This wonderful yet awful thought is seen in Isaiah 53:10, "Yet it pleased the LORD to bruise Him." Here we have the same verb *ḥâpēṣ*, "to bring pleasure, to cause a smile, to enjoy." The Father could not have "enjoyed" the death of His Son. But, because of what that death provides (our salvation), the Father found "pleasure" in it. Isaiah 53:10 ends with the noun *ḥēpeṣ*, "pleasure," thus forming another inclusio (see note 21 below): "And the pleasure of Yahweh shall prosper in His hand." Here *ḥēpeṣ* speaks of the "pleasure" of the Son, after the sacrifice of His own life is accomplished. This amazing truth is the basis for salvation of sinners.

21. When a slave was about to be set free after six years of service, he might wish to remain in slavery in order to remain with his wife and children. In such a case there was a provision for him to decide on voluntary slavery. The mark of such a man was the piercing of an earlobe (Exod. 21:1–6).

22. The term *inclusio* describes a word or phrase used at the beginning

and ending of a section, something like a verbal frame. In Psalm 8, for example, the words in verse 1, "O LORD, our Lord, how excellent is Your name in all the earth," are repeated in verse 9.

23. These words of David were not only the song he sang to God; they were also the words of the Savior as He was about to leave heaven's glory in the Incarnation (Heb. 10:4–6). See Allen, *Lord of Song*, 48–55.

24. For more on this meaning of worshiping God "in spirit" see the section "Restoring the Emphasis on the Holy Spirit in Worship" in chapter 16.

## CHAPTER 9
## WORD, WATER, AND WINE

1. Many mainline churches have lectionaries that prescribe passages from the Bible that are to be read each Sunday of the church year. The idea behind the lectionaries with its elected passages became strongly fixed in the Reformation period as a means of having a balanced teaching ministry and reflecting the church year in an appropriate manner.

2. I use the term "Bible church" as a category that includes other free-church traditions, including Bible-oriented Baptist churches.

3. Ron Owens, with Jan McMurray, *Return to Worship: A God-Centered Approach* (Nashville: Broadman & Holman, 1999), 99. He adds that in one service he attended only two verses were read from the Bible, but that the music went on for thirty minutes, and the service was limited to one hour (ibid., 99–100). The issue of a lack of reading the Bible is not, in my view, simply a result of the increase of music in the contemporary service. It is a matter of priority. Since we have increased the amount of time for music in our services, some have felt that we have had to cut other things. Not so! Churches that have more thoughtful leaders have *lengthened the service*. We don't have to cut other areas of worship to make room for the music that people so strongly desire. Since they desire the music so much, they will happily stay for a lengthened service, *if the rest of the worship elements are presented with as much thought, prayer, and purpose as is the music!*

4. Mazie Nakhro, "The Worship of God in the Apocalypse: Its Function for the Corporate Worship of the Church" (Ph.D. diss., Dallas Theological Seminary, 2000), 82, n. 197.

5. Ibid., 251.

6. Owens writes, "Pastor, remember that your role as shepherd and worship leader is to lead your people to God and to help them respond to Him. The reading of God's Word must be given the prominence it requires in worship if we are going to worship in spirit and in truth, for His Word is truth!" (*Return to Worship*, 101). We may add the troubling question, Pastor, are *you* reading the Word as an active part of your daily life before God? That pastor who makes much of Bible reading in his own life will not need to be encouraged to read it well in the worship services of God's people on Sunday morning.

7. In fact I urge that one should have the habit of reading from a "full Bible," not just from a New Testament, even when one's plan is not to turn to an Old Testament passage. There is something significant in holding the whole Bible, the complete written Word of God. There are times when this may not be necessary, such as a talk at a banquet or an informal youth group meeting on the beach. But when the church is gathered for worship, that most significant symbol of the Protestant faith—the Bible!—should be prominent.

8. In our church, as in many, we have the practice of having two people lead in prayer, one for the bread and one for the cup. Once as I was standing with the other elders waiting my turn as one of those to pray, I was struck with the sense that the prayers for the bread and the cup are the same. Both speak of the death of Christ but in different ways. I then recalled the biblical principle that by two or three witnesses a thing will be established (see, for example, Deut. 17:6). I have since observed that many of the most significant events in biblical history are given in two ways or with two witnesses. For example, the crossing of the Red Sea is recorded in Exodus 14 in prose and in Exodus 15 it is recounted in poetry. God's use of two symbols of Christ's death, the bread and the wine, is the superlative example of the importance of something being established by two witnesses.

9.  By "occasional letters" I certainly do not mean to weaken in any way our appreciation of the significance of the letters of Paul and other New Testament epistles. I simply mean that these letters are not systematic theological writings in the modern sense, developing doctrinal ideas in fullness. Paul's letters to the Corinthians are particularly significant in this regard. He may have written four such letters, of which two have become a part of the New Testament. In each of these he was responding to problems and issues in the church at Corinth. (See David K. Lowery, "1 Corinthians," in *The Bible Knowledge Commentary, New Testament*, ed. John F. Walvoord and Roy B. Zuck [Wheaton, Ill.: Victor, 1983], 505–6.) The most systematic of all of Paul's writings is the magnificent Book of Romans.

10. Beverly and I recall what transpired after the service at the cemetery. We were crammed with our luggage into the car with the pastor and his wife and we experienced a harrowing drive as we hurtled toward the airport for our flight. On that adventure we had many thoughts of cemeteries and cremation on our minds!

## CHAPTER 10
## WORSHIP AS ONE'S MANNER OF LIFE

1.  Diane Winston, "Gallup Says America Has a Shallow Faith," *Dallas Morning News*, 11 December 1999, 1G.

2.  George Gallup, Jr., and D. Michael Lindsay, *Surveying the Religious Landscape: Trends in U.S. Beliefs* (Harrisburg, Pa.: Morehouse, 1999), 2–3; 43–64.

3.  Well, perhaps openness is not given to *everyone*. At times it seems that consideration is given gladly to nearly all religious ideas in our pluralistic times, except to evangelical Christians.

4.  The national "solemnizing" of this neo-festival for black Americans was assured with the release of Kwanzaa stamps along with stamps for Hanukkah and Cinco de Mayo beginning in 1996 by the United States Postal Service. (Fred Greene, "Three Holiday Stamps to Be Reissued in New Thirty-Three-Cent Denominations," *Dallas Morning News*, 6 March 1999, 25A.)

5. Christine Wicker, "Schools Asked to Make Room for Ramadan," *Dallas Morning News*, 9 December 1999, 1A.

6. Roddy Braun, *1 Chronicles*, Word Biblical Commentary (Waco, Tex.: Word), xl.

7. Robert E. Webber, *Worship Is a Verb* (Grand Rapids: Zondervan, 1985).

8. Barry Liesch, *The New Worship: Straight Talk on Music and the Church* (Grand Rapids: Bbaker, 1996), 155–56.

9. This is akin to not reading the key signature correctly in a new piece of music. The Hebrew verb *shāchad* (which we would normally transliterate as *šāḥad*) actually means "to give a present," "to present a bribe" (as in Ezek. 16:33). See Francis Brown, S. R. Driver, and Charles A. Briggs, *A Hebrew and English Lexicon of the Old Testament* (Oxford: Clarendon, 1907), 1005. The verb he means to cite is *šāḥâ*, "to bow down."

10. See Allen and Borror, *Worship: Rediscovering the Missing Jewel*, 127; Ludwig Koehler and Walter Baumgartner, *The Hebrew and Aramaic Lexicon of the Old Testament* (Leiden: Brill, 1994), 295–96; and Terence E. Fretheim, *hāwâ* in *New International Dictionary of Old Testament Theology and Exegesis*, ed. Willem A. VanGemeren (Grand Rapids: Zondervan, 1997), 2:42–44.

11. The new understanding of the biblical verb was made possible because of the discovery of a cognate verb *hwy* in Ugaritic (Fretheim, " *hāwâ*" 2:42).

12. The last couplet presents a wonderful example of unexpected word order in the Psalms. One would expect to read something as follows: "We are the people of His hand, the sheep of His pasture." By inverting the elements, the psalmist heightened the sense of tenderness in the exquisite relationship believers have with God.

13. See Philip Yancey, *The Bible Jesus Read* (Grand Rapids: Zondervan, 1999), 127.

14. The term "idols" in Psalm 96:5 is an example of a wonderful pun in Hebrew language. The term is *'ĕlîlîm*, a word which sounds very much like *'ĕlôhîm*, "God," but which means the opposite! The term means "nothings"! Peoples of the world who worship gods do not

simply worship something that is less than the true God; what they adore is utterly without meaning.

15. John Piper, *Let the Nations Be Glad! The Supremacy of God in Missions* (Grand Rapids: Baker, 1993), 11.

## CHAPTER 11
### ARE THERE STAGES OF WORSHIP?

1. Judson Cornwall, *Let Us Worship* (North Brunswick, N.J.: Bridge-Logos, 1983).
2. This paraphrases Cornwall's chapter 17, "Leading Others into Worship" (ibid., 153–58). To be fair with this godly man, I should observe that he is not sure whether to speak of three or four steps in this verse, but he is certainly fixed on the idea of steps. He writes, "If the leader has been successful in bringing the people step by step into the outer court and on through it into the holy place, there will be a rise in the spiritual response of the people. Instead of mere soulish, emotional responses, there will be responses from the human spirit that have depth and devotion in them" (p. 157).
3. See my book *And I Will Praise Him*, chapter 4, "Poetry—The Language of the Psalms."
4. Cornwall, *Let Us Worship*, 155.
5. The gates of ancient cities in Canaan and Israel were immense, fortified structures. Thus one could "sit at the gates" of the city (see, for example, Ruth 4:1), an expression that really means to sit in the recesses of the fortifications associated with the gate structures of a walled city. Now one may argue that "His gates" in Psalm 100:4 refers to the gates of Jerusalem. In this case one is entering the city first and then the temple second. But this is not the picture that Cornwall and others present. He writes of the "gates" in these words: "It was the home of the priests, who although encamped close to the Tabernacle, could not worship until they had entered the Tabernacle itself. And neither can we. If the song leader will bear in mind that songs about personal condition or experience are songs to be sung when the people are outside the Tabernacle enclosure, he can make excellent use of them to gently get the attention of the singers" (ibid.).

6. Allen, *And I Will Praise Him*, chapter 5, "Praise—The Center of the Psalms."

7. Claus Westermann, *The Praise of God in the Psalms*, trans. Keith R. Crim (Richmond, Va.: John Knox, 1965), 30.

8. Frame, *Worship in Spirit and Truth*, 29.


## CHAPTER 12
## THOSE NEW PRAISE SONGS

1. "Seven words repeated eleven times." But such slurs may lead people on the other side to speak of hymns as "old codgers' music." These and other such derogatory remarks are, in my judgment, not only uncalled for, but are unbecoming.

2. The article is by Michael S. Hamilton, *Christianity Today*, 12 July 1999, 28–35.

3. It is difficult to know what to call this music. Those who do not like this style seem to speak of it (derisively) as "choruses." Many who use this music gladly still use the term "choruses," but that term does not seem adequate for the state of music today. Some proponents of this newer music often use the phrase "praise and worship music." I find this wording also misleading; the suggestion seems to be that the older church music (the hymns) was not for praise and worship! Another term is "contemporary worship music," but that seems misleading as well, for there is a considerable body of new hymns and other worship music that is not a part of the musical style under review. Perhaps the best phrase to use for this new musical style is "new praise songs," an observation I owe to my son Craig.

4. Charles E. Fromm, "New Song: The Sound of Spiritual Awakening, A Study of Music in Revival," a presentation to the Oxford Reading and Research Conference, July 1983, Oxford, England (Santa Ana, Calif.: Institute of Worship Renewal, 1987). Copies of this paper may be obtained from Maranatha! Music; see the "Resources" section near the end of this book for the address.

5. Ibid., 17–18.

6. Ibid., 18.

7. Ibid., 18–19.

8. Ibid., 19.

9. Ibid.

10. Copyright © 1912. Renewal 1940 by Mrs. Howard Smith. Assigned to Singspiration (ASCAP), Division of Zondervan Corp.

11. Copyright © 1978, 1980 House of Mercy Music. Administered by Maranatha! Music.

12. Phil Christensen, "Song Stories: Laurie Klein's "I Love You, Lord,'" *Worship Leader* 6 (May/June 1997): 20–21. This song has been released on more than seventy recordings and in several foreign languages.

13. Many writers learned in the 1970s that the Lockman Foundation, the publisher of this well-received new translation, was difficult to deal with when it came to "fair use" and payment for other use. The New International Version was not yet in publication; when the NIV was published in 1978, there were still issues of payment and "fair use."

14. Martin Nystrom, "As the Deer," copyright © 1984 Maranatha! Music.

15. Of course the licensing agency does not allow changes in wording of copyrighted materials. But there needs to be an exception made (and it can be requested in writing) when there are grammatical issues that are offensive to standards of good writing. A simple solution is to show the song as written, but to teach people to sing it in a consistent grammar.

16. Marcy/Vineyard Publishing, 1995.

17. Marva J. Dawn, *Reaching Out without Dumbing Down: A Theology of Worship for the Turn-of-the-Century Culture* (Grand Rapids: Eerdmans, 1995). Her second book *A Royal "Waste" of Time: The Splendor of Worshiping God and Being Church for the World* (Grand Rapids: Eerdmans, 1999) is more balanced and less acerbic.

18. Ibid., 281. Her book has been reviewed at length by Robert Redman, Jr., in "Friendly Fire: Evangelical Critics Take Aim at Contemporary Worship," *Worship Leader* 4 (November/December 1995): 33–35. Dawn was interviewed in the same publication by Greg Asimakoupoulos, "Sorting through Worship in a Post-Modern Age: An Interview with Marva Dawn," *Worship Leader* 7 (January/February, 1998): 30–33.

19. John M. Frame, *Contemporary Worship Music: A Defense* (Phillipsburg, N. J.: Presbyterian & Reformed, 1997), 155–74.

20. Ibid., 160.

21. Now again, I wish to be careful here. Christians who are older adults and who have had a long history in the church may still love the standard hymns and find in them the very best means for their adoration of God in the singing community. But even for many older Christian adults, the singing of hymns remains a perfunctory chore; for a lot of people, hymns are to be "gotten through," rather than being the means of "getting through" to God. See the next chapter, however, for some balancing thoughts.

22. One of the standard assumptions of many Christian hymn scholars is that the *objective* hymn is on a higher level than the *subjective* hymn. In fact this is just a bias of scholarship; it is without foundation when one turns to the music of the Bible itself. The Book of Psalms has many examples of poems in which the praise of God is given primarily in "You" language (objective). It also has many examples where the psalmist speaks ("I" and "me") to God ("You"), just as in the new praise songs. The reason so many of the new praise songs use the first-person pronouns is precisely because so many of them are adaptations of Scripture itself.

23. Jack W. Hayford, "Majesty," copyright © 1981 Rocksmith Music. Administered by Trust Music Management.

24. *Worship His Majesty* (Waco, Tex.: Word, 1987), 9–14.

25. Ibid., 13.

## CHAPTER 13
## WHAT ABOUT THE HYMNS?

1. Sometimes hymnal publishers have not helped things much in this regard. It is not uncommon among the older hymnals to find dated patterns of layout and design, and the use of Old English script for the titles of hymns. These elements that were once thought to be "classic" speak of something out of date today.

2. Nashville: Word Music/Integrity Music, 1997. Tom Fettke is also the

editor of the popular hymnal of just a few years ago, *The Hymnal for Worship and Celebration* (Waco, Tex.: Word Music, 1986).

3. *Praise*, 4th ed. (Laguna Hills, Calif.: Maranatha! Music, 1997).

4. Ronald Man, "Blended Worship with a Purpose," *Creator Magazine* 20 (July/August 1998): 25.

5. Ibid. Robert Webber has an entire book on this topic: *Blended Worship: Achieving Substance and Relevance in Worship* (Peabody, Mass.: Hendrickson, 1996).

6. Ibid. Man has another helpful article in the same journal, "Congregational Participation: Drawing God's People into Worship," *Worship Leader* 6 (January/February 1997): 30–32. In other unpublished materials which he has sent for me to peruse, he makes strong arguments for "thematic" worship, the point Gordon Borror and I argued in our book, *Worship: Rediscovering the Missing Jewel*, 63–76. When a service is disjointed, it is no wonder that the people have difficulty in joining together in the worship of God.

7. "Sabaoth" is the transliteration of the Hebrew word for "hosts" or "armies." As Commander of the angelic armies, God is sovereign over all He has made.

8. The title of this "catalogue" is *The Great Price Maker*.

9. Michael S. Hamilton, "Triumph of the Praise Songs," *Christianity Today*, 12 July 1999, 28–35.

10. Years ago I was asked to write an article for an "arts" issue of *Moody* magazine. My assigned topic was, "So You Think You Hate the Symphony?" Editor Michael Umlandt said that the article would be acceptable only if it might convince him, although he was not a symphony lover, to think about the possibility of attending a symphony. And he lived in Chicago, the city with one of the finest orchestras in the country! I received many wonderful responses from the article when it was published (*Moody* [December 1984]: 16–18), including an invitation to have a meal with the music director and concertmaster of the Cleveland Symphony (another great orchestra) when his orchestra visited Oregon. Daniel Majeske is now with the Lord; Beverly and I shall never forget his kindness, his musicianship, and his love for Christ.

11. For a fascinating presentation of what we know about musical instruments in biblical times see D. A. Foxvog and A. D. Kilmer, "Music," in *International Standard Bible Encyclopedia*, ed. Geoffrey W. Bromiley et al. (Grand Rapids: Eerdmans, 1986), 3:436–49. Instruments we read about in the Bible are found in regions as diverse as Ur and Ebla, Egypt and Akkad. Foxvog and Kilmer admit that we have fragmentary and somewhat uncertain identification of biblical musical instruments (ibid., 439), but the antecedents of each of the instruments mentioned in the Bible are traced in this very fine article.

    Musical instruments were used for nonreligious purposes in the ancient world, of course. But the association of music and worship was as strong among Israel's neighbors as among the Jewish people.

    Another informative article on musical instruments is by Mary Hopper, "Music and Musical Instruments," in *Baker Encyclopedia of the Bible*, ed. Walter A. Elwell et al. (Grand Rapids: Baker, 1988), 2:1501–12. She regularly compares instruments in the Bible with Egyptian and Mesopotamian examples. The development of Jewish music from late second-temple times is discussed by A. Z. Idelsohn, *Jewish Music: In Its Historical Development* (New York: Schocken, 1967). But he also briefly speaks of the Egyptian and Mesopotamian connections of Israel's temple music and instrumentation (ibid., 3–23).

12. I have reference, of course, to his words of superscription to Psalm 8, calling for the *gittît*, most commonly regarded as an instrument of Gath. See Foxvog and Kilmer, "Music," 448.

13. The text is by Edward Perronet (1726–1792), and the music is by James Ellor (1819–1999).

14. Mark A. Noll, "We Are What We Sing: Our Classic Hymns Reveal Evangelicalism at Its Best," *Christianity Today*, 12 July 1999, 37–41. For a robust champion of Western hymnody, one could find no stronger advocate than Donald E. Hustad. See his several books listed in the bibliography. Also note the recent book on Western hymnody by Paul Westermeyer, *Te Deum: The Church and Music* (Philadelphia: Fortress, 1998).

## INTERLUDE: A CHANGE OF PACE

1. Warren W. Wiersbe, *Real Worship: Playground, Battleground or Holy Ground?* 2d ed. (Grand Rapids: Baker, 2000), 215, n. 1.

## CHAPTER 14
## THOSE SEEKER-SENSITIVE SERVICES

1. This book is consistently presented from the reference point of "white" congregations, because this has been our primary circle of experience. Most works on worship renewal have been oblivious of the tradition of African-American expressions of lively worship of God.

2. See Richard Allen Farmer, "African-American Worship," in George Barna et al., *Experience God in Worship* (Loveland, Colo.: Group, 2000). For the development of music in the black Christian tradition, see the study by Jon Michael Spencer, *Protest and Praise: Sacred Music of Black Religion* (Minneapolis: Fortress, 1990). We may also point to the sense of joy and participation in Hispanic worship tradition. See Justo L. González, ed., *Alabadle! Hispanic Christian Worship* (Nashville: Abingdon, 1996).

3. This seems to be the case in numerous churches where people are seeking to change their patterns. Some people observe significant growth in a church down the road and seek to identify what single magical issue is involved and then to acquire that magical device. Many people conclude that it is "that new music." Actually, however, many elements account for the growth of a church—and God must be included in the matrix! Quick-fix approaches rarely seem to achieve the desired goals.

4. One of the principal worship teams from Willow Creek Community Church repeatedly insisted, "We *love* the lost because God *loves* the lost." These people are truly driven with the zeal of evangelism.

5. While unbelievers cannot worship God, they can observe believers worshiping God. This worship is a genuine form of witness to God's power and presence. As Sally Morgenthaler has put it, real worship witnesses! (*Worship Evangelism: Inviting Unbelievers into the Presence of God* [Grand Rapids: Zondervan, 1993]).

## CHAPTER 15
## LEADING THE CHURCH
## TOWARD CONTEMPORARY WORSHIP

1. ، Some congregations or denominations believe only the first of these questions is relevant. In the Reformed tradition, for example, the "regulative principle" insists that the only worship practices that are permissible are those that Scripture clearly commands. John M. Frame, an Orthodox Presbyterian, attempts to move within this principle, but he makes use of examples as well as direct commands (*Worship in Spirit and Truth*, chapter 4, "The Rules of Worship," 37–49). Frame also presented his approach in "Some Questions about the Regulative Principle," *Westminster Theological Journal* 54 (fall 1992): 367–403. His article received a rebuttal by T. David Gordon, "Some Answers about the Regulative Principle," *Westminster Theological Journal* 55 (fall 1993): 331–42.

   Donald P. Hustad has a very helpful section on the "regulative principle" and contemporary worship in *True Worship: Reclaiming the Wonder and Majesty* (Wheaton, Ill.: Harold Shaw, 1998). See his chapter 4, "Worshiping God in Biblical Truth/In a Strange Land of Differing Interpretations," 103–31.

2. Psalm 150 teaches that all available instruments were to be used by Israel for the praise of God in worship. The range of instruments went from simple flute to complex harp, from soft lyre to loud resounding cymbals. Even though these instruments had been borrowed from neighboring nations with pagan associations, all were to be used rightly in the praise of God. Ultimately He is to be seen as the source of everything good, including music and instrumentation.

## CHAPTER 16
## WHY PURSUE CONTEMPORARY WORSHIP?

1. See chapter 12, "Those New Praise Songs."
2. John Macarthur, Jr., *The Ultimate Priority* (Chicago: Moody Press, 1983). The title of this book on worship is on target.
3. Bruce Shelley, senior professor of church history at Denver Seminary,

wrote a splendid survey of the cultural forces that have impacted worship ideas in America. See his article, "Then and Now," in the series "What's Missing in Our Worship," *Moody* (March/April 1996): 23–25.

4. The older view is not correct when it insists that objective praise is "higher" than subjective. A perusal of the Book of Psalms leads one quickly to a different viewpoint. The praise of God may be "objective," with praise stated in terms of Himself. But often the praise of God is very personal, with numerous uses of first-person pronouns that describe the worshiper. The psalms give us every right to sing about the majesty of the Lord and about the manner in which we have found that He has met our every need.

5. In fact, this wonderful hymn has its origin in the Swedish church. Its use is very wide and rightly so. George Beverly Shea has sung it regularly in his music ministry with the Billy Graham crusades.

6. It was only later when working with Gordon Borror that I (Ron) came to the view that the entire service should have a unified theme! See Allen and Borror, *Worship: Rediscovering the Missing Jewel*, 63–76.

7. See the note on Psalm 33:1 in *The Nelson Study Bible*, 907.

8. One of the meanings of the Greek word *pneuma* ("spirit") and the Hebrew word *rûaḥ* ("spirit") is breath. Perhaps in some mysterious way the "breath" of the believer in true worship is animated by and in concert with the "breath" of God's Spirit.

9. This is the emphasis of James B. Torrance in the Didsbury Lectures, the Nazarene Theological College, Manchester, 1994, published as *Worship, Community, and the Triune God of Grace* (Carlisle, U.K.: Paternoster, 1996).

10. Justo L. González, "Hispanic Worship: An Introduction," in *¡Alabadle!: Hispanic Christian Worship*, 20.

11. It is customary for noncharismatic pastors to chide charismatic brothers by asking why they do not believe that God, who can direct their ministry on Sunday can also direct their planning for that ministry in their office during the week. Well, noncharismatic pastors need to see both aspects of this issue as well.

12. Psalms 11 and 23 are other examples of psalms of trust. Psalm 11:3 is another verse that is often used out of context. "If the foundations are destroyed, what can the righteous do?" Many preachers use this verse to express desperation when things are going badly in our society. The point of the verse in the psalm, however, is precisely the opposite. The words of verse 3 are the words of the wicked who attempt to discourage the righteous. In fact, "the foundations" are *not* destroyed, for "the LORD is in His holy temple" (11:4); in fact the righteous *can do* a great deal. See the notes on this psalm in *The Nelson Study Bible*, 885–86.

13. This is also true of the words of the prophets who called for stillness. When Habakkuk and Zephaniah called for silence before the Lord (Hab. 2:20; Zeph. 1:7), they were not urging people to worship Him in quiet contemplation. Instead, they called for silence in horror before overwhelming judgment! See the notes on these two verses in *The Nelson Study Bible*, 1523, 1527.

14. See chapter 12, "Those New Praise Songs." The wording "Sing praises with understanding" (Ps. 47:7) would rule out mindless repetition. There is no merit saying anything to God without meaning; but to repeat meaningful praise to God is an essentially biblical act of true worship.

15. This "drop" is not total, of course. There are centers in which the exceedingly rich treasures of the heritage of sacred music are still treasured, used, and preserved. But the people for whom this illustration is geared will have little interest in that fact.

16. The impact of Isaac Watts on the English hymn can hardly be overstated. See, for example, the brief but informative discussion by Andrew Wilson-Dickson, *The Story of Christian Music* (Minneapolis: Fortress, 1996), 110–11. He describes the ways in which the hymns of Watts have changed through the centuries, and that the work of the hymn writer is best seen as that of a folk artist.

17. George Barna et al., *Experience God in Worship* (Loveland, Colo.: Group, 2000).

## CHAPTER 17
### HOW TO LEAD IN TRANSITION—PASTORAL ISSUES

1. Wiersbe, *Real Worship*, 120–28.

## CHAPTER 18
### HOW TO LEAD IN TRANSITION—MUSICAL ISSUES

1. See chapter 13 for a discussion of "blended services."
2. On second thought, perhaps they would sing a chant, or at least a form of one.

    The familiar tune for Isaac Watts's hymn "When I Survey the Wondrous Cross" is actually an arrangement of a Gregorian chant by Lowell Mason.

## CHAPTER 20
### NO MORE IDLE WORSHIP

1. This only works, of course, when the preacher actually has his mind on the text and the topic well ahead of time! In homiletics courses we were taught to work on a given sermon well ahead of the preaching event.
2. P. D. James, *A Certain Justice* (New York: Knoff, 1977), 42–43.
3. *Dallas-Forth Worth Heritage*, October 1998, 43. The most astonishing item to me in the article is the observation that on a given Sunday in the United States "more than 75 million adults attend worship services at Christian churches. That is more than triple the number of adults who will tune in football games on a typical Sunday during the regular season."
4. Thor Christensen, "Idle Worship," *Dallas Morning News*, 25 September 1998, 37A. His very caustic review was of the performance of the musical group "Matchbox 20" and its lead singer Rob Thomas.
5. Among older ministers of the gospel the idea of "preliminaries" and "main event" remains the single most significant element in keeping the pastor from being a worshiper with the congregation. Only when the pastor is the lead worshiper will the people see worship as

their greatest task together. Further, when the one who preaches is a worshiper, his sermon becomes a means of encouraging the people to worship. For insights along this line see Davis Duggins, "The Worship Gap," *Moody* (March/April 1996): 19–22.

## CHAPTER 21
### SO LET'S WORSHIP THE TRIUNE GOD!

1. D. G. Kehl, "Worship . . . for the Purpose of Godliness," in *Spiritual Disciplines for the Christian Life*, ed. Donald S. Whitney (Colorado Springs: Navpress, 1991), 90.

2. A. W. Tozer, *Whatever Happened to Worship?* comp. and ed. Gerald B. Smith (Camp Hill, Pa.: Christian Publications, 1985), 105.

3. Some readers may wince at the term *wow*. But interestingly the verb "to wow" has recently been found in an otherwise obscure Canaanite dialect, Alphalphite. The meaning of the ancient term *wow* in Alphalphite is somewhat debated, but it seems to have the idea of "to dazzle, to stun."

4. Tozer, *Whatever Happened to Worship?*

5. Ibid., 55–56.

6. Dawn, *A Royal "Waste" of Time: The Splendor of Worshiping God and Being Church for the World.*

7. Richard Baxter, *The Reformed Pastor: A Pattern for Personal Growth and Ministry*, abridged and ed. James M. Houston (Portland, Oreg.: Multnomah, 1982), 28 (italics his). Ed Hayes, president emeritus of Denver Seminary, quotes these words from Baxter in his chapter on worship, in *The Church: The Body of Christ in the World Today*, Swindoll Leadership Library (Nashville: Word, 1999), 153.

# Bibliography

Allen, Ronald B. *Lord of Song: The Messiah Revealed in the Psalms*. Portland, Oreg.: Multnomah Press, 1985.

_____. *And I Will Praise Him: A Guide to Worship in the Psalms*. Reprint, Grand Rapids: Kregel Books, 1999.

_____. *The Majesty of Man: The Dignity of Being Human*. Reprint, Grand Rapids: Kregel Books, 1999.

_____, and Gordon Borror. *Worship: Rediscovering the Missing Jewel*. Portland, Oreg.: Multnomah Press, 1982.

Barna, George, et al. *Experience God in Worship*. Loveland, Colo.: Group Publishing, 2000.

Basden, Paul. *The Worship Maze: Finding a Style to Fit Your Church*. Downers Grove, Ill.: InterVarsity Press, 1999.

Berglund, Robert D. *A Philosophy of Church Music*. Chicago: Moody Press, 1985.

Berkley, James D., ed. *Word and Worship*. Vol. 1 of *Leadership Handbooks of Practical Theology*. Grand Rapids: Baker Book House, 1992.

Cornwall, Judson. *Let Us Worship*. North Brunswick, N.J.: Bridge-Logos, 1983.

Dawn, Marva J. *Reaching Out without Dumbing Down: A Theology of Worship for the Turn-of-the-Century Culture*. Grand Rapids: Wm. B. Eerdmans Publishing Co., 1995.

_____. *A Royal "Waste" of Time: The Splendor of Worshiping God and Being Church for the World*. Grand Rapids: Wm. B. Eerdmans Publishing Co., 1999.

Frame, John M. *Worship in Spirit and Truth*. Phillipsburg, N.J.: Presbyterian & Reformed Publishing Co., 1996.

_____. *Contemporary Worship Music: A Biblical Defense*. Phillipsburg, N.J.: Presbyterian & Reformed Publishing Co., 1997.

Fromm, Charles E. *New Song: The Sound of Spiritual Awakening, A Study of Music in Revival*. Santa Ana, Calif.: Institute of Worship Renewal, 1987.

Gallup, George, Jr., and D. Michael Lindsay. *Surveying the Religious Landscape: Trends in U.S. Beliefs*. Harrisburg, Pa.: Morehouse Publishing, 1999.

Gillquist, Peter E. *The Physical Side of Being Spiritual*. Grand Rapids: Zondervan Publishing House, 1979.

_____. *Becoming Orthodox: A Journey to the Ancient Christian Faith*. Brentwood, Tenn.: Wolgemuth & Hyatt, Publishers, 1989.

González, Justo L., ed. *¡Alabadle! Hispanic Christian Worship*. Nashville: Abingdon Press, 1996.

Hayford, Jack W. *Worship His Majesty*. Waco, Tex.: Word Books, 1987.

Hustad, Donald P. *Jubilate! Church Music in the Evangelical Tradition*. Carol Stream, Ill.: Hope Publishing Co., 1980.

_____. *Jubilate II: Church Music in Worship and Renewal*. Carol Stream, Ill.: Hope Publishing Co. , 1993.

_____. *True Worship: Reclaiming the Wonder and Majesty*. Carol Stream, Ill.: Hope Publishing Co., 1998.

Johansson, Calvin M. *Music and Ministry: A Biblical Counterpoint*. 2d ed. Peabody, Mass.: Hendrickson Publishers, 1998.

Joseph, Mark. *The Rock & Roll Rebellion: Why People of Faith Abandoned Rock Music—And Why They're Coming Back*. Nashville: Broadman & Holman Publishers, 1999.

Laney, J. Carl. *God: Who He Is, What He Does, How to Know Him Better*. Swindoll Leadership Library. Nashville: Word Publishing, 1999.

Liesch, Barry. *The New Worship: Straight Talk on Music and the Church*. Grand Rapids: Baker Books, 1996.

MacArthur, John Jr. *The Ultimate Priority*. Chicago: Moody Press, 1983.

Martin, Ralph P. *Worship in the Early Church*. Rev. ed. Grand Rapids: Wm. B. Eerdmans Publishing Co., 1974.

_____. *The Worship of God: Some Theological, Pastoral, and Practical Reflections*. Grand Rapids: Wm. B. Eerdmans Publishing Co., 1982.

Morgantholer, Sally. *Worship Evangelism: Inviting Unbelievers into the Presence of God*. Grand Rapids: Zondervan Publishing House, 1999.

Ortlund, Anne. *Up with Worship*. Glendale, Calif.: Regal Books, 1975.

Owens, Ron, with Jan McMurray. *Return to Worship: A God-Centered Approach*. Nashville: Broadman & Holman Publishers, 1999.

Piper, John. *Let the Nations Be Glad! The Supremacy of God in Missions*. Grand Rapids: Baker Books, 1993.

Rayburn, Robert G. *O Come, Let Us Worship: Corporate Worship in the Evangelical Church*. Grand Rapids: Baker Book House, 1980.

Spencer, Jon Michael. *Protest and Praise: Sacred Music of Black Religion*. Minneapolis: Fortress Press, 1990.

Torrance, James B. *Worship, Community, and the Triune God of Grace*. Carlisle, U. K.: Paternoster Press, 1996.

Tozer, A. W. *Worship: The Missing Jewel of the Evangelical Church*. Harrisburg, Pa.: Christian Publications, n.d..

————. *Whatever Happened to Worship?* Compiled and edited by Gerald B. Smith. Camp Hill, Pa.: Christian Publications,1985.

Webber, Robert E. *Common Roots: A Call to Evangelical Maturity.* Grand Rapids: Zondervan Publishing House, 1979.

————. *Worship Is a Verb.* Waco, Tex.: Word Books, 1985.

————. *Worship Old and New: A Biblical, Historical, and Practical Introduction.* Rev. ed. Grand Rapids: Zondervan Publishing House, 1994.

————. *Blended Worship: Achieving Substance and Relevance in Worship* Peabody, Mass.: Hendrickson Publishers, 1996.

Westermann, Claus. *The Praise of God in the Psalms.* Translated by Keith R. Crim. Richmond, Va.: John Knox, 1965.

Westermeyer, Paul. *Te Deum: The Church and Music.* Philadelphia: Fortress Press, 1998.

Wiersbe, Warren W. *Real Worship: Playground, Battleground, or Holy Ground?* 2d ed. Grand Rapids: Baker Books, 2000.

Wilson-Dickson, Andrew. *The Story of Christian Music.* Minneapolis: Fortress Press, 1996.

Wyrtzen, Don. *A Musician Looks at the Psalms.* Grand Rapids: Zondervan Publishing House, 1991.

# Resources

## SONG SOURCES

Integrity's Hosanna! Music
1000 Cody Rd.
Mobile, AL 36695
(334) 633-9000

Maranatha! Music
205 Avenida Fabrincante
San Clemente, CA 92672
(949) 940-7000

Scripture in Song
P.O. Box 525
Lewiston, NY 14092

Vineyard Music
P.O. Box 65004
Anaheim, CA 92815

*Songs of Discovery*

A partner with *Worship Leader* magazine
An annual subscription to the magazine may include a subscription to *Songs of Discovery*, a series of six CDs each year with lead sheet booklets. Write Worship Leader, P.O. Box 747, Mt. Morris, IL 61054-8412.

*Song Stories*, by Phil Christensen. This book (Grand Rapids: Kregel, forthcoming) presents the accounts that Phil Christensen, worship pastor at the Church on the Mountain, Sandy, Oregon, has been telling in *Worship Leader Magazine* about how the new praise songs were written. Just as stories of the writing of the great hymns can bring deeper understanding of that music, so the stories of these praise songs are deeply encouraging.

Craig Allen's music site is www.allenmusic.com.


## PERIODICALS

*Creator Magazine*

Calling itself "The Bimonthly Magazine of Balanced Music Ministry," *Creator Magazine* often has lively articles as well as helpful how-to topics. Contact them at 735 Industrial, San Carlos, CA 94070; 1-800-777-6713.


*Worship Leader*

The magazine is issued six times each year; I have contributed articles since it began in 1992. Articles discuss the theology of worship, the use of new equipment in worship centers, reviews of music and books, and personal stories of worship leaders and the writers of new music. For subscriptions, phone 1-800-286-8099. Or contact www.worshipleader.org.


*Instrumental Instruction*

Psalmist Training Resources
Instructional videos for keyboard and guitar

8929 Old LeMay Ferry Rd.
Hillsboro, MO 63050
(314) 789-4522

*Don Wyrtzen Piano Arrangements*

These arrangements cover a wide variety of styles and forms. The latest to be released in the series are these:

> *Keys of the Kingdom, 7: Piano Arrangements of Gospel Hymns*
> *Keys of the Kingdom, 8: Piano Arrangements of Spirituals*
> The series is published by Abingdon Press.

*Copyright Agency*

Christian Copyright Licensing International (CCLI). This is the licensing agency for Christian music throughout the world. All the information one needs to understand the laws and services is available on their website: www.ccli.com.

## CHURCH MUSIC CONFERENCES

Music California
This conference features new contemporary worship music.

*Maranatha! Worship Leader Conferences*

These conferences, held in various locations, emphasize all aspects of contemporary music.

## BIBLES—SPECIAL EDITIONS

*The Nelson Study Bible.* Edited by Earl D. Radmacher, Ronald B. Allen, and H. Wayne House. Nashville: Thomas Nelson Co., 1997. The extensive notes in this edition of the Bible have a special focus on understanding biblical teaching on the worship of God.

*The Worship Bible.* Edited by Buddy Owens. A joint product of Maranatha! Music and Zondervan Publishing House.

## HYMNALS

*The Hymnal for Worship and Celebration.* Edited by Tom Fettke et al. Waco, Tex.: Word Music, 1986. This superior work is in wide use.

*The Celebration Hymnal: Songs and Hymns for Worship.* Edited by Tom Fettke et al. Waco, Tex.: Word Music/Integrity Music, 1997.

*The Celebration Hymnal; Songs and Hymns for Worship. Worship Resource Edition.* Edited by Tom Fettke et al. Waco, Tex.: Word Music/Integrity Music, 1997. This is a helpful companion volume to *The Celebration Hymnal,* with essays and tools for the use of the hymnal.

*The Worshiping Church: A Hymnal.* Edited by Donald P. Hustad. Carol Stream, Ill.: Hope Publishing Co., 1990.

*The Worshiping Church: A Hymnal—Worship Leaders Edition.* Edited by Donald P. Hustad. Carol Stream, Ill.: Hope Publishing Co., 1990. This book is a "feast" of information for worship leaders.

*Praise.* 4th ed. Laguna Hills, Calif.: Maranatha! Music, 1997. The many editions of Maranatha! Music's *Praise* have done much to bring the new praise songs into many singing communities throughout the English-speaking world.

## HELPFUL AGENCIES

*Artists in Christian Testimony—International.* This is a ministry developed by Byron Spradlin to encourage Christians in their participation in the lively arts. It is both a mission board and a nonprofit umbrella empowerment ministry for Christian artists in a number of countries.

Spradlin been working for indigenous music for worship among new people groups.

Artists in Christian Testimony—International
P.O. Box 395
Franklin, TN 37065-0395
e-mail: ACTNashville@actinternational.org
Phone: 615-591-2598
FAX: 615-591-2599
Website: www.actinternational.org

*Christians in the Visual Arts (CIVA)*. An international association of over fifteen hundred people involved in all areas of visual arts, including producing, promoting, appreciating, and curating art (see John Skillen, "The Art of Being Christian," *Christianity Today*, 24 May 1999, 76–77).

CIVA
P.O. Box 18117
Minneapolis, MN 55418-0117
Website: www.civa.org.

## GRAPHIC ARTS

The industry leader in graphic design in Christian contexts is Church Art Works. The company specializes in apparel products and youth-oriented designs. Here is the prime source for graphic design in youth worship ministries.

Church Art Works/One Way Out
890 Promontory Place S.E.
Salem, OR 97302-1716
Phone: 877-663-9296
Website: Info@ChurchArtWorks.com

## VIDEO SERIES

*The Bible as a Rose*, by Ronald B. Allen (Portland, Oreg.: Western Seminary, 1990). A nine-part video course on three VCR tapes (each session is about thirty minutes), with workbook, suitable for adult Sunday school classes, with a focus on the lines of continuity in the Bible. This is especially important material for new Christians or for those whose knowledge of the Bible is spotty. The series includes instruction in preparation for worshiping God.

## WORSHIP SOURCES ON THE WORLDWIDE WEB

*Worship Map–Resources for Worship*. This website was developed by Bruce L. Johnson, with choice articles on a wide variety of issues relating to the study of biblical worship. Included are extensive annotated bibliographies on worship by Robert R. Redman Jr.

Website: www.worshipmap.com

*Christianity Today Online*. This well-known periodical has a wonderful website with a number of good links to sites relating to worship.

Website: www.christianity.com

*Worship Leader Online*. This magazine's webpage gives access to the current issue as well as to archives of earlier materials of the magazine. There are also links to other sites including Song DISCovery, where new songs can be previewed on line.

Website: www.worshipleader.org

*Creator Magazine Online*. This website includes archived articles, interactive links, clip art, and many other helpful materials from *Creator Magazine*, founded by Marshall J. Sanders in 1978.

Website: www.creativemagazine.com

## PRESENTATION SOFTWARE

*Microsoft "Powerpoint"*™
- · Included as part of Microsoft Office™ 95, 98, and 2000 or separately
- · For Windows 95/98/2000, Windows NT™, and Macintosh®
- · Older versions available for Windows™ 3.1 (16 bit)
- · Dual monitor support with Windows ™ 98

*Tempo Productions "Hymn Show"*™
- · Introduced in 1998. Easy-to-use presentation software
- · Contains thousands of preformatted texts
- · Windows ™ 95 or 98.
- · Designed to interface with Tempo Productions' HymnSearch ™ and other song databases
- · Jump instantaneously between slides or songs via hotkeys and bookmarks
- · Contact Tempo Productions at 1-800-733-5066 or www.tempomusic.com

*R-Technics "Song Show" Plus!*
- · Version 3.0 and Professional Edition available (with slide show, video, and graphics image support, and Nursery call numbers)
- · SongSelect database of over six thousand songs
- · Can work in spontaneous worship setting, can support dual monitor systems, and can log usage activity for CCLI reports
- · Contact R-Technics at 208-898-0756 or www.rtechnics.com, or Fowler Productions at 800-729-0163, or e-mail them at fpi@fowlerinc.com

*Omega Consultants "Worship Song Programmer"*
- · For Macintosh and Windows 98
- · Version 4.0 introduced in summer of 1999
- · Requires dual VGA monitors
- · Supplementary to Powerpoint
- · Contact Dennis Williams at 360-754-7205, or e-mail him at dennis@omegaconsltantsinc.com

*"WorshipBuilder"*
- Introduced in spring of 1999
- Designed specifically for church worship use
- Takes the best features of Word and PowerPoint and makes them easier, faster, and more flexible to use
- See www.worshipbuilder.com, or contact Don Wuebben at 210-913-7137, or e-mail him at donw@worshipbuilder.com

*DesertSoft "DynaVue VCS"*
- Windows 98 and Windows NT versions
- Run automatic slide shows or complex multimedia presentations
- Includes fonts, gradient backgrounds, 3-D effects, special effects
- Edit songs even while projecting other songs
- Auto cue lists or manual operation, prepares CCLI reports, Nursery Paging system
- NT features include multichannel video control and operates up to three projectors from one PC
- Contact DynaVue Central at www.desertsoft.net

## WEBSITES AND LINKS

- *Soundcheck* Magazine: www.churchsoundcheck.com/ and links
- Technologies for Worship: www.tfwm.com
- Church Media Resources: home.gs.verio.net/~pswindal/
- www.worshipmusic.com and links at www.praise.net/worship/links/index.html

# Scripture Index

# Subject Index

as quality of God, 46–51.
  *See also* Love
Hodges, Zane, 18
Hoffman, Nancy, 160
Hoffmans, 3
Holiness of God, 41–44
"Holy"
  meaning of term, 43–44
Holy Communion, 267.
  *See also* Lord's Supper
*Holy God, We Praise Thy Name,*
  148–49
*Holy, Holy, Holy! Lord God Almighty,*
  149, 161
Holy Spirit, in worship, 184–85
Houston, James, 246
"How Great Thou Art", 183
Hustad, Donald, 6
Hymnals
  limitations, 154–55
  wornout hymnals, 154–55.
  *See also* Contemporary hymnals;
    Hymns
Hymns
  as treasure of church, 147
  contemporary, 147–50
  contrasted with praise songs, 156–57
  effective accompaniment, 229–32
  extending their life, 227–32
  favorites slow to change, 219–20
  new generation's response, 209–10
  out-of-date feeling, 156
  sense of history, 153
  their role, 227–29
  theological content, 153
  vanished hymns, 189–90.
  *See also* Blended services;
    Contemporary hymnals; Hymns

—I—

"I Love You, Lord", 150–51
"I Sing Praises", 149
International Council of Biblical
  Inerrancy, 46

Isaiah
  his vision, 253–54
  his vision interpreted, 41–46
  on worship, 85–86
Israel
  Israel's confession, 54–56
  salvation of Israel, 63–64, 66–67,
    258–59

—J—

James, P.D., 235–36
Jesus Christ
  as Prophet greater than Moses, 81
  as Servant, 24–25
  as Teacher of Righteousness, 81
  exaltation of Christ, 23
  fulfilling Moses, 81–82
  hesed as quality, 50–51
  his ministry model, 195
  on worship, 91–93
  preincarnate, 47–48, 250
  Psalm 118, 75
Jesus Movement, 182
  and new praise music, 131, 132
Jews. *See* Israel
Johnston, Julia H., 64
Jonah, 50
Joshua (high priest), 9–13, 18–19,
  249–50

—K—

Kaiser, Walter K, Jr., 74
Kehl, D.G., 243
Kelly, Thomas, 149
Kendrick, Graham, 142
King James Version
  in praise music, 136
Kirkland, Camp, 149
Klein, Laurie, 57, 134, 150

—L—

Lafferty, Karen, 142
Lane, Eddie, 128
Laney, J. Carl, 41, 53, 67

teaching function in worship, 202–7
theology of worship, 239–40
view of worship, 238–39
Patience of God, 49, 50
Patterson, George, 131
Paul, on God's glory, 21–23
Pentateuch, rose analogy, 82–95
Perrins, Wayne and Cathy, 246
Phylacteries, 58, 257
Piano, 224
Pillar Cloud, 47–49, 255–56
Piper, John, 118
Place of worship, 191–93
Platform, as barrier to worship, 4–5
Praise, 150
Praise
  as beauty of God, 72–73
  beauty of praise, 69–79
  in Exodus 15, 73–79.
  *See also* Church music; Praise music;
    Worship
Praise music
  contrasted with hymns, 156–57
  historic battles, 128–29
  objective vs. subjective, 278
  origins of praise music, 130–33
  progression idea, 121–25.
  *See also* Contemporary hymnals;
    Praise music controversy; Worship
Praise music controversy
  blending as compromise, 174
  criticism of praise music, 127–28
  "dumbing down" issue, 141–42
  incorrect modern grammar, 138–39
  incorrect older grammar, 137–38
  King James usage, 136–38
  "meaningfulness" issue, 139–41
  older choruses, 129–30
  repetition issue, 135
  strengths of praise music, 134–35
  weak lyrics as issue, 133–34.
  *See also* Blended services; Church
    music; Worship

*Praise My Soul, the King of Heaven,* 148
*Praise the Savior,* 149
Prayer
  leading congregational prayer,
    193–94.
  *See also* Worship
Predestination, 22, 257
Priests
  wicked priests, 32–35
Promise Band, 229
Prophets, 35–36
Psalms
  "stages of worship" idea, 121–25
  problems with idea, 123–25

—R—

Ralston, Timothy, 106, 107
Rayburn, Robert, 6
*Reaching Out Without Dumbing Down,*
  141
Redempto–centrism, 21
Reed, John, 104
*Reformed Pastor, The,* 246
Ritual, 31–37
  empty ritual, 31–33
Romanov, Demitri, 105, 145–46
Romanov, Julia, 145–46
Rose analogy, 82–95
Rosen, Moishe, 138
Rowe, James, 133
Rucker, Robert, 158

—S—

Salvation
  and God's glory, 21–23
  in gospel, 64–66
  in Old Testament, 62–64
Samaritan woman, 72–73, 81, 82, 85,
  91–92
Samuel, 86–89
Sanchez, Peter Jr., 77, 78
Sarah, 62, 64
Saul, 86–89, 264, 265
  his rejection, 87–88

# Additional Selections from
# Dr. Ronald Allen (contributing author)

## THE ROAD TO ARMAGEDDON (BOOK)

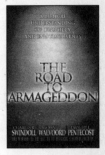

The end of the century. A new millennium. For Christians everywhere, there is little doubt that these are the last days, as we move down the road to Armageddon. This book features six of the most respected scholars and teachers on Bible prophecy and coming world events. An important tool for understanding the future.

## THE ROAD TO ARMAGEDDON AND BEYOND SERIES (CURRICULUM)

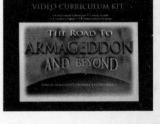

A series of six sessions designed to help Christians understand biblical prophecy. Each video in the series provides a wealth of solid Bible teaching on such topics as the Tribulation, the Rapture, the Antichrist, and the Second Coming. A must-see for every Christian concerned about the future.

## THE ROAD TO ARMAGEDDON AND BEYOND SERIES, VIDEO 6: THE SECOND COMING (VIDEO)

At the Second Coming, what should we be looking for? Ronald Allen answers this question, helping the listener understand the full implication and impact of the Second Coming—the cataclysmic changes that will take place in the world and the great comfort and peace that will follow.

# The
## Swindoll Leadership Library

## ANGELS, SATAN AND DEMONS
### Dr. Robert Lightner

The supernatural world gets a lot of attention these days in books, movies, and television series, but what does the Bible say about these other-worldly beings? Dr. Robert Lightner answers these questions with an in-depth look at the world of the "invisible" as expressed in Scripture.

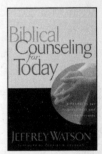

## BIBLICAL COUNSELING FOR TODAY
### Dr. Jeffrey Watson

Written by veteran counselor Dr. Jeffrey Watson, this handbook explores counseling from a biblical perspective—how to use Scripture to help others work through issues, choose healthy goals, and work toward those goals for a healthier, more spiritually grounded life. In *Biblical Counseling for Today,* both professional and lay counselors will find insightful, relevant answers to strengthen their ministries.

## THE CHURCH
### Dr. Ed Hayes

In this indispensable guide, Dr. Ed Hayes explores the labyrinths of the church, delving into her history, doctrines, rituals, and resources to find out what it means to be the Body of Christ on earth. Both passionate and precise, this essential volume offers solid insights on worship, persecution, missions, and morality: a bold call to unity and renewal.

## COACHING MINISTRY TEAMS
### Dr. Kenn Gangel

When it comes to effective discipleship, it takes a discipler, a coach, who is capable of not only leading by example, but also empowering his "players" to stay the course. In fifteen practical chapters, Christian education expert Kenn Gangel examines, among other topics, the attitudes in "The Heart of a Champion," leadership modeling in "Setting the Standard for the Team," and strategic planning in "Looking Down the Field."

### COLOR OUTSIDE THE LINES
*Dr. Howard G. Hendricks*

Just as the apostle Paul prodded early Christians "not to be conformed" to the world, Dr. Howard Hendricks vividly—and unexpectedly—extends that biblical theme and charges us to learn the art of living creatively, reflecting the image of the Creator rather than the culture.

### EFFECTIVE CHURCH GROWTH STRATEGIES
*Dr. Joseph Wall and Dr. Gene Getz*

*Effective Church Growth Strategies* outlines the biblical foundations necessary for raising healthy churches. Wall and Getz examine the groundwork essential for church growth, qualities of biblically healthy churches, methods for planting a new church, and steps for numerical and spiritual growth. The authors' study of Scripture, history, and culture will spark a new vision for today's church leaders.

### EFFECTIVE PASTORING
*Dr. Bill Lawrence*

In *Effective Pastoring*, Dr. Bill Lawrence examines what it means to be a pastor in the 21st century. Lawrence discusses often overlooked issues, writing transparently about the struggles of the pastor, the purpose and practice of servant leadership, and the roles and relationships crucial to pastoring. In doing so, he offers a revealing look beneath the "how to" to the "how to be" for pastors.

### EMPOWERED LEADERS
*Dr. Hans Finzel*

What is leadership really about? The rewards, excitement, and exhilaration? Or the responsibilities, frustrations, and exhausting nights? Dr. Hans Finzel takes readers on a journey into the lives of the Bible's great leaders, unearthing powerful principles for effective leadership in any situation.

## END TIMES
### Dr. John F. Walvoord

Long regarded as one of the top prophecy experts, Dr. John F. Walvoord now explores world events in light of biblical prophecy. By examining all of the prophetic passages in the Bible, Walvoord clearly explains the mystery behind confusing verses and conflicting viewpoints. This is the definitive work on prophecy for Bible students.

## THE FORGOTTEN BLESSING
### Dr. Henry Holloman

For many Christians, the gift of God's grace is central to their faith. But another gift—sanctification—is often overlooked. *The Forgotten Blessing* clarifies this essential doctrine, showing us what it means to be set apart, and how the process of sanctification can forever change our relationship with God.

## GOD
### Dr. J. Carl Laney

With tenacity and clarity, Dr. J. Carl Laney makes it plain: it's not enough to know *about* God. We can know *God* better. This book presents a practical path to life-changing encounters with the goodness, greatness, and glory of our Creator.

## THE HOLY SPIRIT
### Dr. Robert Gromacki

In *The Holy Spirit*, Dr. Robert Gromacki examines the personality, deity, symbols, and gifts of the Holy Spirit, while recapping the ministry of the Spirit throughout the Old Testament, the Gospel Era, the life of Christ, the Book of Acts, and the lives of believers.

## HUMANITY AND SIN
### *Dr. Robert A. Pyne*

Sin may seem like an outdated concept these days, but its consequences remain as destructive as ever. Dr. Robert A. Pyne takes a close look at humankind through the pages of Scripture and the lens of modern culture. As never before, readers will understand sin's overarching effect on creation and our world today.

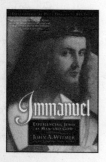

## IMMANUEL
### *Dr. John A. Witmer*

Dr. John A. Witmer presents the almighty Son of God as a living, breathing, incarnate man. He shows us a full picture of the Christ in four distinct phases: the Son of God before He became man, the divine suffering man on Earth, the glorified and ascended Christ, and the reigning King today.

## A LIFE OF PRAYER
### *Dr. Paul Cedar*

Dr. Paul Cedar explores prayer through three primary concepts, showing us how to consider, cultivate, and continue a lifestyle of prayer. This volume helps readers recognize the unlimited potential and the awesome purpose of prayer.

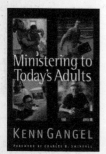

## MINISTERING TO TODAY'S ADULTS
### *Dr. Kenn Gangel*

After 40 years of research and experience, Dr. Kenn Gangel knows what it takes to reach adults. In an easy-to-grasp, easy-to-apply style, Gangel offers proven systematic strategies for building dynamic adult ministries.

## MORAL DILEMMAS
### J. Kerby Anderson

Should biblically informed Christians be for or against capital punishment? How should we as Christians view abortion, euthanasia, genetic engineering, divorce, and technology? In this comprehensive, cutting-edge book, J. Kerby Anderson challenges us to thoughtfully analyze the dividing issues facing our age, while equipping believers to maneuver through the ethical and moral land mines of our times.

## THE NEW TESTAMENT EXPLORER
### Mark Bailey and Tom Constable

*The New Testament Explorer* provides a concise, on-target map for traveling through the New Testament. Mark Bailey and Tom Constable guide the reader paragraph by paragraph through the New Testament, providing an up-close-and-to-the-point examination of the leaders behind the page and the theological implications of the truths revealed. A great tool for teachers and pastors alike, this exploration tool comes equipped with outlines for further study, narrative discussion, and applicable truths for teaching and for living.

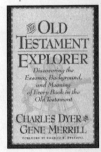

## THE OLD TESTAMENT EXPLORER
### Dr. Charles Dyer and Dr. Gene Merrill

Imagine the deep blackness before the dawn of creation. Wander with the Jews through the wilderness in search of the Promised Land. Stand outside the gates as Daniel is led to the den of lions. With *The Old Testament Explorer*, Charles Dyer and Gene Merrill guide you step-by-step through the depths of each Old Testament book and provide a variety of tools for understanding God's message. In contemporary and understandable language, you'll learn valuable information about the stories, people, and life-truths in each Old Testament book.

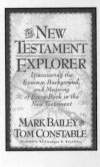

## SALVATION
### Earl D. Radmacher

God's ultimate gift to His children is salvation. In this volume, Earl Radmacher offers an in-depth look at the most fundamental element of the Christian faith. From defining the essentials of salvation to explaining the result of Christ's sacrifice, this book walks readers through the spiritual meaning, motives, application, and eternal result of God's work of salvation in our lives.

## SPIRIT-FILLED TEACHING
*Dr. Roy B. Zuck*

Whether you teach a small Sunday school class or a standing-room-only crowd at a major university, the process of teaching can be demanding and draining. This lively book brings a new understanding of the Holy Spirit's essential role in teaching.

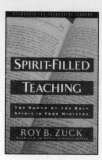

## TALE OF THE TARDY OXCART AND 1501 OTHER STORIES
*Dr. Charles R. Swindoll*

In this rich volume, you'll have access to resourcing Dr. Charles R. Swindoll's favorite anecdotes on prayer or quotations for grief. In *The Tale of the Tardy Oxcart,* thousands of illustrations are arranged by subjects alphabetically for quick-and-easy access. A perfect resource for all pastors and speakers.

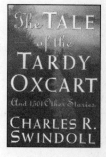

## THE THEOLOGICAL WORDBOOK
*Campbell, Johnston, Walvoord, Witmer*

Compiled by four of today's best theological minds, *The Theological Wordbook* is a valuable, accessible reference guide to the most important theological terms. Definitions, scriptural references, engaging explanations—all in one easy-to-find, applicable resource—for both the lay person and serious Bible student.

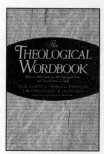

## WOMEN AND THE CHURCH
*Dr. Lucy Mabery-Foster*

*Women and the Church* provides an overview of the historical, biblical, and cultural perspectives on the unique roles and gifts women bring to the church, while exploring what it takes to minister to women today. Important insight for any leader seeking to understand how to more effectively minister to women and build women's ministries in the local church.

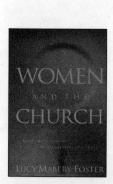